Contents

Inclusive Language Education and Digital Technology

MIX
Paper from
responsible sources
FSC® C014540
www.fsc.org

NEW PERSPECTIVES ON LANGUAGE AND EDUCATION
Series Editor: Professor Viv Edwards, *University of Reading, Reading, UK*
Series Advisor: Professor Allan Luke, *Queensland University of Technology, Brisbane, Australia*

Two decades of research and development in language and literacy education have yielded a broad, multidisciplinary focus. Yet education systems face constant economic and technological change, with attendant issues of identity and power, community and culture. This series will feature critical and interpretive, disciplinary and multidisciplinary perspectives on teaching and learning, language and literacy in new times.

Full details of all the books in this series and of all our other publications can be found on http://www.multilingual-matters.com, or by writing to Multilingual Matters, St Nicholas House, 31–34 High Street, Bristol, BS1 2AW, UK.

Inclusive Language Education and Digital Technology

Edited by
Elina Vilar Beltrán, Chris Abbott and Jane Jones

MULTILINGUAL MATTERS
Bristol • Buffalo • Toronto

Educ.
P
53.855
.I54
2013

*To Gabriela
from Eli*

Library of Congress Cataloging in Publication Data
Inclusive Language Education and Digital Technology/Edited by Elina Vilar Beltrán,
Chris Abbott and Jane Jones.
New Perspectives on Language and Education: 30
Includes bibliographical references and index.
1. Language and languages—Study and teaching—Technological innovations. 2. Language
and languages—Computer-assisted instruction. 3. Children with disabilities—Education.
I. Beltrán, Elina Vilar, editor of compilation.
P53.855.I54 2013
418.0078–dc23 2013001854

British Library Cataloguing in Publication Data
A catalogue entry for this book is available from the British Library.

ISBN-13: 978-1-84769-973-2 (hbk)
ISBN-13: 978-1-84769-972-5 (pbk)

Multilingual Matters
UK: St Nicholas House, 31–34 High Street, Bristol, BS1 2AW, UK.
USA: UTP, 2250 Military Road, Tonawanda, NY 14150, USA.
Canada: UTP, 5201 Dufferin Street, North York, Ontario M3H 5T8, Canada.

The policy of Multilingual Matters/Channel View Publications is to use papers that are
natural, renewable and recyclable products, made from wood grown in sustainable for-
ests. In the manufacturing process of our books, and to further support our policy, preference is given to printers that have FSC and PEFC Chain of Custody certification. The FSC
and/or PEFC logos will appear on those books where full certification has been granted
to the printer concerned.

Typeset by Techset Composition Ltd., Salisbury, UK.
Printed and bound in Great Britain by Short Run Press Ltd.

Contributors

Chris Abbott is Reader in e-Inclusion at King's College London. He taught in mainstream and special schools, mostly in the London area, for twenty years before becoming Director of the Inner London Educational Computing Centre. Since joining King's College London, he has specialised in teaching and research around literacy, language and assistive technologies, especially with regard to students identified as having learning difficulties. He is the Programme Director of the MA Inclusive Education & Technology, and of the Foundation Degree/BA Education Studies. He has led a number of research projects on aspects of technology and disability, and is the author of ICT: Changing Education (2000) and SEN and the Internet: Issues for the Inclusive Classroom (2002). He is the Editor of the Journal of Assistive Technologies.

Email: Chris.abbott@kcl.ac.uk

John Connor A former head of a language faculty and local authority adviser, John worked for a time as a team inspector for OFSTED, specialising in modern languages and special educational needs in mainstream settings. He has worked on national languages projects, and latterly on developing languages in primary schools. He has led training and teaching and learning quality audits across the UK, Europe, the Middle East and the Far East. He is an Assessor for the Advanced Skills Teacher programme for the Department for Education.

Email: johnfconnor@aol.com

Margaret Crombie is currently an Educational Consultant with a specialism in Literacy Difficulties and Dyslexia. She is an Associate Lecturer with the Open University (Difficulties in Literacy Development course) and supervises a number of doctorate students. Margaret has considerable previous experience of working in the dyslexia field as a Specialist Teacher and as a Manager and Lecturer. She has researched into dyslexia and the learning of a foreign language in schools in Scotland, and is co-author of the book, *Dyslexia and Foreign Language Learning* (Schneider & Crombie, 2003). She has contributed to many other publications. She has chaired the Working Group for Dyslexia Scotland, which has produced an online Toolkit for the assessment and support of those with literacy difficulties in a Scottish school context – The Addressing Dyslexia Toolkit.

Email: margaretcrombie@me.com

Ewa Domagała-Zyśk, since 1998, has been working as a Researcher and Lecturer at the Pedagogy Department of the John Paul II Catholic University of Lublin and at the Centre for Deaf and Hard of Hearing Education at KUL. She was a pioneer of teaching English as a foreign language to deaf university students in Poland, starting her work in 1999. She is the author of more than 30 empirical papers on that issue, both in English and in Polish, a co-author (with K. Karpinska-Szaj) of *Uczeń z wadą słuchu w szkole ogólnodostępnej. Podstawy metodyki nauczania języków obcych* [Hearing impaired student in mainstream school. Basics of methodology of teaching English]. She participated in more than 30 international conferences presenting papers on teaching English as a foreign language to deaf and hard of hearing students.

Email: ewadom@kul.lublin.pl

Andreas Jeitler has been a specialist in the field of universal accessibility at Klagenfurt University's Library since 2004. Beside other tasks, he supports and trains students, teachers and other library users in the process of creating and understanding how to use digital-accessible learning materials. Owing to his own visual and hearing impairments, he knows and understands the barriers that arise for people with disabilities. Andreas is Chairman of the Advisory Board on the Equalisation of People with Disabilities of the city of Klagenfurt and also long term Chairman of Uniability, the workgroup for the equalisation of people with disabilities and chronicle illnesses at Austria's Universities and colleges.

Email: andreas.jeitler@uni-klu.ac.at

Jane Jones is Senior Lecturer in MFL Teacher Education at King's College London. She taught languages for many years in comprehensive schools. She is subject specialist in the Assessment for Learning Group at King's. Her research interests include the development and embedding of effective formative assessment practices in language teaching and learning, especially with student teachers, and the promotion of self-regulatory strategies by pupils of all abilities and all ages to manage their own learning. Jane has participated in many EU funded international research projects on language learning, assessment and inclusion as well as the management and leadership of schools and within these, has been interested to promote critical teacher research and the pupil voice.

Email: jane.jones@kcl.ac.uk

Lynne Meiring taught French and German in a range of secondary and Further Education colleges for 17 years. She has worked in Higher Education for 20 years, teaching on the PGCE programmes (primary and secondary) at University of Wales, Swansea and Swansea Metropolitan University. She has also taught on Masters' programmes. She is an ESTYN section 10 inspector and has worked as a Modern Foreign Language Consultant in schools. Her research interests include developing literacy through modern foreign languages and the use of technology in the teaching and learning of modern foreign languages. She has several publications related to the teaching of modern foreign languages.

Email: lynne.meiring@smu.ac.uk

Nigel Norman was formerly Senior Lecturer in Education (Modern Foreign Languages) at Swansea Metropolitan University School of Education. His research interests include the methodology of language teaching, grammar and literacy, and information technology in languages. Previously he was Advisory Teacher in Wiltshire, where he was involved in curriculum development, in-service training and resources management. Prior to that he spent seven years as Head of Modern Languages in a comprehensive school and ten years in a boys' grammar school, including a year's exchange teaching in Germany. He has published course materials for German teaching and a variety of book contributions and articles in academic journals. He is the Reviews Editor for *Language Learning Journal*.

Email: nigel.norman@smu.ac.uk

Auxiliadora Sales Ciges is Senior Lecturer in the Department of Education at Universitat Jaume I, Castellón, Spain. She is the coordinator of the research group MEICRI (*Mejora Educativa y Ciudadanía Crítica*). Her research focuses on intercultural and inclusive education, attitudes and values training and planning, developing and evaluating measures of attention to diversity in schools. Her latest projects examine teachers' professional development through action research and school change. Her research has resulted in publications in national and international refereed journals.

Email: asales@edu.uji.es

Elina Vilar Beltrán is a language instructor at Queen Mary, University of London. Modern languages education and accessibility have been her main areas of study since she started her post-doctoral training at King's College London. She held the Batista i Roca fellowship at Fitzwilliam College, University of Cambridge for three years and was part of a Young Researchers Programme from the Spanish Ministry of Education at Universitat Jaume I; researching inclusive education policies in different countries and designing materials for practising and aspiring language teachers. Other areas of interest include digital literacies, intercultural communication and language development in the study abroad context.

Email: e.vilar@qmul.ac.uk

Mark Wassermann is Head of the Department for the Support of Students with Disability and Commissioner for Persons with Disabilities at the University of Klagenfurt. As a visually impaired person, he acts as Vice Chairman of the advisory board on accessibility for the city of Klagenfurt and Vice Chairman of the Independent Living Movement of Carinthia. As a member of the committee for the accessibility of vending machines at the Austrian Standard Institute, Mark represents the interests of blind and visually impaired persons. As an independent contractor he provides accessibility consulting and training for companies and organisations with the focus of accessible information technology.

Email: mark.wassermann@uni-klu.ac.at

David R. Wilson, BA (Leeds), Grad.Cert.Ed., MA, MEd. (Newcastle), Adv.Dip. Ed in Special Needs in Education (Open), now retired, works voluntarily in the Equal Opportunities Department at Harton Technology College in South Shields in the North East of England, where, for 37 years, he taught French, German and latterly secondary school students with learning difficulties. His research interests and specialeducationalneeds.com website focus on school curriculum accessibility, with particular reference to modern foreign languages, special educational needs and appropriate use of information and communications technology. He has published articles, delivered teacher-training workshops and presented papers at international conferences in Europe, Asia and North America.

Email: davidritchiewilson@compuserve.com

Introduction

Elina Vilar Beltrán, Chris Abbott and Jane Jones

The Purpose of the Book

Globalization of business, improved travel opportunities and ever grow-ing means of communication have made it even more necessary for people of different linguistic and cultural backgrounds to communicate with each other in a wide variety of contexts and for a wide variety of purposes. Communication is richer, culturally as well as linguistically and economi-cally, when it is possible in more than one language; having competence in languages is also personally enriching and generates enjoyment as well as growth; as has been shown by McColl (2000: 5): *'foreign language learning, far from interfering with language development as was once thought, stimulates its devel-opment, and gains can be detected right across the curriculum'*. This statement provides a very solid theoretical basis for the implementation of teaching languages to all pupils and a powerful rationale for the expansion of this activity within the context of special educational needs (SEN). Digital tech-nologies are ever more present in our lives and language-teaching contexts need to exploit the potential of these technologies in order to raise barriers to learning modern foreign languages (MFL). This book aims to show how this can be achieved with those individuals for whom language learning is more challenging, in a variety of contexts and from varying perspectives, and with a strong focus on the role of digital technologies. This is not an attempt to summarize developments worldwide, but a UK-based book with illumina-tive case studies from several European countries. Our exemplar chapters are not parochial, but carefully chosen to provide illuminative case studies within an area where very little has been published.

The book is aimed at teachers, advisers and researchers with an interest in the field of MFL teaching and learning, SEN and digital technologies. It may also be of interest to those studying the most effective approaches to inclusive language education. We also address postgraduate students looking for new and inclusive ways to teach MFL and heads and governors with responsibility for SEN/inclusion and for languages, as well as trainee teachers and teaching assistants.

Outline of the Book

The book is divided into two parts. The first part identifies and draws out the key issues of inclusive education, languages and digital technologies. These are not considered separately but are seen as inextricably interwoven, and each chapter takes a different emphasis and a different perspective. Part 2 comprises a set of case studies of current and emerging practices in a range of cultural contexts. The methods and the initiatives to meet those challenges have clear international currency.

Part 1: The Key Issues

Jones, in the first chapter, reviews recent policy changes regarding SEN and MFL, and reminds readers how learners with SEN were, for a long time, excluded from language learning. While the development of the National Curriculum strongly promoted inclusion in MFL, a suitable pedagogy has been elusive and teachers have lacked the necessary training, knowledge and resources in terms of materials and specialist support staff, a situation that is only slowly being remedied. Drawing on the insights and practices of three experienced and committed language teachers, Jones discusses the scope for the inclusion of pupils in a new culture of collaborative classroom language learning, a community in which all can achieve something on an identifiable 'can do' basis. A formative approach to assessing and progressing learning is considered central to learning. It is argued that learners with SEN need to develop a new language learner identity that empowers them with a measure of self-agency in such a learning community.

In Chapter 2, Abbott takes a personal view of the history of technology use by teachers of languages, first centred around audio and then in response to the availability of a wide range of digital technologies. Where once such technologies were found only in the classroom, learners now have access to mobile and other devices that offer sophisticated language tools. At the same time, the rapid development of the semantic web and social networking has offered fertile contexts for genuine linguistic engagement. A central focus of this chapter is the response of teachers and schools to these developments.

Wilson, in Chapter 3, identifies the challenges confronting teachers over recent years as they have differentiated their MFL lessons to include learners with SEN through information and communication technology (ICT). He argues for a more critical appraisal of the educational benefits of leading-edge technologies before their classroom adoption. SEN and ICT quite recently became priorities of MFL as a foundation subject within England's first National Curriculum. While MFL, SEN and ICT experts collaborated in the early years to pioneer good practice, the onus moved to MFL teachers working alone or, more recently, with a learning support assistant (LSA). Outside the classroom, Wilson argues, some adults expect too little from some learners, while assuming too much about the potential of ICT. The chapter includes a set of 10 practical scenarios for the readers to give thought to possible solutions.

Part 2: Case Studies

Vilar Beltrán and Sales Ciges, in Chapter 4, explore the languages classroom of the 21st century in English and Spanish schools. Drawing on research in the field, the authors focus in particular on beliefs and practices of language teachers with regards to context, pedagogical approach and differentiation and modification in response to diversity. In addition to exploring language teachers' perceptions, Vilar Beltrán and Sales Ciges analyse case studies of the implementation of digital technologies in language-teaching contexts. Digital technologies, they argue, not only form the reality for most students of this era but they could also be powerful tools that have the potential to enhance language teaching for all.

Chapter 5, by Domagała-Zyśk, focuses on the use of technology for teaching English as a Foreign Language (EFL) to the deaf and hard of hearing. For such people, as with all others, online environments offer the potential for building and maintaining social networks, enabling alternative communication without using speech. The internet has replaced previous modes of communication used by people who are deaf or hard of hearing, such as letters, faxes or text telephones. Using computer technology often requires the ability to use English. Many of the students described in this chapter have to learn EFL in order to update their knowledge and skills, and to access technology. Domagała-Zyśk describes the ways in which ICT can support the process of learning EFL, including a case study of the author's experience of using ICT during English classes for deaf students.

In Chapter 6, Meiring and Norman advance a case for ICT as an instrument for developing inclusive practice in the training of MFL teachers. They cite recent changes in legislation in Wales that have led to stronger demands for learners with SEN to have access to language learning. Using this policy requirement as a starting point, the authors consider the role and benefit of ICT in the curriculum, whether for access or enhancement. They consider the extent to which there may be a case for a distinctive pedagogy for SEN learners within MFL lessons, and the implications of this for teacher education. Using examples from their own practice in initial teacher education, the authors explore issues of pedagogy and resourcing, providing several practical examples.

The particular special needs of the learner with dyslexia are explored by Crombie in Chapter 7. In this chapter, Crombie, who has previously researched foreign language learning and dyslexia in schools in Scotland, considers a range of examples of inclusive practice. Building on her previous publications in this area, and her experience of working with teachers and learners, she considers how the use of technology in the foreign language classroom can benefit dyslexic and other learners. The chapter provides current and ready-to-use technologies for the classroom, and explains how these can be useful for language teachers.

The focus of Chapter 8 is an investigation by Connor into the extent to which interactive, creative resources can be a way to engage and motivate children who find learning difficult in the languages classroom. According to the author, the availability of interactive Web 2.0 tools has opened up new dimensions in the motivation and engagement of pupils who find learning languages difficult for various reasons. He argues that certain tools can provide students with an authentic purpose for their work, and if linked to a bespoke blog or wiki, can also provide them with an audience that could theoretically be global. Connor claims that blending digital technologies with other tried and tested approaches, such as making the learning active and kinaesthetic, affords students a much broader range of meaningful language learning opportunities.

Wassermann and Jeitler reflect on the conflicts between real-time resources and the storage of digitized materials including issues of copyright. Universities and other higher education institutions have been dealing with the complexities of digital resources for some time, but this has now become an issue for schools. This is particularly the case for teachers of languages who may wish to use authentic materials from digital versions of journals and magazines. In some cases, particular issues have arisen for learners with disabilities, for example visually impaired young people who need access to raw text for screen-readers. Without changes in the law of the kind that has recently occurred in the UK, such processes risk infringing copyright. From their experiences of grappling with these issues at their own institution, the authors consider all aspects of digitizing, from proofing to publication and dissemination. They also consider different emerging and actual legal solutions to this important area of resource provision.

Looking Forward

In the conclusion, Vilar Beltrán, Abbott and Jones bring together the issues outlined in Part 1, which are detailed and exemplified in Part 2, to outline a blueprint for the immediate future. Here they balance the evident enthusiasm for technology-mediated language learning with a nuanced recognition of the constraints that exist, whether these are related to the provision of resources at a time of recession, the need for effective teacher education or the appropriate response to a socially networked learning community. The challenges for teachers with often conflicting demands are not underestimated. Despite acknowledging these complex and challenging areas, the editors tentatively indicate a shift from an experimental to a mature phase of development as technology becomes an invisible but vital tool for the 21st century languages teacher.

A Word About Terminology

Our three areas of focus: technology, learning difficulty and language teaching, lead us into a complex field with regards to terminology. In a book with many contributors it would neither be appropriate nor helpful to insist on one standard terminology throughout, especially since many of the terms in use are not truly synonymous and may reflect varying understandings and policies. ICT – information and communication technology – is the name of a curriculum area in the UK and is widely used across Europe. However, this may be changing, and recent announcements in the UK suggest that the term may fall out of use in England, at least in the revised curriculum to be launched in 2014. Technology – and its component part digital technology – are in more general use and are used for this reason by several contributors. The term special educational needs (SEN) has been widely used in the UK since the late 1970s, although not often elsewhere. Those learners identified in the UK as having SEN may be given other designations in other contexts, with terms such as additional support needs (ASN), learning difficulties, learning disabilities and intellectual difficulties all in use.

Whatever the term used, our focus throughout is on those learners who need extra support to achieve and understand. Our curriculum context, of course, is the teaching of languages, and this has been traditionally named MFL in many curricula. Whether the term used is MFL or foreign language learning or simply language learning, our context remains the same.

We would like to express our gratitude to all the educators and the schools who provided examples and participated in the case studies that follow.

Acknowledgement

Elina Vilar Beltrán is very grateful for the support and financial input from the Batista i Roca Fellowship, Fitzwilliam College, University of Cambridge and the Young Researchers Programme from the Spanish Ministry of Education for giving her the opportunity to complete this work.

Reference

McColl, H. (2000) *Modern Languages for All*. London: David Fulton.

Part 1

The Key Issues

1 Modern Foreign Languages as an Inclusive Learning Opportunity: Changing Policies, Practices and Identities in the Languages Classroom

Jane Jones

Introduction

There has been a considerable change in attitude and in classroom practices regarding the teaching of modern foreign languages (MFL) to children with special educational needs, also referred to as children with learning differences and those with additional support needs (ASN). Where exclusion for many from the opportunity to embrace fully a language learning experience as part of regular school curriculum provision was widespread in previous decades, nearly all children have been included in language learning at some stage of their school career in recent times. This change has taken place in the light of policy frameworks of inclusion, especially with mainstreamed education as the status quo, and with concurrent and interlinked changes in approaches to, and views about, teaching and learning of MFL. Recent developments in MFL classrooms have proffered potential inclusive scenarios of many kinds. To explore these developments, this chapter is divided into two sections.

Section 1:
- Identifies briefly important policy changes concerning inclusive practice that provide a backdrop for such developments.
- Highlights key changes in approaches to languages teaching, learning and assessment, and the impact for children with learning differences.

Section 2:
- Proposes a language classroom collaborative learning community emphasising personalised learning that would include digital technologies, and formative assessment as a way to transform the learning experience for learners.
- Suggests redefining the language learner's identity as empowered and with agency.

In the conclusion, I discuss teacher training needs and the benefits of working in partnership, and I emphasise the need for leadership to support a whole school structure of effective provision for inclusive practices. I stress the importance of the wider goals of MFL learning for learners with special educational needs (SEN) and the need to monitor and research critically developing practice in MFL

As part of a learning conversation about issues in this chapter in order to provide concrete examples for points raised, I incorporate at all junctures the views and suggestions of three MFL teachers selected for their avowed commitment to inclusion and MFL, their insights into the need to personalise learning and for the creative strategies they have developed for personalised learning. The term 'SEN' is ubiquitous in the English context as can be seen in the verbatim comments from the teachers, and also in European Union documentation cited.

Section 1

Policies of inclusion

The 'Education for all' (EFA) agenda asserted in the 1990 Jomtien Declaration provides an important backdrop to understand the approach to inclusion in the UK. EFA aims to support all children everywhere in accessing good quality, basic education in an environment where they feel safe and welcome. The EFA inclusive philosophy has framed international and national policy approaches to education, including the Salamanca Statement on Principles, Policy and Practices in Special Needs Education

(UNESCO, 1994). Within this framework, it is understood that the education of all children should take place within the mainstream where all learners with their diversity of needs, experiences and backgrounds, come together, not just within the four walls, but in the *'putting into action values based on equity, entitlement, community, participation and respect for diversity'* (Booth *et al.*, 2003: 1), thus breaking down barriers to learning and participation.

The inclusive approach to education that is dominant in mainstream schools today has its origins in the Warnock Review of Special Education (1978), the ensuing Education Act of 1981 and the fundamental changes consequent to this Act, based on the concept of integration of learners with SEN into mainstream schools and social inclusion. The changes have been reflected in subsequent policy and iniatives that have sought to promote education for all. The National Curriculum has been central to this aim in addressing broader concerns of inclusion, for the 'gifted and talented', those for whom English is an additional language and those with SEN *inter alia*. The revised National Curriculum (QCA, 2007), emphasised personal development and well-being, and encouraged learners to become enterprising and responsible citizens as part of the broader concerns for the development of the whole child, physically, mentally and socially. These reflect the objectives of the Common European Framework of Reference for Languages: Teaching, Learning and Assessment (CEFR) that provide a framework for all languages teachers across Europe, aiming to: *'promote mutual understanding and to learn respect for identities and cultural diversity through more effective communication'* (2001: 3), and emphasising the scope of the value of MFL learning. One teacher describes the scope thus: *'MFL is an inclusive subject as it appeals to multiple skills – it is NOT exclusively about writing, speaking. It improves students' abilities to develop social skills, comprehend others, look beyond the written word in front of them.'* It is a view that resonates with McColl's (2005) perspective on language learning, inclusion and citizenship.

Change in MFL teaching, learning and assessment policy and practice

The teaching and learning of MFL extends far beyond the mere act of learning language, indeed, the centrality of language learning to promote social cohesion according to the CEFR (2001) and to build citizenship is strongly expressed in the executive summary of the report entitled 'Languages for Life: A Strategy for England', which states: '... language competence and intercultural understanding are not optional extras; they are an essential part of being a citizen' (Department for Education and Skills (DfES), 2002: 5).

This strategy has had considerable influence on the way MFL has been justified as part of the essential school curriculum and MFL has been seen as central to the development of a wide range of social and cultural as well as linguistic skills. The more inclusive approach to education in general, that began to develop at the end of the 1980s, was potentially very helpful in promoting foreign language learning, when the study of modern foreign language became a statutory entitlement following the implementation of the National Curriculum (NC) and the introduction of the programmes of study for Key Stage 3 (learners aged 11–14) in 1992 and Key Stage 4 (learners aged 14–16) in 1995. The National Curriculum has subsequently experienced changes and refinements over the last 20 years, critically with MFL at Key Stage 4 designated as no longer compulsory in 2004, and the introduction of a revised and more flexible National Curriculum in 2007 (QCA, 2007). Nonetheless, the introduction of a statutory requirement to study MFL was a significant measure. It confirmed the importance of the study of MFL in schools in England and Wales, by including MFL as a foundation subject and defining it as the right of every pupil. This represented a considerable shift from a position earlier in the 20th century, when the learning of any foreign language was reserved for a small élite (Anderson, 2000). The current approach to the teaching of MFL in the UK, as reflected in the revised National Curriculum (QCA, 2007) is understood as an inclusive one, promoting the study of languages for all. The study of a foreign language continues to be compulsory at Key Stage 3 for all learners under the revised National Curriculum (QCA, 2007) and is very likely to become compulsory at Key Stage 2 in the top end of the primary school for pupils aged 7–11. However, at Key Stage 4, MFL is likely to remain an 'entitlement' subject, that learners may choose to study as a GCSE (General Certificate of Secondary Education) option. The GCSE examination has provided differentiated options for entry level, higher and foundation, assessment in the four skills and a wide variety of tasks. The National Curriculum approach is supported by the aims of the CEFR (2001: 3) in seeking to:

> Promote, encourage and support the efforts of teachers and learners at all levels to apply in their own situation the principles of the construction of language learning systems ... and promote research and develop programmes of learning to the introduction, at all levels, of methods and materials best suited to enabling different classes and types of student to acquire a communicative proficiency appropriate to their specific need.

In very recent years, and in the light of alarming 'drop-out rates' from languages (CfBT, 2012), the stance schools have adopted towards entitlement has been monitored by the inspection body OFSTED. The inclusion of children in the study of MFL, while responding to an undeniable right to be involved in the wider agenda of foreign language study, has put considerable pressure on teachers (Hargreaves, 1994), who have, at the same time, to take into account the standards agenda and meet curriculum targets (MacBeath *et al.*, 2006). It has been found by researchers, such as Florian and Rouse (2001), that these conflicting pressures are influential in shaping teachers' attitudes to learning differences, and there remains some tension between the desire to provide inclusive education and the ability to provide effective support for all learners, some of whom may have a range of very specific needs requiring specialist tuition. Dyson (2001: 25) writes that while in practice, all children follow a common National Curriculum within common schools and are taught using widely accepted pedagogic practices, at the same time it needs to be recognised that all learners are different in that they have diverse learning styles and needs. In order to meet the needs created by these differences, schools respond by varying the teaching groupings, varying the teaching methodology and, to some degree, the content of the common curriculum. Dyson stresses the dilemma that this creates for schools and policy makers, in the struggle to '*reconcile the dual imperatives of commonality and difference*' (ibid). Richardson (2011: 27), echoing the views of Warnock, argues that: '*blanket acceptance of an inclusion model, that suggests "a one size fits all" approach to schooling, is unsupportable and far from a sustainable solution*'.

MFL in the curriculum

After the Education Act of 1944 (The 1944 (Butler) Act) establishing secondary education for all and a tripartite provision of grammar, technical and secondary modern schools, MFL came within the scope of more children. This was more prevalent in the grammar schools and, indeed, HMI (Department of Education and Science (DES), 1977: 4) reported on the restriction of MFL to '*perhaps 60–80 per cent of the pupils*'. With the advent of comprehensive reorganisation of schools, languages became increasingly politicised and began to be considered an entitlement of all children as part of the increasing equal opportunities debate and aforementioned policy shifts (Hodgkinson & Vickerman, 2009). The then Inner London Education Authority, the ILEA, in the 1970s, for example, disseminated a booklet entitled 'French for us all? Why not?' (1977) written by a group of MFL teachers, and the 'Languages for all' policy was implemented in London schools with some considerable success. A high level of accompanying training and resourcing that included considerable investment in technology, was made available. Technology, aspects of which are proposed as powerful tools to support learners and MFL learning in this volume, was thus not lacking in language learning (indeed the specialist MFL journal of the time was entitled *'The Audio-Visual Language Learning Journal'*), with language teachers making use of, for example, large reel to reel tape recorders, slide carousels and language laboratories. For those of us teaching at the time, it seemed very avant-garde and we believed the multi-sensory aspects of the approaches helped to create a more inclusive learning environment in supporting a wider range of learning styles. With training and resources, teachers became exponentially committed to the right of children with learning differences to engage in language learning. One teacher illustrates this view:

> By and large, I can think of very few circumstances when MFL teaching would not be possible and to the advantage of the student. I have worked in a comprehensive environment for many years now and most students have been able to follow MFL lessons or at least MFL-based activities. One of the reasons I am in favour of MFL for students is simply to follow the principle of inclusion as far as possible and not take SEN students out of lessons within a school environment. This means they can stay part of the school/class/form community.

Towards a communicative approach

Language teaching methods have changed over the years, not just in response to the inclusion agenda but also to developments in education systems at large, changes in society, the demands of the global economy and widening participation. Ideas about teaching and learning generally are products of their times and as Mitchell writes (1994), bringing in comprehensive education in the 1970s led to the teaching of a foreign language to almost all children, for the first time, for at least the first stage of secondary education. She associates a shift towards the communicative approach with a 'broadening of the "market" for foreign languages [that] created pressure for change in teaching methods and curricula, to suit the needs of non-traditional groups of learning (1994: 33)'. However, Mitchell (1994: 37) asserts that the rise of the communicative approach was not simply a reaction to the recognition of the inadequacies of grammar/translation and structural approaches, but new thinking and linguistic influences in formulating: *'a new expanded definition of what it means to "know" a language, on the one hand, and new ways of defining the content and goals of language syllabuses on the other hand'*, (see, for example, Mitchell & Myles, 1998).

In a critical review of language teaching trends, Klapper (2003), discussing communicative language teaching (CLT), suggests that a 'weak' version of CLT predominates in language classrooms, characterised by structured tasks, controlled practice and a gradual build-up towards stated objectives. The general claims of the approach include a focus on learner activity, all four skills but prioritise speaking, pupil as well as teacher target language use, authentic materials, tolerance of error and using language for real communicative purposes in collaborative scenarios *inter alia*. These signal benefits and options for a wide spectrum of learners, although Mitchell and Myles (1998: 195) warn that there is *'no best method'* that will apply *'at all times and in all situations with every type of learner'*. Nevertheless, many language teachers claim this is their preferred approach (and my 40 years of observing in language classrooms bear this out), interpreting it in a multiplicity of ways, in the belief that the flexibility of the approach caters best for the needs of mixed ability classes.

As with all initiatives, the best intentions and planning for inclusive practice are, however, sometimes thwarted depending on factors relating to class size, the resources available and level of support needed. In the past, MFL examination provision at 16+ was often limited in restricting the language offer to French only (no 2nd FL offer), or to a European Studies type course (with minimal language content) or to Short Courses at GCSE that put a cap on possible achievable grade. The previous policy of 'disapplication' for some pupils from MFL study and examination also excluded some learners from continuing their language study (see Chapter 4 for some examples of cases of disapplication).

Nowadays, provision is much more equal and versions of CLT prevail, but the interpretation of the communicative approach as largely oral has led to perhaps unintended consequences of 'closing down' options once again in marginalising reading and writing, especially for learners with SEN. It is not uncommon to hear languages teachers say things such as: *'It's mainly speaking, no writing'*, or *'We don't do grammar with that group'*, thereby, in a sense, making decisions that 'disapply' certain children from developing some competence in some of the four skills. It may be that we do a disservice to both the written word and to grammar, albeit topics of endless contestation in the MFL community, as well as underestimating the learners' capability to function in all four skills.

The inclusion of all four skills

In my work over many years with student teachers, it is noticeable that they invariably plan reading and writing tasks with great care and with all manner of learning props, including technologies, as part of their differentiated support for learning difference, but neglect to do the same for speaking and listening. One trainee explained her reasons for this: '*My SEN pupil feels secure in the tasks and I give him the time he needs to do them. I monitor carefully and at the end of the lesson he has achieved something*'. The European Commission Report (2005) on Special Educational Needs in Europe: Insights and Innovation, is a product of cross-European debate by specialists on common issues and sharing of workable strategies for SEN. Of relevance for this discussion is one of the report's findings that some children felt secure with activities that involved reading and writing programs on a PC because they had a visible result and immediate feedback that was confidence-giving. Such activities also gave pupils time to think, plan and check their work. A teacher finds agreement with this and stresses its importance with regard to writing:

Well with writing, it depends on the SEN – if they don't grasp the link between sounds and writing in L1 this causes issues with L2. Providing a language book such as a carnet de vocab (for French), or a Mappe (for German) for them to use as a resource can overcome this and most importantly, they might not always need to ASK during a lesson. I can contrast high ability lazy students who ask for words like 'the' or simple topic vocab, with SEN who – whilst they don't remember – are resourceful enough to find this out without using teacher. I train them to use brain, book, buddy, boss (BBBB): brain – think; check in book – is it there?; buddy – ask your neighbour; boss – ask the teacher – last resort. My pupils with SEN like the structure.

The teacher also commented on the supportive role of writing:

Providing writing frames and checklists generally reassures the pupils [with SEN]. They can complete whatever they need to (using glossary/dictionary/BBBB). They often do not think to look back in their books as they see each lesson as discrete and cannot link up what we're looking at today with what we did yesterday so they need to be able to refer back to something. It is useful to help them have good page layout for this to work – like a textbook. The date and title also have a purposeful and reference meaning (maybe in L1 for some students) and can help provide continuity of learning.

Writing can serve a multiplicity of functions in providing support for other language skills, learning skills and the development of confidence. Alexander

(2008: 108–109) found from his research in Yorkshire primary classrooms that 'the less able' benefited from a larger amount of pupil talk combined with shorter, but more concentrated, periods of writing in improving their reading and writing skills. Some students are capable of very good achievement in writing, with the appropriate support and target, as in the following example supplied by a teacher:

A Y10 student with autism and limited attention span – writes and generally works in 'chunks', he has learnt to put chunks together and completed writing and speaking controlled assessments. He also, through the SEN manager, completes German enrichment tasks (writing 3 sentences a night, which I mark for him once a week). This has extended and supported his writing. He is now up to 1000 words in 3 months!!

The key issue would seem, then, to be identifying suitable reading and writing tasks and providing support to enable the learner to undertake these. Teachers need to be aware of what is involved in reading and writing – motor skills, hand writing, sequencing and directionality, decoding, speed of processing, grapheme–phoneme connection for example, and provide targeted support (Crombie, 1997). Finding ways to develop all four skills to the best of each learner's ability and being attentive to support needed, provides the learner with options in their language use. A teacher describes how she supports the learners in a variety of skills:

Some students are excellent at listening and reading and can be challenged but they may find it difficult to speak for example because of a speech impediment. Likewise students may be hearing impaired. I then give them the transcript, a walkman or MP3 player to avoid background noise, occasionally if support is available (learning support assistant or a language assistant) they can read out and students can lip-read. Underlining keywords in case that literacy is an issue helps as well. Differentiating the task is helpful, i.e. a student underlines key words or finds pictures rather than working with whole texts, etc.

Deane (1992) suggests teachers need to be aware of the potential difficulties of speaking (remembering what to say and how to formulate it) and listening (the time needed for absorption and to react), which it should not be assumed are, *de facto*, she asserts, any easier than reading and writing.

The teachers who were part of the conversation around this chapter were completely at ease with technology of all kinds and made extensive use of the interactive whiteboard in particular, and a variety of software packages as well as some digital technology. However, there was limited pupil use of digital technology although one used a dictaphone with a child and another MP3 players for pupils to record lessons to take away for further study. One teacher reflected on the possibility of extending the sort of group work that she already did to include pupil use of technology:

> I haven't made much use of technology in groups. Here's how it could go. Groups put on task, each table uses a laptop or mobile phone to make a video-recording of their conversation. They self-assess first. Then the pupils move round to different work stations and evaluate the other groups' work. An extension could be to set a further task for another group.

It is also important to be aware that many younger secondary learners will have experienced some MFL learning in the primary school, mainly through a ludic approach emphasising oral skills, but in an approach where, in fact, there is often extensive exposure to the written word, e.g. with flashcards, story books and computer program (Department for Education and Skills (DfES), 2004). A dimension of reading for pleasure should remain central to the learners' reading schedule and might include comics, cartoons and big books. Useful supportive writing tasks might include scrapbook comments and notes, and topic-webs, for example. Johnstone (2008) suggests that introducing reading and writing early in language learning not only supports linguistic development but maintains motivation, in extending learners' opportunities to make links between their developing literacy in the mother tongue and the new language. A teacher gives an example: '*Spelling tests are motivating. Give 5 words (common words) usually L2 to L1 to improve literacy in English. The sense of pride in improving is always evident*'.

Deane (1992: 45) asserts that it is important to '*give frequent and positive feedback on [learners'] achievement and not measure their failure*'.

Grammar as a scaffold for learning

With regard to grammar, the conceptual obstacle teachers raise for pupils with SEN is perhaps rooted in a stereotypical construct of grammar teaching of the formal, prescriptive kind, prevalent in a generation of traditional text books. Typically, grammatical structures would be introduced in the abstract (verb paradigms, for example, or a list of cases), followed by examples then exercises. In the 1980s, at time of the introduction of the National Curriculum and the 'great grammar debate' that was taking place animatedly at the time, Heafford (1993: 55) writes that: '*most modern linguists were happy to move along with the times: functional–notional syllabuses replaced grammatical ones and the primacy of "communicative competence"'*. This necessitated a rethink of the place of grammar.

Arguably, in most classrooms today, grammar is now introduced in line with a broadly communicative and task-based approach and elaborated as a 'pedagogical grammar' or what Mohammed (1993: 59) calls a 'practical grammar' or 'teaching grammar', that is to say: *'one that is simplified and presented to the learners in such a way that it can easily be digested and used as a means rather than as a end in itself'* (see Heafford, 1993, for an elaboration of this approach to teaching grammar). In this approach, in brief, learning scenarios enable pupils to practise and, through deduction, to transfer their learning into new contexts. It could be described as a kind of linguistic Lego-building to provide a useful scaffold for the pupils' learning. The learners with the most difficulties need the most scaffolding of all. This is the approach of one teacher:

> Grammar is much trickier. I generally teach a limited set of phrases and show adaptations, e.g. singular to plural. Those at Key Stage 3 who are capable of achieving Level 5+ in the National Curriculum can usually show attempts at moving from 1st to 3rd person singular and plural. Starting with the L1 and comparing the item in the foreign language is often a good starting point if the foreign language is similar (e.g. the German imperfect), but confusing if not (French perfect tense – most compound tenses). I plan activities which give weaker/SEN students time to plan. They may not ever be able to give 'off-the-cuff' responses – but they will be able to use pre-learned vocabulary and structures and adapt these if given time and resources.

It will be crucial to build on the learners' previous experiences and, while it is unlikely that learners in the primary school will have learnt grammar in any formal way, it *is* likely that the children will have been sensitised to patterns and language awareness in their literacy development. The teacher's comments, above and below, focus on addressing how the learners, with the right support and resourcing, can make some sense of and use grammar. To this end, the teacher shows how the pupils can be supported to engage with grammar:

> Yes, I am teaching grammatical terms (nouns, verbs, adjectives, adverbs) but giving more student-friendly vocabulary to work with so a noun is a (person/place/thing, and a verb is a 'doing word',) if they find writing/saying the grammatical terms challenging. This is tricky with German and the case system so I provide example verb patterns, e.g.

Ich habe einen Hund but eine Katze and ein Pferd. I get students to cat-egorise and try to solve this, and provide alternatives using their ideas.

To conclude this point, Grenfell (2000: 24) asserts that: *'The "to grammar or not to grammar" question always obscured the crucial issue on these aspects of language learning, which are: what grammar? when grammar? why grammar? how grammar.'* Similarly, Montgomery (1990: 23) writes: *'it is not necessarily the curriculum but the pedagogy which is the barrier to the participation of children with learning difficulties (sic)'.*

As part of ongoing teacher reflection on practice, a re-positioning on the pedagogical approach for pupils with SEN, which focuses on what is enabling for pupils at different levels and in different ways, would allow teachers to think about how to operationalise the new imperative of personalised language learning (which I explore in the next section) and how this might translate to practice. One teacher identifies 'personalisation' as key:

MFL can also be very visual and includes a variety of skills, i.e. speaking, listening … this means it lends itself well to personalisation based on the students' needs. The lesson or structure of the lesson and differentiation obviously depend on the stage and nature of SEN. I have taught a student with Asperger's Syndrome who produced excellent work but needed more time writing, etc.… and students with severe SEN needs may be given a differentiated assessment. I had to plan my teaching around these needs.

Section 2

Classroom learning and inclusive language teaching pedagogy

The field of language teaching has been an unsettled one, one subject to pendulum swings as Hawkins (1996) put it, and subject to a plethora of suggested panaceas that has frequently included technology. Even today, language learning is not always seen by all as a key skill or necessity in a world where English is the lingua franca, and MFL is not always given wholesale and unqualified support, such as is given to maths and science, for example. There is much rhetoric and moral exhortation about the teaching and learning of MFL, and the inclusion of all pupils. A broadly communicative approach has enabled teachers to be much more flexible about encouraging pupils to learn in their own way at their own rate, albeit within certain boundaries of whole school planning, targets and available support. More often than not, the streamed classes of previous decades, although still in existence in some schools, have given way to gentler and more flexible setting arrangements and 'internal' streaming or setting within class groups, that is to say ability grouping. Ireson and Hallam (2001) found that languages, alongside maths and science, were highly likely to be taught in ability groups where ability was defined in terms of the perception that 'you can either do it or you can't'. Children with ASN, even if they were good at an aspect of language, would, they found, *de facto* find themselves in a less able or 'slower' group. Since, however, there is invariably quite a range of ability in sets, a learning community approach has the potential to enable the communicative approach to be better exploited in giving teachers the time and space to personalise learning and provision.

The MFL classroom as a learning community

A learning community creates conditions for pupils to develop trust and be trusted, and to function in a predominantly collaborative format, with a commitment to the learning of all in the group. The move from teacher-led to more pupil-centred learning facilitates organising pupils to work on tasks to which all learners can make a contribution and that acknowledge learner preferences and differences. One teacher gives an example of such collaboration:

> The upper ability had to order vocabulary and include in a sentence. The weaker ones had to sort and link using simple connectives and time phrases. They all interacted with the vocabulary in some way, therefore getting the best from what has been presented. You can then use either task as an extension for the others.

The languages classroom that incorporates this type of activity chimes with what Alexander (2008: 105) calls the 'dialogic classroom' in which teaching is dialogic and not transmissive. Dialogic teaching is defined, according to Alexander, by certain criteria:

- *Collective* – addressing learning tasks together.
- *Reciprocal* – listening to each other and sharing ideas.
- *Supportive* – articulating ideas freely without the fear of embarrassment and helping each other.
- *Cumulative* – building on each other's ideas.
- *Purposeful* – where teachers orientate classroom talk towards specific goals.

The 'collective' and the 'purposeful' criteria are much in evidence in language classrooms, while there is probably scope to exploit the other criteria.

In dialogic classrooms, pupil talk predominates. A teacher gives an example of how this might look:

> After some pre-teaching and practice, and setting up of task, pupils are engaged in text dissection in groups – the teacher decides mixed groups ahead of time and provides groups with texts, dictionaries and a glossary in various formats of new vocabulary. Students have to 1 – translate texts in groups, 2 – find key vocabulary and highlight it, 3 – use glossary words to create new language after dissecting and discussing text (either enlarged or typed up double-spaced for those with SEN). All work together and have a role in the task.

Learners, here, are supported by well managed teaching, guiding and formative feedback, make full use of each other as resources for the other's learning as Black and Wiliam (2009) urge; the aforementioned teacher's 'BBBB' format is also very much in evidence. In the dialogic classroom, the children with learning differences are part of the class learning dialogue and not outside of it. Teachers employ a responsive, watchful style of teaching and assessment where learners are enabled to include themselves in the range of structured yet flexible learning situations. Coyle's (2007) concept of the strategic classroom as one in which the establishment of a language learning community that nurtures the development of learner strategies is useful in attempting to draw a portrait of the inclusive languages classroom. Coyle's (2007: 66) classroom is *'a physical and social place where learners not only learn a foreign language but "learn how to learn" in order that they can become effective future learners'*. While there are many (Harris, 1997; Jones & Coffey, 2006; Macaro, 2001) who have argued for the explicit teaching and practice of learning strategies, Coyle suggests that strategic behaviour can grow out of the learning context in which scaffolding, seeking opportunities, mediation and self-regulation are key ideas. For the learners, strategy training to aid the development of metacognitive skills as well as the creation of learning contexts in which the pupils can take their learning forward in a personalised way are essential.

Personalisation

Learning, as with teaching, is personal. Personalisation, while not entirely new, was given prominence in a speech given in 2004 by the then Minister for Schools that emphasised the need to tailor education to individual needs, interests and aptitudes. The introduction of the Department for Children, Schools and Families (DCSF) (2008) document on personalised learning requires teachers, in adopting a personalised learning approach, to:

- Involve children as joint partners in the design of their learning.
- Meet children's learning needs in and beyond the school environment.
- Provide additional support for children who are not fulfilling their predicted potential.
- Enable children to respect others and their learning needs and develop self-esteem through learning in a mutually supportive environment.

Nothing has been stipulated in terms of how these translate to programmes of learning, for these will themselves be personalised according to the learning context. Although teachers have interpreted the agenda in a variety of ways, research undertaken by Sebba et al. (Department for Education and Skills (DfES), 2007) found that personalisation built on much existing good practice, such as Assessment for Learning (AfL), effective differentiation and high expectations, as well as individualised curriculum provision to meet learners' needs. Their research identified the importance of the role of learning mentors, raising aspirations, consulting and hearing the 'genuine pupil voice' and crucially giving pupils skills to learn independently. Robinson et al. (2008) in their research into personalisation and SEN identified digital technologies as something that really motivated and engaged learners. They emphasised the need to shift from teacher-led personalisation to learner-led personalisation, recognising the many challenges that this poses for teachers, not least the need for personalised provision. They concluded (p. 37) that 'learner-influenced' personalisation provided a workable and more manageable strategy for teachers.

Knowles (2009: 103) emphasises the need for time for learners to talk to adults about their learning and for the school to involve all learners in the wider work of the school in a 'well developed inclusive ethos'. Knowles' (2009: 94) definition of personalised learning as *'a partnership with the setting or school rather than something that is "done to them" however sensitive and sympathetic to their needs'* is a powerful one. As part of essential classroom dialogue and negotiation between learners and teachers, this definition meshes well with the learning community concept in that it has an individualising and not an isolating focus. It requires teachers to take on board the following:

- Prior knowledge and learning experiences.
- Different starting points and pace for learning.
- Learner preferences, strengths and particular needs.

- Learner interests and choices in terms of curriculum content.
- Different ways to demonstrate learning in a variety of ways and through a range of media.

Personalisation, then, goes some way beyond traditional differentiation strategies (learning objectives on three levels: most will … some will … a few will …). It provides quite some challenge for teachers as they work with different skills, levels, preferences and needs. One teacher illustrates this challenge:

This very much depends on the type of SEN. There may be cognitive issues which may prevent SEN students to progress beyond a certain stage (English and Welsh National Curriculum Levels 1–3) or, for example in the case of dyslexia, it may be difficult for students to access texts (but this is also the case for other subjects and at least, as mentioned above, MFL covers four skills). Students with speech impediments may find it difficult to speak (and be self conscious) but, again, may be good at writing, reading and listening. In very severe cases, in-classroom learning may not always be appropriate. All need different resources.

A crucial point here is that the teacher recognises the strengths and challenges of the particular type of SEN. Another teacher showed a similar responsiveness to varying needs:

For visually impaired students I copy larger font or instead of A4 onto A3. I don't expect students to read off the board, depending on the severity. Sometimes sitting at the front is fine. Same for hearing impaired or strategies as above. Also standing in the right place not covering one's face, looking at the class or particular student can be important. I taught a student with Asperger's. I realise that there are different forms. The main issue I found was that I needed to allow for more writing time and slightly more explanation. The best thing is to be fully informed about the students with an IEP (individual education plan) and talk to the SEN department who can give advice. Lessons or work needs to be prepared thoroughly otherwise the learning experience is frustrating for the student.

Personalisation is not without considerable challenge also to pupils, as one teacher commented: *'Some students require a lot of attention and support (ideally, in serious cases a teaching assistant is present to work with the student). It can also be difficult to provide challenge without alienation'.* The potential for learner stress needs to be borne in mind and here a teacher highlights the importance of breaking learning down into manageable steps:

> Include some short and focused listening. You can re-use listening clips with SEN pupils – get them to listen for different things, i.e. the first time for cognates, the second time for verbs, the third time they can attempt the exercise as presented in textbook. Alternatively, you can give a transcript, for them to highlight first things they know, and things they don't know, they look up in textbook glossary/dictionary. This way there are fewer surprises and it is less stressful.

Part of the classroom dialogue between pupils and teacher and pupils with pupils concerns responsibilities as well as needs. Stobart (2008: 179) claims that it is the learner's responsibility to become independent and it is the teachers' task to use appropriate methodology to enable learners to become autonomous: *'Part of being a self-regulated learner is to accept responsibility for learning, just as teachers must take responsibility for creating a context which helps learning'.* Rudduck and McIntyre, (2007) suggest that communicating with the learners is key and that teachers should make time to listen to their pupils talking about their learning rather than making assumptions. A learner-centred culture and community provide an arena in which to validate the pupil voice and hear pupils' views on learning and other contributions. In classrooms where learners have the opportunity to make certain choices about their learning, all can be included in valuable cooperative and collaborative learning and assessment activities with their peers and approach challenges with confidence.

Assessment of a formative kind

All the aforementioned are completely in tune with a formative assessment approach where formative assessment is defined as 'the frequent assessments of student progress to identify learning needs and shape teaching' (OECD, 2005: 1). It is an approach, geared towards promoting progression for each learner through, for example, feedback, collaborative learning, support and targets for learning that I want to emphasise as being helpful to all learners (Black & Wiliam, 1998). A formative approach is not antithetical to summative assessment but can support it. The type of languages classroom in which formative assessment would be to the fore includes and nurtures learners in providing constructive feedback to give the learner a sense of achievement and identifying ways to propel learning forward, however modest the steps. A teacher stresses the importance of tangible achievement:

> SEN students' boost from being class experts is massive. They need to be in charge of how to succeed just like all other students and be able to support their peers. Teachers need to plan activities that will enable SEN students to develop some expertise.

Formative assessment is often visible in practices teachers may recognise as being in congruence with an AfL cross-subject approach and that MFL has embraced (Jones & Wiliam, 2006). According to cross-European research into cultural interpretations of formative assessment, the OECD (2005: 21) asserted that:

> Teachers using formative assessment approaches and techniques are better prepared to meet diverse students' needs- through differentiation and adaptation of teaching to raise levels of student achievement and to achieve a greater equity of student outcomes.

This is an important point since, in England at least, many pupils are left with little identifiable achievement in terms of internal tests and national tests, for example. Across Europe, language teachers are increasingly adopting the CEFR as a frame to guide learning, teaching and assessment in MFL, and the most recent interpretation for teachers (Council of Europe, 2011; by Piccardo *et al.*) strongly encourages critical teacher reflexivity about their assessment practice to enable it to support learning needs. Assessment in the CEFR is absolutely driven by a 'can do' philosophy and structure (see Chapter 9 of the CEFR), and to this end a variety of levels have been created. The 'breakthrough' general level, A1, provides 'a manageable task for all learners in establishing "simple, general tasks ..." that can constitute useful objectives for beginners' (Council of Europe, 2001: 31). It is suggested that at this level, learners can:

- Make simple purchases where pointing or other gestures can support the verbal reference.
- Ask and tell day, time of day and date.
- Use some basic greetings.
- Fill in uncomplicated forms with personal details; name, address, nationality.
- Write a short, simple postcard.

These would seem to constitute basic and useful pedagogic tasks for all learners and put a recognisable and creditable level of achievement in the reach of all learners. All of these tasks can be done with the aid of digital technologies where this is useful or the learner preference. The level provides clear, simple and achievable targets. Most pupils will be able to take their language learning forward by negotiating targets and establishing the steps necessary to move to another level. However, where this is not possible, the learners end their language learning journey with a description of what they can do and with a credit, rather than a deficit, a low grade or 'disapplication' of some kind.

The pendulum has swung where exams are concerned too. Significantly, the Graded Objectives Movement in Modern Languages (GOML) of the 1970s, and that was the precursor to CEFR-style levels provided opportunities for flexible assessment in tune with the learner's needs and capabilities and contributed to the framing of national curricula and assessment. The languages ladder (asset languages), the current national recognition scheme for languages with accrediting national certification, provides flexibility for teachers and learners, although the scheme is patchily used at present. It is currently in the throes of redevelopment and, rather worryingly, the most recent report from Centre for British Teachers (CfBT, 2011) shows a decline in the take-up of the Asset Languages scheme and GNVQs, examinations that would favour certain pupils with SEN.

Portfolio assessment, fortunately, remains very much in the hands of teachers and learners. The individual child's language learning journey can be well documented with the use of a portfolio and can work alongside any formal assessment scheme. The European Language Portfolio (ELP) exists for such a purpose, but it is not used extensively in England. Some teachers find the ELP a rather passive tool in its filling-in format of ready-made tick lists that go against the idea of the learners' active construction of their portfolios. Other teachers have taken the idea of the portfolio and developed their own version of portfolio, paper versions or e-portfolios (Jones, 2012). Hebert's (2001) view of the portfolio as 'a companion to learning' provides a useful frame for both creating a personalised record of achievement and as a platform for more personalised feedback in a process of dialogue with the learner whose voice in this is essential.

Flutter and Rudduck (2004: 7) are of the view that pupils have the capacity '*to discuss their learning in a considered and insightful way, although they may not always be able to articulate their ideas in the formal language of education*'. This view stresses the value of the quality of interactions between teachers and learners and the importance for teachers of creating a purposeful and trustful learning environment where students can be effectively supported in developing their learning skills and an identity as an empowered language learner.

Redefining the language learner identity

Motivation and self-belief are important in the creation of the empowered learner identity. Research by Boekarts (2002), for example, indicates that motivational beliefs, which provide a frame of reference for pupils' feelings and actions in a given subject or task, result from learning experiences and serve either as a favourable context for learning or negatively to students who are not motivated to learn in the face of failure. Students who have strong positive beliefs about their capacity to learn achieve more highly. Self-regulatory skills are all about the learners' capacity to control and manage their own learning. Boekarts distinguishes between meta-cognitive skills (learning goals that refer to the learners' capacity to generate cognitive strategies in a context-specific way), meta-motivational and self-management skills. These are skills we want the learners to develop within the classroom community to enable them to become increasingly responsible for and independent in their learning. Teachers need to plan activities to encourage independent thinking and decision-making, so that the pupils can become more independent and self-reliant. Pupils who are encouraged by their teachers through feedback and well planned learning activities involving peer-work and assessment, self-assessment and other activities conducive to developing self-reliance and self-worth according to Linnenbrink and Pintrich (2002), can become well-motivated learners capable of substantial achievement. One pupil is cited by a teacher in this respect:

This is a student with confrontational behaviour issues who when he had the confidence, asked for extra work to support his application to take GCSE French. He got a National Curriculum level 7 when a level 4 was predicted. His confidence and belief in himself shot up.

Given the necessary support (Reid (2005), for example, is in favour of teachers paying attention to different learning styles or learner preferences; Nel (2008) suggests teachers need to be flexible in their teaching styles), then it becomes possible to redefine the language learners' identity as active agents in their learning. In this, learners have an awareness of their difficulties, but also of the range of self-regulating and self-supporting learning options available to them. In this way, the learners would be in a position to move from a state of passivity, sometimes helplessness and dependency on the judgment of others, to having a measure of agency, control and independence. They develop a positive sense of self-worth and capability.

Boaler's (2008: 167) research with maths students in the US can be insightful here for she asserts that teachers' pedagogic practices that engendered pupil talk and interactions, promoted what she terms *'relational equity'* through *'respect for other people's ideas leading to positive intellectual relations; commitment to the learning of others; and learned methods of communication and support'*. Such methods shaped learner identities as both active and sensitive to the needs of peers. This approach is equally valid for our budding linguists, I would suggest. In this way, learners could contribute to the task in hand in their own way, using a range of strategies and both supported by peers and supporting their peers, enhancing confidence and self-belief resulting from successes of varying kinds in the classroom.

Conclusion

Many language teachers, as a matter of course, include the majority of children into the language learning project because they believe that all learners are able to profit from and make a contribution to the classroom community, as suggested by the teachers' comments throughout this chapter. Teachers also need to feel secure that they can meet the challenge and have adequate support (Jones & McLachlan, 2009) and to demand appropriate, job-embedded and imaginative training that would include teamwork and networking (see European Commission Report, 2005, for examples in different countries that have transfer value). Teachers also need to plan the necessary support for use in class – as the teacher examples show – to avoid creating undue pressure or anxiety for learners in situations. One teacher stressed the need to: *'Have realistic expectations. Play towards the strength of the student. It is always important to know exactly what the student needs are and plan accordingly'*.

Talking to colleagues and pupils can provide useful insights into planning needs:

I talk to the SENCO a lot, and ask for advice for specific students (e.g. student with profound difficulties but no Learning Support Assistant – providing glossaries, preparing individualised copies of texts, giving thinking time, suggesting ways to work with a partner, etc).

Consulting pupils

Rudduck and McIntyre (2008) state that consulting the pupils about their learning experiences can give direct feedback that can help teachers to reflect on their practice and how to improve it. One teacher builds this into her practice on a regular basis thus: *'I ask the pupils 3-1, that means three things they like about my lesson, one they don't. I pay particular attention to the SEN students who need help sometimes to express themselves'*. Rudduck and McIntyre (2008: 30) suggest that this process would enable teachers to answer the following questions for the pupils: 'What is helpful and unhelpful for them in *my* classroom?' and 'What kinds of modifications to my lessons, to *my* ways of managing their learning, would make learning more attractive, easier, more effective for them?'. Fielding and Bragg (2003: 15–18) identify benefits for the pupils of a consultative dialogue about learning thus: *'a positive sense of self-agency ... new skills ... new social competences and new relationships ... a chance to be active and creative'*.

From teacher rhetoric to expertise

Reaping full benefits from pupil consultation requires pupil self-awareness and teacher knowledge of the specifics of SEN. Richardson (2011) points out that language teachers are often inadequately trained in the specifics of SEN, the needs of children with dyslexia, for example, or those on the autistic spectrum. Her research showed that the language-teaching community is generally functional in the general rhetoric of inclusion, but not always in the detailed knowledge required to make inclusion of varying needs a reality. The European Commission report (2005: 9) asserts that:

> There is a prevailing view that SEN children are somehow different and thus require different educational solutions. It is obviously true that some SEN learners need very specific language learning approaches. But it is also true that the same logic applied to good foreign language learning for non-SEN learners applies to those with SEN.

Working in partnership

The teachers sharing their views in this chapter have stressed the need to work in partnership with colleagues, even if this is rather 'last minute' (see quote below), be they in class as Teaching Assistants, or in the school community as leaders of SEN/ASN provision. This aspect of partnership cannot be over-emphasised in providing sustainable and cohesive support. A teacher comments:

> It is important to involve any Learning Support Assistants (LSA) in the LEARNING (*sic*). They may know even less than your SEN students! Give them resources ahead of time (or at least at the door). Give them a guide to phonetic pronunciation. Give a quick breakdown of the rule/ structure being focused on and, that way, if a student asks the LSA (and

they should feel able to do so!) they do not feel out of their depth. When I had an LSA in lessons I got a different one each time so pre-planning was impossible.

Another crucial aspect of partnership is that of effective primary–secondary liaison involving primary and secondary MFL teachers liaising to ensure a coherent and continuous learning experience building on individual strengths and successes. SEN in language learning, in addition to a child's strengths and achievements, would usefully be a feature of children's learning records that were part of transfer arrangements. This would assist secondary teachers in the process of continuing inclusion given that MFL learning in the primary school is entirely inclusive.

New technologies, new learner identities

Technology offers a range of new learning opportunities that are increasingly used in language classrooms, but it does not in itself provide a panacea to enable successful language learning for any learners, as one teacher said: 'Technology is not the be all and end all'. While significant advances have been made in technology, and languages classrooms often have the appearance of hi-tech, teacher access to and confidence with appropriate technology approaches and support are often problematic. The European Commission Report (2005: 17) claims that in many of today's classrooms: 'Although ICT learning programmes are available, there is often a problem with compatibility and the fact that they may rely on standard pedagogical approaches and methods', underlining the fact that new technologies require a rethink of pedagogy; technology cannot just be an add-on.

A teacher frame of mind that focuses on identifying strength and potential rather than weakness can aid learners to develop the confidence to be active and responsible learners as far as each is able. One teacher commented on the need thus to 'play to the strengths of the learner with SEN', and another in a similar vein said: 'I try to take the strengths of the student into account rather than focus on what they struggle with'. This supports the idea of learners embracing a new learner identity as capable linguists and at least part agents of their own learning, contributing their ideas and developing their strategies, especially in the face of their known limitations. Within such a framework that needs to be part of a whole school culture in which collaborative learning and formative assessment are well embedded (Ozga, 2002), technologies can have more prominence not just for teacher-controlled whole class navigation of learning (for this is still important in language learning where teacher models are necessary at strategic points), but also as options for all pupils as a way to make the learning their own, in their own way, in their own time, according to their own needs and in a way that is completely in tune with the way they, as youngsters, appropriate technologies in their daily lives and exploit language for their own purposes. Languages are also windows into other cultures and technologies can enable learners to enlarge their cultural horizons through virtual culture on the internet, for example, and more adventurously, to engage interactively with creating culture and sharing with youngsters in other cultures. uScreen (www.uScreen.co.uk), set up and run by Screen South, is part of Accentuate, The London 2012 Legacy Programme for the South East, and has created opportunities for accessible film making, collaboration and sharing on a global scale. These activities, designed for youngsters with disabilities as well as for those without, provide a platform for cross-curricularity (languages, culture, technology, film, drama, citizenship, social skills) and offer real authentic cultural and linguistic contexts for language learning and collaboration. They also meet the broader aim of intercultural engagement in language learning to which all learners have an entitlement.

Leadership and whole school involvement

Yet, pupils cannot undertake these endeavours alone, nor can their teachers: even rich resourcing that includes all manner of new technology and other support is alone inadequate to promote real and sustainable change in effective inclusive practice in MFL. For change to occur, effective leadership is a prerequisite (Harris & Lambert, 2003), and those leaders must build capacity for whole school improvement of inclusive practice, providing opportunities for all staff involved to work together in partnership to improve inclusive practice in general. Only within this context can language teachers respond to the question of *how better* and not *whether* to teach MFL to all. In so doing, in order to prevent what Grenfell (2000: 23) called *'something of a mirage'* of languages for all, teachers need to engage in ongoing exploratory and reflective research on their practice and monitor developments in the pedagogy of personalisation and in pupil achievements to ensure the sustainability of the inclusive language learning project.

References

Alexander, R. (2008) Culture, dialogue and learning: Notes on an emerging pedagogy. In N. Mercer and S. Hodgkinson (eds) *Exploring Talk in School*. London: Sage.
Anderson, J. (2000) Which language? An embarrassment of choice. In K. Field (ed.) *Issues in Modern Languages Teaching*. London: Routledge Falmer.

Black, P. and Wiliam, D. (1998) *Inside the Black Box: Raising Standards Through Classroom Assessment*. London: King's College London.

Black, P. and Wiliam, D. (2009) Developing the theory of formative assessment. *Educational Assessment, Evaluation and Accountability* 21 (1), 5–31.

Boaler, J. (2008) Promoting 'relational equity' and high mathematics achievement through an innovative mixed ability approach. *British Educational Research Journal* 34 (2), 167–194.

Boekarts, M. (2002) *Motivation to Learn. Educational Practices Series*. Paris: International Academy of Education-International Bureau of Education (UNESCO).

Booth, T., Nes, K. and Strømstrad, M. (eds) (2003) *Developing Inclusive Teacher Education*. London: Routledge Falmer.

Centre for British Teachers (2011) accessed 16 January 2013. http://www.cfbt.com/evidenceforeducation/our_research/evidence_for_government/national_policy_reforms/language_trends_survey.aspx.

Council of Europe (2011) In Piccardo, E., Berchoud, M., Cignatta, T., Mentz, O. and Pamula, M. *Pathways Through Assessing, Learning and Teaching in the CEFR*. ECML: Graz.

Council of Europe (2001) *Common European Framework of Reference for Languages: Learning, Teaching, Assessment*. Cambridge: CUP.

Coyle, D. (2007) Strategic classrooms: Learning communities which nurture the development of learner strategies. *Language Learning Journal* 35 (1), 65–79.

Crombie, M. (1997) The effects of specific learning difficulties (dyslexia) on the learning of a foreign language in school. *Dyslexia – An International Journal of Research and Practice* 3 (1), 27–47.

Deane, M. (1992) Teaching modern languages to pupils with SEN? With pleasure. *Language Learning Journal* 6, 43–47.

Department for Children, Schools and Families (DCSF) (2008) *Personalised Learning*, accessed 1 August 2012. http://www.Standards.dfes.gov.uk/personalisedlearning/about/

Department of Education and Science (DES) (1977) *Modern Languages in Comprehensive Schools*. London: HMSO.

Department for Education and Skills (DfES) (2002) *Languages for All: Languages for Life – A Strategy for England*. Nottingham: DfES.

Department for Education and Skills (DfES) (2004) In P. Driscoll, J. Jones and G. Macrory (eds) *The Provision of Foreign Language Learning for Pupils at Key Stage 2*. DfES Research Report 572. London: DfES.

Department for Education and Skills (DfES) (2007) In J. Sebba, N. Brown, S. Steward, M. Galton, and M. James (eds) *An investigation of Personalised Learning Approaches used by Schools*. DfES Research Report 843. London: DfES.

Dyson, A. (2001) Special needs in the twenty-first century: Where we've been and where we're going. *British Journal of Special Education* 28 (1), 24–29.

European Commission (2005) *Special Educational Needs in Europe: The Teaching and Learning of Languages: Insights and Innovations*. Brussels: European Commission DC EAC.

Fielding, M. and Bragg, S. (2003) *Students as Researchers: Making a Difference*. Cambridge: Pearson.

Florian, L. and Rouse, M. (2001) Inclusive practice in English secondary schools: Lessons learned. *Cambridge Journal of Education* 31 (3), 399–412.

Flutter, J. and Rudduck, J. (2004) *Consulting Pupils: What's in it for Schools?* London: Routledge Falmer.

Grenfell, M. (2000) Modern Languages – beyond Nuffield and into the 21st Century. *Language Learning Journal* 22 (1), 23–29.

Hargreaves, A. (1994) *Changing Teachers, Changing Times: Teachers' Work and Culture in the Post-Modern Age.* London: Continuum.

Harris, V. (1997) *Teaching Learners How to Learn; Strategy Training in the Modern Languages Classroom.* London: CILT.

Harris, A. and Lambert, L. (2003) *Building Leadership Capacity for School Improvement.* Maidenhead: Oxford University Press.

Hawkins, E. (ed.) (1996) *30 Years of Language Teaching.* London: CILT.

Heafford, M. (1993) What is grammar, who is she? *Language Learning Journal* 7, 55–58.

Hebert, E. (2001) *The Power of Portfolios.* San Francisco: Jossey Bass.

Hodgkinson, A. and Vickerman, P. (2009) *Key Issues in SEN and Inclusion.* London: Sage.

Inner London Education Authority (1977) *French For Us All? Why Not?* London: ILEA.

Ireson, J. and Hallam, S. (2001) *Ability Grouping in Education.* London: Sage.

Johnstone, R. (2008) Teaching a modern language to children at primary school: Making it work for all. *English Teaching and Learning* 32 (4), 1–40.

Jones, J. (2012) Portfolios as 'learning companions' for children and a means to support and assess Language Learning in the primary school. Education 3–13. *International Journal of Primary, Elementary and Early Years Education* 40 (4), 401–416.

Jones, J. and Coffey, S. (2006) *Modern Foreign Languages. A Guide for Teachers.* London: David Fulton Publishers.

Jones, J. and McLachlan, A. (2009) *Primary Languages in Practice. A Guide to Teaching and Learning.* Maidenhead: OUP McGraw-Hill Education.

Jones, J. and Wiliam, D. (2006) *Modern Foreign Languages Inside the Black Box.* London: GLA Assessment.

Klapper. J. (2003) Taking communication to task? A critical review of recent trends in language teaching. *Language Learning Journal* 27, 33–42.

Knowles, G. (2009) *Ensuring Every Child Matters.* London: Sage.

Linnenbrink, E.A. and Pintrich, P.R. (2002) Motivation as an enabler for academic success. *School Pyschology Review* 31 (3), 313–328.

Macaro, E. (2001) *Learning Strategies in Foreign and Second Language Classrooms.* London: Continuum.

MacBeath, J., Galton, M., Steward, S., MacBeath, A. and Page, C. (2006) *The Costs of Inclusion: A study of inclusion policy and practice in English primary, secondary and special schools.* Cambridge: University of Cambridge.

McColl, H. (2005) Foreign language learning and inclusion: Who? why? what? – and how? *British Journal of Language Support* 20 (3), 1–10.

Mitchell, R. (1994) The communicative approach to language teaching. In A. Swarbrick (ed.) *Teaching Modern Languages.* London: Routledge.

Mitchell, R. and Myles, F. (1998) *Second Language Learning Theories.* London: Arnold.

Mohammed, A. (1993) Towards a learner-centred technique of teaching grammar. *Language Learning Journal* 7, 59–63.

Montgomery, D. (1990) *Children with Learning Difficulties.* London: Cassell.

Nel, C. (2008) Learning style and good language learners. In C. Griffiths (ed.) *Lessons from Good Language Learners.* Cambridge: CUP.

OECD (2005) *Formative Assessment: improving learning in secondary classrooms.* OECD. Centre for Educational Research and Innovation.

Ozga, J. (2002) *School Culture and Policy Action in Educational Settings: Contested Terrains.* Buckingham: OUP.

QCA (2007) *The new secondary curriculum: what has changed and why?*, accessed 1 August 2012. http://dera.ioe.ac.uk/6564/1/qca-07-3172-new_sec_curric_changes.pdf

Reid, G. (2005) *Learning Styles and Inclusion*. London: Paul Chapman Publishing.

Richardson, C. (2011) Supporting the dyslexic pupil in the curriculum: Exploring inclusive practice in mainstream schools with special reference to dyslexic learners in the modern foreign languages classroom. Unpublished PhD thesis, King's College, London.

Robinson, C., Sebba, J., Mackrill, D. and Higgins, S. (2008) *Personalising Learning: The Learner Perspective and Their Influences on Demand*. Coventry: BECTA.

Rudduck, J. and McIntyre, D. (2007) *Improving Learning through Consulting Pupils*. London: Routledge.

Screen South (2011) accessed 31 January 2013. http://www.uScreen.co.uk.

Stobart, G. (2008) *Testing Times: The Uses and Abuses of Assessment*. London: Routledge.

The Education Act of 1944, The Butler Act. London: HMSO.

UNESCO (1994) *Salamanca Statement and Framework for Action on Special Needs Education*, accessed 15 January 2009. www.unesco.org/education/pdf/SALAMA_E.PDF

UNESCO (2003) *Overcoming Exclusion Through Inclusive Approaches in Education: A Challenge and a Vision*. Conceptual paper. Paris: UNESCO.

2 Technology Uses and Language – A Personal View

Chris Abbott

Introduction

> ...the search for pedagogical applications of new technologies ...has been a common challenge ... for many years. The careful assessment of the prospects provided by technologies of yesteryear and the extent to which those capabilities were actually harnessed may lead to a more judicious assessment of the pedagogical potential of modern technologies for future applications in L2 teaching and learning. (Salaberry, 2001: 52)

For those of us who were involved with education before the arrival of classroom computers, it was through audio that technology entered our language learning. Those who were pupils in the 1960s will remember the rapid rise of the Language Laboratory in what has been described as the 'Audiolingual Era' (Salaberry, 2001: 42), where communication seemed technologically mediated and the teacher could sometimes appear to be sitting on the flight deck of a spacecraft; perhaps not an unexpected phenomenon at the time. Such technology was didactic in nature, with the teacher very much in control and setting tasks for pupils. Any suggestion of technology as a tool for learners was still some way in the future, with these technologies privileging vocabulary over meaning, and promoting repetition and the regurgitation of set phrases.

By the 1970s, young teachers – and it was often the younger ones who got involved – could make use of a range of audio devices. Some made use of flash cards with magnetic backing, so that the word on a card could be heard in spoken form. With this technology, teachers could prepare resources at word level, choosing which words to pre-record on one side of the card and to write on the other. Inevitably, use of this type of technology privileged a vocabulary-building approach to language rather than any more holistic or communicative approach. The amount of speech that could be recorded was very limited until the next technological advance came along, and offered the amazing (for the time) possibility of a whole sentence of recorded speech on the reverse of an A4 card. This technology was far less widely taken up than the word-card devices, and the difficulties faced by teachers who wanted to create resources tended to result in the technology being seldom used to its full potential.

By the beginning of the 21st century, modern foreign languages (MFL) teaching was already in a position to look back at a long and informed use of a wide range of technologies, with one author reviewing this area as far back as 1916 (Salaberry, 2001). If indeed the *potential pedagogical uses of radio were naturally perceived as an extension of the benefits previously advanced for the use of the phonograph*' (Salaberry, 2001: 40), then it is clear that the use of technology has a long and distinguished history in the languages classroom. By the 1960s, he suggests, television was seen as '*a natural extension of the use of radio broadcasts*' (Salaberry, 2001: 41). In a fascinating diversion, he later discusses, not only the use of what he terms conventional technology, but also unconventional devices, such as voice reflectors, enabling learners to listen to their own pronunciation, and spectrographs that could present learners' language outputs in pictorial form. He also suggests that, when computers began to appear in classrooms more widely from the 1980s, technology tools for language learning developed further and their potential became clearer, and this was seen as change of a nature not seen before, as '*new technologies – revolutionary as they may be from a strictly technological point of view – are normally regarded as revolutionary from a pedagogical standpoint as well*' (Salaberry, 2001: 39).

Initially identified with maths and science departments, these computers eventually migrated from those subject bases to wider curriculum use as software tools developed and, crucially, as countries such as the UK and Denmark chose to promote the use of technology across the curriculum. From the beginnings of the UK National Curriculum in 1998, a requirement to use information and communication technology (ICT) across the curriculum in the UK led to rapid, if sometimes piecemeal, development of resources and working practices in this area. This was enthusiastically taken up by many teachers, particularly in view of the experience of technology on the part of MFL teachers, and it was noted in a major UK survey of computer use across the curriculum (Sutherland *et al.*, 2004) that MFL teachers were neither techno-phobic nor techno-positive as a community. They were, however, often willing to experiment and to be open to using new tools, and had *'developed productive ways of integrating ICT into their subject teaching'* (Sutherland *et al.,* 2004: 416).

ICT and Language Learning

For this writer, computers became available just in time, as I was moving from writing a Masters dissertation (on an electric typewriter) to the rather more daunting prospect of a PhD thesis. Access to a word processor began to change the way I write, so that – at least in my case – thoughts and ideas were inscribed on the screen far earlier in the composition process than they would have been with other writing tools. I have written elsewhere (Abbott, 2000) about the complex and developing relationship between literacy – especially schooled literacy – and digital technology. I would suggest that the summary of key aspects of the relationship put forward then still seems relevant more than 10 years later:

- ICT is changing our notion of what schooling consists of and how it should be delivered.
- Notions of literacy have changed and developed as a result of ICT, and literacy is central to most definitions of education.
- ICT in the classroom can be seen as part of a continuum dealing with the use of previous forms of instructional technology.
- Aspects of ICT offer access to information or the means of publication which may prove threatening to historically privileged individuals or states.
- ICT is becoming less related to the word-based text and is now essentially multimedia, involving sound, pictures and the moving image. (Abbott, 2000: 11)

If producing this summary today I would suggest that all these aspects of the relationship remain valid, although they might be couched in a language of intertextuality and multimodality, both of these being key foci of late 20th and early 21st century literacy (Kress & van Leeuwen, 2001). Society continues to see potential in ICT as an enabler of radical change within models of schooling, though these changes have remained stubbornly theoretical and extremely limited in practical implementation. Literacy today is rarely seen as related only to reading and writing, even by those policy makers and others who might have adhered to such reductionist definitions in the past. It not only remains central to education, but its successful mastery is seen by many as the paramount indicator of a successful education.

Recognition of changes in the nature of literacy, however, tends to be represented more often among education practitioners than policy-makers. As has been shown above, and will be further considered below, the use of ICT can, in many ways, be seen as a further development of previous practice in what was sometimes known as instructional technology or the use of audio-visual equipment, though with ICT – and in particular its use online and within networks – the line of development is perhaps blurred by the scale of change. The emancipatory and liberating possibilities of access to all through online publication have perhaps been problematised, ten years or more later, by those aspects of access that have resulted in the publication and dissemination of inappropriate or even harmful material; but the potential is still there for the sharing of real texts, with real audiences, across national and geographical boundaries. Finally, where the 2000 statement indicated a shift towards a multimedia environment, we now find ourselves in an almost wholly media-enhanced world – augmented reality rather than virtual reality – particularly through the rapid and widespread adoption of mobile technology and social networking.

As has been shown, the first use of technology within language classrooms tended to be related to practising the skills of listening and speaking. In the early days, writing was the focus, more often, for first language teaching than for MFL; although this changed as the word processor, and the demand for it, became ubiquitous. Early computer keyboards could not support writing in anything other than the Roman alphabet, with accents causing problems, and the other scripts required for some of the languages being studied in schools were impossible to produce on that early technology. Eventually, the education sector began to address this deficiency through the development of multi-lingual word processors, such as *Allwrite* in the Inner London Educational Authority, and this was followed by rapid development of built-in script changing options for all the main computer systems.

Reading was not a focus for technology-related teaching and learning except in a few specific instances, but it was a use of computers to support reading that opened the eyes of many teachers to the possibilities offered by digital technologies. *Devtray* (Developing Tray) was a very early computer program designed to enable teachers to prepare and manage a range of text prediction exercises. It turned out to be much more than mere cloze procedure however, since the combination of the affordances of the software and the changing dynamic of a collaborative group around a computer screen often led to a playful and sophisticated interaction with language. This was encouraged by its developers, who made much of the intention that there was no *'proper way to run a Devtray session . . . powerful users can make quite radically different uses of it'* (Moy, 1985: 3).

Based on a series of teacher workshops and rooted in the psycholinguistic understandings of reading that were current in its day (Smith, 1982), *Devtray* has survived to the present day, and a version is still sold to schools (www.2simple.com/devtray). It was *Devtray* that first showed something of the potential of technology tools for reading, for example when I used it to explore the text of a World War One sonnet with a group of reluctant learners in a special school classroom. Many of the group had considerable difficulties related to literacy and none of them had more than a limited understanding of the context of the set war poem, which was Wilfred Owen's *Anthem for Doomed Youth*. However, by encouraging them to focus on the text and to make full use of the contextual understanding that could be shared among the group, the program both enabled and encouraged a far more sophisticated engagement with the text than I could easily have encouraged without such a tool. Since then, *Devtray* and many other programs have been used in a wide range of languages to enable learners to explore, understand and interact with texts; indeed the very first release of the program in the 1980s included examples of MFL texts for use with the software.

As digital storage improved, multimedia resources became more accessible to schools, with texts in many languages, and associated images and video, stored on CD or DVD. It was with the arrival of the internet, however, that learners could much more readily have access to real texts in the language they were learning. For the first time, language teachers could access the day's news in a target language on the day of publication, as well as finding other articles of interest to young people and which might encourage them to become more proficient in the language they were learning.

In addition, the easy availability and reproduction of image, video and sound alongside text has led to a new understanding of the visual aspects of language (Heath & Wolf, 2004; Kress & van Leeuwen, 1996; Kress & van Leeuwen, 2001; Shaikh & Abbott, 2005). Indeed, for some learners, the use of images in the form of graphical symbols has enabled access to literacy – in first and other languages – for those to whom such resources were otherwise unattainable (Abbott *et al.*, 2006; Detheridge & Detheridge, 2002). Such graphical symbols, and the software to produce them, have proved to be a valuable tool for those enlightened teachers who have worked to bring MFL teaching to children with learning disabilities in special schools, offering them curriculum enhancement of a nature and extent not previously available.

Access to a wider range of speech engines has also transformed the potential of educational software that might previously have been of use in English alone. A speech engine is a software component that allows the computer to match particular words or combinations of letters with the sounds to which these are associated in a particular language. Without such a speech engine, text-to-speech programs would be unable to read aloud text in another language, at least not without sounding like the least impressive teenager in a French class. With the appropriate speech engine installed or accessible, learners are able to choose to have selected text read aloud to them, to listen to particular texts or phrases, or to listen to a whole newspaper news item to assess and develop their ability to acquire meaning from a spoken text. Speech engines are more sophisticated now with regard to accent in many languages, with the Scottish Government, for example, funding Scottish-accented voices that were launched as a free resource in 2011. Machine translation, once derided by many and unaffordably expensive, is now available to all through free tools such as Google Translate, and to a surprisingly high level of effectiveness and usability.

Faster networks and freely available tools such as Skype and FaceTime have brought what was once described as video-conferencing to a level of accessibility that enables its affordable use in the classroom. Provided teachers have the contacts and willingness to do so, it is now much easier to set up live language exchanges with native speakers in classrooms. Such tools can be used to waste time or for less appropriate purposes too, which has led some schools to block them from use on their networks. Language teachers may need to put forward a clear and justified case for the use of such video chat tools and for them to be enabled on school networks. That same issue may also arise with the use of online virtual environments such as Second Life; although there are many educationally owned or oriented areas in that environment, there are others that may not be suitable for classroom use. The potential of avatar creation for language learning is clear, however, and tools aimed at educational institutions in particular, such as Voki, may provide a more secure environment (see Chapters 7 and 8 for examples of Voki in use).

In addition to these developments based on aspects of social networking and powered by online access, some teachers and pupils also have access to technology such as interactive whiteboards (IWBs). Although originally seen, at least by policy makers in the UK, as didactic tools, these devices have been used by teachers to develop innovative group activities and to engage learners. Mobile technologies like phones, messaging devices and tablets have enabled online learning to continue outside the temporal and geographical confines of the classroom, a development that has been seen as an opportunity by some schools and a threat by others. Trying to hold back the tide of mobile technology use would seem to be a hopeless task however, and even the most hardline 'no mobiles' school will have to cave in as wearable devices become the norm.

Virtual reality, on the other hand, seems to wax and wane in fashion. Although the technical possibilities are much greater now, the playful virtual environments beloved by gamers and others seem to be giving way to augmented reality experiences, with the technology providing extra ways of experiencing a particular environment. In many ways, this is what assistive technologies have always done for those with special educational needs, particularly when used to support those with sensory or language impairments.

Social Networking and Languages

In addition to access to information, the internet has enabled an explosion in the communication and interaction technologies variously described as social networking, Web 2.0 or the semantic web. Just as the Web offered the means of worldwide publication to all in the 1990s, so the tools that have followed, like Twitter and Facebook, have made this publication easier, faster and even more pervasive. Although the use of these tools for social interaction among young people has been well documented (Abbott & Alder, 2009; Boyd, 2008), their use within formal education has been the subject of much less research (Buckingham, 2005; Milton, 2002; Snyder, 2002), although digitally supported collaboration in the classroom space has long been a subject for scholarly writing (Crook, 1994). At first, the emphasis was on the extent to which these new technologies might be creating new forms of language (Collot & Belmore, 1996; Crystal, 2001), but more recently the focus has shifted to the ways in which existing language power discourses and interactions are reproduced – or not – online, and new genres of writing, such as blogs and wikis, have developed (Knobel & Lankshear, 2006). Several of the other contributors to this volume have addressed this area, especially Vilar Beltrán in Chapter 5, who looks in some detail at language teachers' responses to learners today.

It is within this broad area of social networking and online collaboration that many teachers see the potential for far-reaching changes in the ways in which learners experience language in all its forms. The long-lasting dominance of English is increasingly challenged by a Web in which the number of sites in Chinese is fast approaching those in English. This is, however, a tentative assertion and difficult to support, not just because of the dynamic nature of the resource, but also because of the widely varying estimates that have been made by various sources. In addition, most of these sources are themselves consultancy companies working in the field of e-business, and sometimes keep their information behind firewalls for their customers only.

An examination of some of the statistical data that has been published online will give a picture that is illuminative and probably broadly representative. One website (www.internetworldstats.com) that offers a detailed set of statistics about languages found on the web is owned by a consultancy company, the Miniwatts Marketing Group. The data on this site suggest that, as of October 2011, there were more internet users who speak English as their main language than any other language. Chinese was in second place, followed by Spanish, Japanese and then Portuguese (www.internetworldstats.com/stats7.htm). These figures are not achieved by counting websites, but by comparing national populations with the percentage of known internet users for that group.

It is even more difficult to measure the number of websites in each language. Many different methodologies have been tried and most are in agreement that English is the language of less than half of the websites in the world, although beyond that there is little consensus. Despite the considerable challenges involved, a UNESCO report in 2010 attempted to use a combination of the existing datasets in order to estimate the proportion of websites in each language (Pimienta *et al.,* 2010). The authors are clear that there is a need to correct what they see as the mistaken impression that English is dominant on the web, and they make their case by reference to a wide range of methodologies. They suggest that, by the end of 2007, 45% of web content was in English, compared with 75% in 1998 (Pimienta *et al.,* 2010: 33). However, the particular languages studied did not include Chinese, and, as the authors acknowledge, there is '*a massive Chinese online presence*'. Unfortunately, the methodology adopted by the authors of this report could not assess web content in ideographic languages such as Chinese.

Within Europe, many EU-funded research projects have explored issues related to the use of technology for language learning, although all too often the outcomes of those projects, worthy though they may be, have sunk without trace within the vast number of such activities. Listings do exist, however, for example at the EU Language Policy site (http://ec.europa.eu/languages/eu-language-policy/studies_en.htm) and at CORDIS, the home of the EU Research and Development Information Service (http://cordis.europa.eu/projects/home_en.html). All past EU funded projects are listed here, together with links to their outcomes and the tools, guides and findings made available.

How, then, might we describe the opportunities that have opened up for teachers of languages? As with other areas of technologies, it is possible to classify the possibilities according to the level of support they offer. A taxonomy put forward as a means of classifying assistive technologies use in general (Abbott, 2007) could also be applied to the use of technology – especially online technology – to support language teaching:

- Technology uses to practise language learning.
- Technology uses to assist language learning.
- Technology uses to enable language learning. (Adapted from Abbott, 2007)

Technology Uses to Practise Language Learning

It was often the case in the early years of technology use within education that there was confusion between learning and practice. As far ago as the 1960s, developers were selling microfiche readers with multiple choice tests, possibly of use for revision before exams, but described by their makers as teaching machines. Often termed drill and practice products by their developers, these technologies have sometimes been given less positive names such as *'Computer Aided Instruction: Drill and (S)kill'* (Salaberry, 2001). With their origins in a Skinnerian model of behaviourist learning, these technologies held sway for some years in the classroom in the absence of alternatives marketed as enthusiastically, being used as what has been described as *'a substitute for human drillmasters'* (Lambert, 2001: 359).

There is certainly a place in the classroom, however, for technology that will continue to provide opportunities for practice without learners tiring, growing irritable or losing interest. Whether the learner develops any of those responses will depend upon the degree of interest, variety and response built in to the practice tool. Early software too often fell into the category of what was then called drill and practice, and much of it failed to find a sustainable place in the classroom precisely because the variety of activities was not wide enough, the examples not numerous enough and the responses required of the learner were not sufficiently varied. Pedagogical practices for the use of such technology were often given little attention, with teachers and learners given little guidance as to the appropriate amount of time to use such tools, whether to do so individually or in groups and how these activities could be integrated into the daily life of the classroom.

Loucky (2002) investigated the use of digital dictionaries, in his case with Japanese students learning English, and found that a range of such devices were available even at the time of his study, and that their effective use depended on their integration into a clear strategy for vocabulary learning. Focusing on *'short-term gains in passive recognition and active productive vocabulary'* (Loucky, 2002: 297), and using a range of different devices, he found that the devices were most effectively used by the most able students. He also noted that the weight of Japanese–English and English–Japanese dictionaries was such that no students carried both in printed form, so any digital tool offered a considerable advantage.

Technology Uses to Assist Language Learning

A use of technology that has increased rapidly in recent years is that of assisting learning; in effect, the technology is used as a tool to help a learner by providing information, support or guidance. This change is reflected in the terminology; in his history of the use of technology in MFL teaching, Salaberry (2001) notes the change from computer-aided instruction (CAI) to computer-assisted language learning (CALL), and the associated development in understanding on the part of teachers. He also reminds us of the claims made for CAI and the very limited evidence base for these, since there is *'little or no empirical evidence – let alone theoretical analysis – supported such a categorical contention in favour of the effectiveness of CAI at the time'* (Salaberry, 2001: 49).

For example, at the simplest end, an online dictionary could be seen to fulfil this role, or a learning framework that is designed to guide the learner through a particular activity. Many technologies that assist learning are essentially teacher tools, in a sense the 21st century equivalent of audio-visual support or language laboratories. With the aid of such tools, teachers are able to prepare and store materials, offer differentiated tasks to learners and provide extension activities for those able to undertake them. The rapid development of technology as a teacher support tool is evident in the changing shape of staffrooms, most of which have transformed from something resembling a club lounge to a cross between a computer laboratory and a busy back office. For learners, technology to assist is too often reliant on parental support and access to funding, although initiatives such as the Home Computer Scheme in the UK have made inroads, as have the various initiatives to develop low-cost computers for classroom use, especially in countries with no widespread ICT infrastructure. An example of the latter is the development of the *Aakash* tablet computer in India, launched in 2012 and claimed to be the world's cheapest tablet PC. Tablet PCs themselves – and the smartphones to which they are generically related – are likely to become the technology of choice for the next few years for the digital resources that learners need regular and easy access to, as they undertake classroom tasks.

Technology can also assist in the assessment of modern language teaching, and this was the focus of a paper by Hunt et al. (2007), who conducted a European survey of technology use in the assessment of language skills and compared this with the UK context. They noted that the piecemeal development of technology use in the sector had increased pace more recently, with access to the internet and multimedia resources being driving factors. Turning to computer-aided assessment (CAA), they then describe the benefits of ICT for formative assessment in particular, and the continuing move to various forms of e-assessment. Hunt *et al.*, together with their European partners, developed a tool that could enable comparison of language achievement across national boundaries, something not possible previously. The project also collected data about the electronic resources in use in each of the partner countries (Denmark, England, Finland, Italy, Norway, Poland and Romania), and then assessed the value of each resource for the key language skills of reading, writing, listening and speaking. They also noted the potential of ICT for assessment for learning (rather than assessment of learning), but also showed that this was more marked in England than elsewhere.

> Two major differences between the English scene and the European scene are the range of languages used and the relative importance of formative versus summative assessment.
>
> In other European countries, English tends to be the most commonly taught MFL, ... the traditional dominance of French in England has been challenged, and there is also demand for teaching in the home languages of English as an additional language (EAL) learners. Commercial providers, especially, are likely to find the demand for these languages less rewarding than providing resources for TEFL, where adult learners require fluency for work or training purposes. The nature of this demand for TEFL also affects the type of assessment demanded. It was notable that respondents to the ON-LANG survey placed greater emphasis on summative, as compared to formative, assessment, and less emphasis on interaction and creativity, than might be expected in English practice. The resources were also most commonly suited to individual learning rather than group or class work. (Hunt *et al.*, 2007: 210)

Technology Uses to Enable Language Learning

Technology can do more than enable learners to practise or even to provide essential tools to assist learning; in certain circumstances and with the enthusiastic and expert support of technology-aware teachers, it can enable learning where it would otherwise not take place. In a further development of terminology, this is often within the area described as CMC – computer-mediated communication.

Online automated instant translation as described earlier, imperfect and unreliable though it may be, is also improving all the time and it is easy to forget that such tools needed extremely powerful computers and very deep pockets only a few years ago, but are now available free of charge to all with an internet connection. Although many remain sceptical of the potential of this area, it is important that educators are involved in developing these technologies, which has not always been the case, as was noted more than ten years ago.

> ... [The language teaching] community was unrepresented and, more generally, has participated very little in the development of machine translation. When language professionals do participate, they are often linguists interested in 'natural languages' and transformational grammar, not in the specifics of particular languages. The widely held belief among Foreign Language teachers that machine translation does not and cannot work inhibits their participation in what is a major development.... (Lambert, 2001: 359)

Online chat and forum discussion systems – used within education to discuss academic points and put forward hypotheses – have traditionally been limited not by geography but by language, although synchronous communication such as real-time chat has also, to some extent, been constrained by time zones, and, in the past, expense.

> ... [Technology has been used as] a means of providing opportunities to communicate with native speakers through the Internet, although the expense of real-time, face-to-face electronic interaction is so high [this was the case in 2001 although not an issue today] and the proficiency level of the American learners is so low that sustained communication is limited. Perhaps student exposure to new, emerging forms of language use like cyber-Spanglish will spur interest in learning. (Lambert, 2001: 359)

The advent of almost instantaneous translation is already enabling some degree of communication across language barriers, with each respondent pasting texts into a translation tool and then sending the outcome. This produces a somewhat stilted conversation, but should be seen only as the early form of what will become a vital tool for international dialogue. Already it is possible, even with free tools, to see the phrase appearing in the target language as it is being typed in the native one, with the result changing and re-building as the software attempts to deal with idiom and grammar. Automated translation is also much more representative of current speakers than is the human translator, although the latter is much more correct since s/he has learned the language rather than derived it from many millions of examples of how it is used.

Automated translation could prove truly revolutionary when married to other technologies moving from the research laboratory to the marketplace. Brain–computer interfaces are one example, with the possibility of a user sending messages to a computer through brain activity resulting in words appearing on a computer screen. Linking this to automated translation could result in a thought in, say, English appearing on a computer screen in Spanish – perhaps therefore enabling the originator to learn about the language and experiment with alternative modes of expression.

Conclusion – What Does This Mean For Inclusion?

Digital technologies for language learning – including online technologies – are now at a level of maturity where they can be used both widely and with informed understanding on the part of educators. It is essential, therefore, that these valuable tools are made available to all learners and not just to those who are adept at language learning. All learners deserve to benefit from a learning environment that is more than monolingual, but as Salaberry suggests below, this requires that teachers have a nuanced and rich understanding of the affordances of the technology.

> Although matters of research design and empirical analysis are important, it is possible that the most important challenge posed by technology-assisted language learning will be the identification of the pedagogical objective that technology-based teaching is intended to fulfil....I argue that the concept of the pedagogical objective of technology-based instruction must be identified as a separate theoretical construct from the features that define technological resources. (Salaberry, 2001: 50)

No country can afford to ignore the potential of technology for language learners, and some countries previously denied access to these tools are now rapidly acquiring the necessary skills and resource, for example in Central and Eastern Europe (Wetzl, 2010). Focusing on Romania in particular, she describes how technology was seized upon enthusiastically following the change of regime after 1989, with resources such as mobile phones and computers being much sought after. Changes in languages teaching followed, with the traditional dominance of Russian as a second language in schools being lost to English, although many of these developments were related to urban rather than rural areas. As with so many countries, minority communities – in this case the Romani – were most deprived of access. More recent governments in Romania saw access to technology – and to the teaching of English – as a route out of poverty, and a challenge to the increasing tendency for citizens to move abroad.

> ...technology was welcomed by Romanians as a possible answer to the problems created by forty-five years of communism. The access to modern technology was denied to Romanians for so long that they equated access with freedom. Updating the technology infrastructure was also a prerequisite to the much coveted a ccession to the EU. Besides the drive for modernization, politicians also called for ...competency in ...English and French. It was believed that digital literacy and English skills increased the chances for Romanian graduates to gain employment as Western companies started investing in Romania; promoted communication and learning about the world through the Internet; and allowed the former communist nations, through their young representatives, to participate in the globalized world. (Wetzl, 2010: 121)

As we begin to see the potential of new ways of controlling computers, such as brain interfaces, the vastly improved accuracy of speech recognition, and as we acknowledge the rapid development of much improved and freely available automatic translation, we can begin to glimpse the possibilities afforded by a combination of these developments. The language learner of the future, as we have suggested, will be able use technology to turn speech into text, and will be able to reply by thinking a response onto a computer screen in another language, where rapid translation tools will be able to assist in proofing and tidying the results. All of these tools exist; we await only their joining together into a suite of technologies that, with the assistance of informed and expert teachers of language, will enable all our learners to be included in a multilingual future.

References

Abbott, C. (2000) *ICT: Changing Education*. London: RoutledgeFalmer.

Abbott, C., Detheridge, T. and Detheridge, C. (2006) *Symbols, Literacy and Social Justice*. Leamington: Widgit.

Abbott, C. (2007) *e-Inclusion: Learning Difficulties and Digital Technologies*. Bristol: Futurelab.

Abbott, C. and Alder, W. (2009) Social networking and schools: Early responses and implications for practice. In S. Hatzipanagos and S. Warburton (eds) *Handbook of*

Research on Social Software and Developing Community Ontologies (pp. 18–26). Hershey, New York: IGI Global.

Boyd, D. (2008) Why youth (heart) social nework sites: The role of networked publics in teenage social life. In D. Buckingham (ed.) *Identity*. USA: MIT Press.

Buckingham, D. (2005) *Schooling the Digital Generation: Popular Culture, New Media and the Future of Education*. London: Institute of Education.

Collot, M. and Belmore, N. (1996) Electronic language: A new variety of English. In S.C. Herring (ed.) *Computer-Mediated Communication: Linguistic, Social and Cross-Cultural Perspectives*. Amsterdam: Benjamins.

Crook, C. (1994) *Computers and the Collaborative Experience of Learning*. London: Routledge.

Crystal, D. (2001) *Language and the Internet*. Cambridge: Cambridge University Press.

Detheridge, M. and Detheridge, T. (2002) *Literacy Through Symbols: Improving Access for Children and Adults* (2nd edn). London: David Fulton Publishers.

Heath, S.B. and Wolf, S. (2004) *Visual Learning in the Community School*. London: Creative Partnerships.

Hunt, M., Neill, S. and Barnes, A. (2007) The use of ICT in the assessment of modern languages: The English context and European viewpoints. *Educational Review* 59 (2), 195–213.

Knobel, M. and Lankshear, C. (2006) Weblog worlds and constructions of effective and powerful writing: Cross with care, and only where signs permit. In K. Pahl and J. Rowsell (eds) *Travel Notes from the New Literacy Studies: Instances of Practice* (pp. 72–92). Clevedon: Multilingual Matters.

Kress, G. and van Leeuwen, T. (1996) *Reading Images: The Grammar of Visual Design*. London: Routledge.

Kress, G. and van Leeuwen, T. (2001) *Multimodal Discourses*. London: Arnold.

Lambert, R. (2001) Updating the foreign language agenda. *The Modern Language Journal* 85 (3), 347–362.

Loucky, J.P. (2002) Improving access to target vocabulary using computerized bilingual dictionaries. *ReCALL* 14 (2), 295–314.

Milton, J. (2002) *Literature Review in Languages, Technology and Learning*. Bristol: NESTA Futurelab.

Moy, B. (1985) Introduction. In J. Stephens (ed.) *Devtray Teaching Documents* (pp. 2–3). London: ILEA.

Pimienta, D., Prado, D. and Blanco, A. (2010) *Twelve Years of Measuring Linguistic Diversity in the Internet: Balance and Perspectives*. Paris: UNESCO.

Salaberry, M.R. (2001) The use of technology for second language learning and teaching: a retrospective. *The Modern Language Journal* 85 (1), 39–56.

Shaikh, A. and Abbott, C. (2005) Visual representation in the digital age: Issues arising from a case study of digital media use and representation by pupils in a multicultural school setting. *Language and Education* 19 (6), 455–466.

Smith, F. (1982) *Writing and the Writer*. New York: Holt, Rinehart and Winston.

Snyder, I. (ed.) (2002) *Silicon Literacies: Education, Communication and the New Technologies*. London: Routledge.

Sutherland, R., Armstrong, V., Barnes, S., Brawn, R., Breeze, N., Gall, M., Matthewman, S., Olivero, F., Taylor, A., Triggs, P., Wishart, J. and John, P. (2004) Transforming teaching and learning: Embedding ICT into everyday classroom practices. *Journal of Computer Assisted Learning* 20, 413–425.

Wetzl, A. (2010) Digital education in Eastern Europe: Romania's modern affair with technology. *Computers and Composition* 27, 112–213.

3 Meeting Special Educational Needs in Technology-Enhanced Language Teaching: Learning from the Past, Working for the Future

David Wilson

Introduction

In our digital age, information and communication technology (ICT) is routinely deployed as a strategy to reach and teach all students within modern foreign language (MFL) classrooms around the world. Some two decades have elapsed since the terms 'special educational needs' (SEN), 'sonderpädagogischer Förderbedarf', 'besoins éducatifs particuliers' and 'bisogni educativi speciali' entered European educational 'officialese', signalling a change of direction to accommodate the implications of learner diversity and educational inclusion for the delivery of school curricula across the continent. Half a century ago, the world's first computer-assisted language learning (CALL) program was successfully trialled in the United States of America. Truly, ICT for learners of MFL with SEN is an international phenomenon with a proud history. However, challenges persist, as long as certain adults still expect too little from MFL learners with SEN while assuming too much about what ICT can do to deliver the subject.

The present chapter highlights, among many, six key points to be considered when introducing, delivering and reviewing ICT-enhanced MFL courses for those that find learning difficult. The moral of Lessons One and Two is that good practice in the field lies neither in a single geographical area nor in a single historical period. Lessons Three and Four dissect the roles of SEN professionals, MFL teachers and other stakeholders in providing a broad and balanced curriculum for every learner with additional needs. Lessons Five and Six discuss how learners with SEN challenge our preconceptions and how modern technology enriches everybody's lives when it is harnessed by MFL teachers whose primary concern is the welfare of their human charges, not how cutting-edge their choice of computer hardware or software might be.

Lesson One: Compare and Adapt

No single nation, institution or individual has the monopoly of knowledge and wisdom when developing technology usage to reach and teach every foreign language learner. It is therefore essential to import best practice from the world's centres of excellence, making adjustments to suit our circumstances.

ICT usage in teaching MFL to learners with SEN has an extensive geography. Although CALL originated in the USA in the early 1960s, it gradually spread around the English-speaking world, from Canada and the UK in the north to South Africa, Australia and New Zealand in the south, where a 'Canterbury Monograph for Teachers of French' entitled *Computers in Language Teaching* (Collett, 1980) appeared in 1980. In the mid- and late-1980s, among other continental European countries, France (Janitza, 1985), West Germany (Langenscheidt-Redaktion, 1985), Italy (Mazzotti, 1987), Denmark (Böss *et al.*, 1988), Hungary (Kecskés, 1987) and the Netherlands (Bongaerts *et al.*, 1988) spawned CALL publications of their own.

The journals, conferences and online forums of national and international CALL organisations, e.g. CALICO, EUROCALL, AsiaCALL and WORLDCALL, have also played their part in propagating knowledge and good practice to the four corners of the world. In the summer of 2000 I flew to the Japanese city of Kobe to present a paper on building bridges to inclusive foreign language education through appropriately applied technologies (Wilson, 2001a) at FLEAT IV, the Fourth Conference on Foreign Language Education and Technology, hosted by the Japan Association for Language Education and Technology, the North America-based International Association for Language Learning Technology and the Korea Association of Multimedia-Assisted Language Learning. The overwhelming majority of the speakers at FLEAT IV hailed from the Far East and their presentations in

English as a second language testified to the success of CALL in countries such as Japan, Korea and Taiwan. Technology-enhanced language learning is now a worldwide phenomenon.

Many authors of printed CALL publications tend to concentrate less on school students and more on an academically talented élite enrolled in higher education, but they often come up with advice applicable to learners of every nationality, age and ability: *'In addition to being a promoter of positive interactive and social experiences, the computer can sometimes encourage a form of "anti-social behaviour" that amounts to working in isolation from others'* (Pennington, 1996: 10). At the turn of the new millennium, a desire to use computers to enable language learners with sensory impairments to interact, not only with courseware but also with able-bodied and disabled peers, inspired individuals to conduct computer-based learning projects within educational institutions in two different continental European countries. Such initiatives, *mutatis mutandis*, appear to be replicable anywhere and exemplify how groundbreaking CALL also thrives outside the Anglophone world.

In the first continental European project, a teacher with a doctorate in visually impaired CALL deployed computers as communication tools to promote inclusion in English classes at Laski School for the Blind in Poland. This research arose from his conviction that:

Visual impairment may, and in numerous cases does, hinder social communication. Limited use and perception of body language become hurdles lined up along the communication track. Frozen postures and expressionless faces discourage sighted speakers to continue their turn in a dyadic discourse. Adding to it Braille, which is illegible for the majority in any community, the visually impaired, and the blind in particular, end up neglected and often underestimated. (Wiązowski, 2002: 2)

Computer-mediated communication (CMC), still relatively novel back then, proved to be a versatile digital solution to the problem of social exclusion for visually impaired Polish learners of English. Synchronous (chat) and asynchronous (electronic mail) communication tools in particular empowered these students to launch an exchange of messages and documents with individuals and schools abroad and to engage them in a collaborative enterprise centring on the construction of an 'online multilingual dictionary of sounds and noises'.

The use of CMC to benefit learners of English with a sensory impairment was also at the heart of the second continental European initiative, which ran between March and May 2000 (Hilger, 2000). This 'intercultural cooperation project' involved senior students at a deaf school in southern

Germany exchanging emails with their hearing peers at a high school in the US state of North Carolina. As a pilot project, the email exchange lasted just six weeks and covered just two pre-agreed topics – 'Getting to know each other' and 'Presenting our school' – but the experience not only gave the German hearing-impaired students' English a good workout, but also circumvented the barriers arising whenever the lip-reading skills of the deaf and the sign-language skills of the hearing leave something to be desired. An article confirming that email writing helped to improve the written English of German deaf school students appeared two years later (Költzsch, 2002).

Lesson Two: Look Back and Remember

Although the so-called 'state of the art' in digital technology, learning theory and subject methodology sounds like a good starting point, obsolescence and flux have already compromised its integrity. Our future prospects in the field depend on us understanding better how technology, theory, methodology and not least we classroom practitioners, have evolved over time, as we teach languages in general and learners with SEN in particular.

The use of digital technology in the teaching of MFL to students with SEN has a long history, subsumed not only in the development of CALL since the 1960s, but also enshrined in the personal experiences of teachers who learned foreign languages with the occasional help of technology. I maintain a bibliography of online and printed articles supporting inclusion in MFL through information and communications technologies (Wilson, 2007). Most of the 100-odd references are synchronic studies describing projects, materials and small-scale research exercises, written during the 1990s and the first decade of the new millennium. Retrospective and diachronic studies in the field are sparse.

The professional literature of CALL dates back half a century to the proceedings of an American conference of 10–12 October 1961 on 'Application of Digital Computers to Automated Instruction', which featured a paper describing how a mainframe computer was programmed to accept typed English renderings of German words, to keep a record of wrong answers, to print scores and to make comments varying from 'Dummkopf' to 'hot dog' (Licklider, 1962). Though methodologically and technologically innovative then, the principle of computer-delivered drill-and-practice, often thinly disguised as game-playing, still dominates task-setting in our modern age when courseware developers aspire to meet the diverse needs of all learners within the context of a more communicative approach to MFL teaching.

Technology in the form of language laboratories found its way into the foreign language education of the visually impaired as early as the mid-1960s:

> The teachers who conducted language laboratory experiments at Liverpool's Royal School for the Blind in 1966 hailed the particular advantages of using the tape recorder for blind students. Despite reservations that the language lab machinery created a barrier (especially pertinent to blind children who received much individual tuition anyway and risked feeling isolated), they valued especially the opportunity recordings gave for 'active listening' whereby pupils would follow the tape with a Braille transcript. (Couper, 1996: 7)

By way of contrast, my own introduction to the language laboratory was a disabling experience. During my year abroad in France in the late 1960s, I opted for an advanced French for foreigners course at the local university. I was keen to improve my listening skills and was excited at the prospect of using a language laboratory for the first time. All I remember of the session, however, was my sense of isolation and frustration as I grappled vainly in my booth with pattern drills requiring thirty-word sentences in the present tense to be heard and reproduced at speed from memory in the imperfect tense while a disembodied voice intoned 'Vous êtes britannique, n'est-ce pas?' Although my training in the grammar-translation school of language learning had equipped me to cope with the transformation of written French verb forms, the unfamiliar audio-lingual method implicit in the language laboratory drills required the manipulation of extended spoken French utterances without the support of a written French text. The students at the Royal School for the Blind at least had their Braille transcript.

When BBC microcomputers appeared in UK schools during the early 1980s, the Centre for Information on Language Teaching and Research (CILT) published a ground-breaking guide to computers, language and language learning, which embraced the idea of using computers to support struggling learners challenged by traditional language teaching. Using the historically appropriate terms 'slow learner' (a student with learning difficulties) and 'remedial class' (a group of students withdrawn for specialist interventions) that SEN professionals routinely employed in the early 1980s, the author, a British pioneer of CALL, wrote:

> The computer (...) has the patience of Job, does not mind how many errors the learner makes and does not laugh at stupid mistakes. Moreover,

the slow learner is no longer sent to the remedial class but to a piece of sophisticated hardware which is not associated with any particular skills that may be lacking. (Davies, 1982: 23)

By the mid-1980s, this vision of 'CALL for struggling learners' became more of a reality. For example, *Granville*, a leading-edge computer simulation of a French town, was trialled by one comprehensive school modern language department in rural Eastern England with a 'remedial group' of 13–14 year olds:

Each pupil has a diary in which he records how to operate the program and useful French words met within it. Two groups of six pupils are then formed and take a computer each, being assisted by either their regular teacher or the French assistant. Each team member accomplishes one task on the computer, and all six tasks and their consequences, price, time, weather, transport, for example, are noted down by the other team members. Then the diary in the 'Journal' is printed out, and the pupils use the print-out and their notes to write a newspaper account in English on 'Lucky Prizewinner's Day Out in Granville'. (Council for Educational Technology, 1986: 52)

Most of the learners had been identified as in need of help, especially in their writing, yet their computer and problem-solving skills and their ability to reach group decisions were most encouraging.

Lesson Three: Identify, Assess and Provide

Although SENCOs (Special Educational Needs Coordinators) and other SEN professionals have overall responsibility for the identification and assessment of children with SEN and for the special educational provision made for them, these access arrangements will affect the classroom practice in general, and the technology usage in particular, of MFL teachers of such students with SEN.

According to the current *Special Educational Needs Code of Practice* (CoP), the 'manual' of the English primary and secondary school SENCO, school-age children have SEN:

if they have a *learning difficulty* which calls for *special educational provision* to be made for them. Children have a *learning difficulty* if they: (a) have a significantly greater difficulty in learning than the majority of children of the same age; or (b) have a disability which prevents or hinders them from making use of educational facilities of a kind generally provided for children of the same age in schools within the area of the local education authority. (. . .) *Special educational provision* means (...) educational provision which is additional to, or otherwise different from, the educational provision made generally for children of their age in schools maintained by the LEA, other than special schools, in the area. (Department for Education and Skills, 2001: 6)

The CoP also introduced three stages of provision: School action, where all provision is 'in-house'; School action plus, where outside agencies, e.g. educational psychologists, are involved; and Statement, where the local authority draws up a legally enforceable document of entitlement. Over the years, for school census purposes, the British government proposed official categories of additional needs:

- Cognitive and learning difficulties: moderate learning difficulties (MLD), severe learning difficulties (SLD), profound and multiple learning difficulties (PMLD); specific learning difficulties.
- Social, emotional and behavioural difficulties (SEBD).
- Communication and interaction difficulties: autistic spectrum disorders (ASD), speech, language and communication needs (SLCN).
- Sensory and physical disabilities: hearing impairment (HI), visual impairment (VI) and physical disabilities (PD).

Although the school SENCO is responsible for identifying and recording a school student as having SEN, both language teachers and digital technology have a part to play in the identification process. If students attend lessons in the subject, their MFL teacher will be asked about the progress they have made. SENCOs may also set a computer-based battery of tests to determine whether students meet the criteria of being 'at risk'. After administering assessments in the guise of games, these general 'screeners' typically output a bar-chart profile of learners' relative strengths and weaknesses in visual and auditory memory, sound-letter correspondence, general intelligence and other key areas with implications for education in general and language learning in particular. Other narrower-focused computer software may be deployed in the case of a particular condition; by way of example, after screening individuals with Irlen Syndrome, one program will recommend a colour for the translucent plastic overlay to be used by sufferers when reading printed text on white paper. Although such technology is a routine instrument in the modern SENCO's toolbox, the human dimension remains paramount because an appropriately qualified person must still observe/assist the learner at work, interpret the results and draw the conclusions.

Special educational provision is about equalising learning opportunities for otherwise disadvantaged students by providing them with human and material resources to meet their additional needs. When this provision involves technology, the training needs of the student, the teacher and the classroom assistant, if applicable, must be factored into the procurement of the necessary hardware or software. As with screening, the initial decision-making about cross-curricular computer support rests with the SENCO, who may seek the advice of the school's ICT subject teachers and technicians, particularly if software has to be installed on the school's computer network. In matters of SEN-specific electronic resources, e.g. input devices, portable word processors and literacy development programs, the SENCOs themselves may be prepared to 'cascade' training to all the interested parties, including the students, who will want to use their new acquisitions across the school curriculum. Other, non-SEN-specific equipment, such as portable computers, will require some cross-curricular pooling of knowledge and expertise to ensure that, say, a laptop's package of word processing, presentation and, if applicable, online communications software not only meets the additional needs of the student but also matches the subject-specific expectations of a broad, balanced and age-appropriate curriculum. Sometimes a little tweaking of computer settings is all that is required to increase font sizes for the partially sighted, to switch background colours for someone with specific learning difficulties or to make foreign character generating alt-key combinations easier for an individual with manual dexterity issues.

The special assessment needs of otherwise disadvantaged public examination candidates must also be met. According to the rules:

> access arrangements are not intended to give candidates an unfair advantage, but to give all candidates a level playing field in which to demonstrate their skills, knowledge and understanding (…) Centres should request access arrangements which reflect the candidate's normal way of working and for which there is evidence of need, (…) unless such arrangements would affect the integrity of the assessment. (Joint Council for Qualifications, 2010: 1, 3)

Such access arrangements may involve the use of technology, e.g. a word processor, or the substitution of human support for technology, e.g. the use of a live speaker instead of an audio recording to enable a candidate with hearing loss to lip-read during an aural test.

Procedures and interventions designed to meet special educational and assessment needs are subject to regular review involving all interested parties, including the SENCO, outside agencies, local authority SEN officers, subject teachers, classroom assistants, parents and, last but not least, learners themselves, who may outgrow an electronic resource or require further training in its use as they progress to more challenging work.

Lesson Four: Differentiate, Support and Collaborate

A school's SENCO can provide vital information and advice for MFL teachers working with students with SEN in general and delivering computer-based learning in particular. However, while the SENCO starts from the additional needs of the individual student, the MFL teacher's point of departure is the curriculum subject for which they are responsible. Both approaches are complementary and necessary for successful professional teamwork.

When teaching a heterogeneous class of learners, ranging from the gifted and talented to those with marked mother-tongue literacy problems, MFL classroom practitioners will often meet the challenge by differentiating their delivery to match the needs of particular groups of students. In the case of computer-based MFL lessons, there will be a need for multi-step extension work to stretch the more able students and for single-step tasks designed to be within reach of those that find learning difficult. Off-computer follow-up activities will also be necessary for all to ensure that everybody remains on task and consolidates the knowledge and skills acquired through the teacher presentation and the computer-based work.

MFL teachers who have taken the time to read the records of students with SEN in their charge will be forearmed when devising and setting computer-based tasks for them. The following ten case studies serve to exemplify the major categories of SEN as they apply to MFL classroom practice with lower secondary school students. Each scenario presents not only a challenge but also an ICT opportunity.

Case study 1: Anna – a modern foreign language native speaker with literacy difficulties

Anna has just arrived from Switzerland, where she attended primary school. One of the country's three major languages is her mother tongue, which also happens to be taught as a foreign language within your school. Anna's mother believes her daughter has literacy difficulties in her mother tongue and she wants Anna to study her native language at school as the family may later return to Switzerland.

Potential linguistic talent and SEN are not mutually exclusive. ICT can come to the rescue here: Swiss school diagnostic reading tests in

Anna's mother tongue may be purchased online, while she can be found more advanced tutorial software to promote her native language skills.

- It would be useful to explore online SEN practice in Swiss Schools.
- Challenging but age-appropriate tutorial software needs to be identified.

Case study 2: Ben – a foreign language learner with moderate learning difficulties (MLD)

Ben has been referred to an educational psychologist who has diagnosed MLD. Ben's basic literacy and numeracy skills are all very poor. He also suffers from low self-esteem, short attention spans and temper tantrums. He has difficulty in making and sustaining friendships.

During his MFL lessons, he enjoys drawing and recently produced a passable though misspelled poster on the computer with the help of a classroom assistant. Unlike copywriting and rote learning, ICT in MFL lessons manifestly offers this boy a creative, collaborative and kinaesthetic experience to which he responds positively.

- Word-processing tasks with simple language content will need to be devised.
- Adoption of primary school MFL courseware whose content and approach are secondary school age-appropriate might be considered.

Case study 3: Caroline – a foreign language learner with severe learning difficulties (SLD)

Caroline's cognitive impairments are such that she attends a nearby school for students with SLD and PMLD. The teachers at this special school have asked your department for advice about introducing MFL into the curriculum. They believe the subject would enhance the learning experience of Caroline and her peers if taught appropriately.

Having been asked to devise ICT-based MFL activities for Caroline, you arrange to observe her at work on the computer during a routine life-skills session in the presence of her teacher and classroom assistant. You will also interview teaching and support staff, none of them MFL specialists, to find out which computer programs they regularly use, how they integrate such technology into classroom practice and what they do to match the pace and scope of learning to their students' needs. When your research is complete, you will deliver a demonstration computer-based MFL lesson.

- What might you be looking for during your observation of Caroline at work?
- It would be important to think about the questions you will ask when you interview the special school staff.

Case study 4: Darren – a foreign language learner with Specific Learning Difficulties (Dyslexia) (SpLD)

Darren's educational psychologist has diagnosed Specific Learning Difficulties (Dyslexia). Darren has average to above-average intelligence and a wide range of interests. He plays for the town under-13 football team. He has a reading age at least three years below his chronological age while his spelling skills are poor in both English and his MFL.

During the early months of learning the MFL he appeared to be enjoying the subject and making good progress, but you have noticed that he has difficulty with certain aspects of the subject and particularly with written work. Controlled MFL writing assignments are particularly challenging for him as he finds the target-language text he has prepared hard to memorise and recall. As an *aide-mémoire*, Darren might type what he has composed into text manipulation authoring software, which will then display the text with blanked-out words to be entered. He might also benefit from a program that reinforces how spoken utterances match their written representation in the MFL.

- Programs that will store text and convert it to a cloze test need to be identified.
- What features are desirable in a software package whose functions include drilling sound–symbol correspondence in MFL?

Case study 5: Emma – a foreign language learner with social, emotional and behavioural difficulties (SEBD)

Emma is recorded as having SEBD. Although her primary school excluded her for misconduct on several occasions, it also provided her with class-room support so far as resources allowed. Your secondary school intends following this inclusion route.

Emma is known to have good literacy and numeracy skills. During the early stages of learning the MFL she appeared to cope with her studies well enough. Indeed, some of her oral work shows a lot of promise. However, she fidgets, seeks attention and distracts other students in class. In the ICT room, nobody is prepared to work near her and she has developed the habit of pressing keys on other students' computers, deleting their work. Her behaviour grows more troublesome and disrupts your lesson.

- It would be useful to devise an ICT activity with short-term goals and very specific outcomes.
- A point of focus could be to consider how working with a laptop computer might improve her behaviour.

Case study 6: Frank – a foreign language learner with speech, language and communication needs (SLCN)

Frank has a pronounced stammer and an immature vocabulary. A speech therapist withdraws him occasionally for individual tuition. A learning support assistant comes into some of his lessons to help him improve his word knowledge. Frank struggles to express himself verbally and he often falls out with his peers. Whether learning MFL will boost or damage his self-esteem remains to be seen.

Frank finds the learning environment better when seated at the computer, making his mistakes more discreetly and avoiding being 'wound up' by his classmates. He requires a MFL vocabulary-building program with which he can interact at his own pace and which will reinforce memorisation and recall.

- It would be important to think about dedicated or authoring soft-ware to build Frank's vocabulary.
- There is a need to identify online MFL games that might help improve his self-esteem.

Case study 7: Gavin – a foreign language learner with autistic spectrum disorders (ASD)

Gavin has a medical diagnosis of Asperger Syndrome, a condition on the autistic spectrum, entitling him to a classroom assistant. Albeit computer-literate and an excellent grammarian, he lacks the social skills taken for granted in a mainstream MFL classroom. As he prefers to work alone and cannot see the point of pretending that he is in the target-language country, he dislikes role-playing with a partner.

The school's MFL scheme of work features an ICT activity focusing on rail travel in continental Europe. Working in groups, the class is expected to research train connections for an imaginary journey using an online rail planner and to word process a travel brochure containing the information, all using the target language.

- It would be useful to explore what Gavin may find stressful in this assignment.
- A point of focus for observation would be envisaging ways in which the activity could be modified to include Gavin.

Case study 8: Harriet – a foreign language learner with hearing impairment (HI)

Harriet has profound hearing loss. She is highly intelligent and responds very positively to music, dance and visual stimuli. Your school's SENCO approaches you and asks whether you know of any teaching materials, including multimedia, which would lend themselves to additional MFL support work. The SEN department has arranged for a signer, who is not a linguist, to come into your lesson to assist Harriet. You meet before the first supported lesson to discuss what you intend to teach the class in general and how you are going to include Harriet in particular in the learning process.

- It would be useful to brief Harriet's signer on the use of the interactive whiteboard (IWB).
- Productivity software to develop her writing skills needs to be identified.

Case study 9: Ivor – a foreign language learner with visual impairment (VI)

Ivor, who is very intelligent, suffers from sight loss. The local authority VI service has provided the school with guidance about the use of ICT with partially sighted students. When compiling presentations, the emphasis is on sharp focus and high contrast, while font type, size, colour and background should be appropriately, sensitively and consistently deployed. In the case of IWBs the advice is to seat visually impaired learners at wireless or networked laptops or computers where they can view the IWB display on a small screen. Ivor will also require large-print versions of worksheets and test papers.

- To what extent should existing ICT-based MFL resources be modified?
- The feasibility of word processing MFL materials in larger print merits consideration.

Case study 10: Jessica – a foreign language learner with medical and physical disabilities

Jessica suffers from a debilitating illness that means spending long periods at home or in hospital. When she attends school, she is often tired and sometimes confined to a wheelchair. She is an intelligent student who is keen to do her best in MFL, but she is in danger of falling behind with her work because of her protracted absences.

The school's MFL department conducts an audit of existing hardware and software to determine how appropriate they are for vulnerable students such as Jessica. Email, websites and the school's virtual learning environment (VLE) are all considered as well as the wheelchair accessibility of electronic whiteboards and computer benches.

- There is a need to explore what home-school communications technologies can help Jessica progress.
- It would be important to think about how she can access MFL classroom-based technology from a wheelchair.

The use of technology with MFL students who have SEN will provide not only a learning experience for the students but also an opportunity for their teachers to reflect on their own practice. A lesson leaving a teacher with a sense of professional failure and frustration can often be a much more powerful instrument of self-improvement than a session where everything goes according to plan. The 'wow' factor in digital technology can also blind both learners and teachers to the fact that the technology itself ultimately matters much less than the way it is used when working with MFL. 'Cutting-edge' technology will have little impact in the MFL classroom without equally effective strategies and methodologies to ensure that the additional needs of vulnerable learners are also served. Matching technology with methodology requires a partnership between teachers, students, parents, classroom assistants, ICT technicians, SEN professionals and, ideally, software developers. For their collaboration to be successful, a problem-solving process involving definition, intervention and review, with plenty of opportunity for information exchange along the way, is crucial.

Lesson Five: Observe and Verify

Reflective practitioners should temper a positive outlook with healthy scepticism, refraining from premature celebration when a computer-based intervention apparently succeeds. Matters are not always as they seem when a language learner with SEN works with technology.

Vigilance pays dividends when using an ICT resource to support MFL learners with SEN. The conventional wisdom is that multimedia applications not only engage both eyes and ears but also boost motivation, self-esteem and concentration. Judicious monitoring will determine whether this is always the case in practice.

In the mid-1990s, my secondary school purchased a tutorial package designed for use by 11–14-year-old learners of French. The software featured not only text and images, but also authentic audio recordings and video sequences. I planned to use one of the units to teach direction-giving to two groups of low attainers in their third year of studying French. The unit introduced new language through a listening activity and then practised it through a game during which the learner's score of right and wrong responses was displayed. Learners answering all the questions correctly were rewarded with a video clip of a group of young people applauding.

The presentation activity displayed a town plan with named streets and places identified solely by symbols. The user was invited by a native speaker and an on-screen message to 'Choisissez une image, cliquez, écoutez et répétez...'. Clicking the mouse pointer over the icon of a building flying the tricolour elicited the spoken and written explanation 'C'est l'hôtel de ville'. The game invited the player to select and drag each of the place symbols from the right of the screen to its correct location on the map: 'Écoutez et mettez le symbole au bon endroit'. If the town hall icon was selected, the message 'L'hôtel de ville est sur la Place du Marché' was heard but not seen. When the player released the icon over one of the ten map locations now identified by large dots, either 'Faux' or 'Bravo – Un point' was heard. I demonstrated the presentation and the practice stages of the unit.

The resource's audio component, particularly the applause awarded after gaining full marks in the follow-up game, intrigued both French sets. One learner, who had formerly displayed behaviour problems, was so engrossed that he insisted on playing the game on his own in several subsequent lessons. However, as I watched my learners, I also noticed that they manifestly paid little heed to the spoken French clues in the game, e.g. 'L'hôtel de ville est sur la Place du Marché.' They relied instead on their visual memory of the locations of the church, post office, café, tourist office, town hall, supermarket, stadium, school, railway station and swimming pool from the presentation phase.

While tutoring a colleague's nine-year-old daughter in French – a bright student with a diagnosis of specific learning difficulties – I found that she too ignored the spoken clues when using the software because she had instant recall of the location of each place on the street grid. Though one of the four attainment targets since the introduction of the National Curriculum, listening comprehension is reputedly the least liked and developed skill in MFL learning. Learners, particularly those with SEN, will compensate for this weakness by enlisting their comparative strengths, in this case spatial awareness. The moral for software developers is to give learners a degree of control over audio delivery, allowing them not only to listen to the spoken French as many times as they want, but also to hear the text read aloud at a slower pace if they wish. Aural test reliability would also have improved if the programmers had randomised the location of the amenities on the town plan, so that they changed position whenever the game was replayed.

Lesson Six: Research, Develop and Network

These days, all teachers are expected to be reflective practitioners and every teacher has become a special needs teacher. MFL teachers working with low attainers cannot rely on conventional methods and textbooks when delivering their subject. Ideas, resources and strategies must be shared within and between educational institutions for the benefits of vulnerable learners.

At the heart of every pearl lies one tiny, sharp, piece of grit, which invades the host oyster's shell, irritating and inducing the creature over a period of time to coat the foreign body with a lustrous secretion of high value. Similarly, when MFL teachers working with students with SEN find their well-planned lessons going awry, they can turn their negative frustration into a positive research proposal. A number of years ago, my class pestered me because they were unable to read their French correspondents' handwritten letters, not because the language was beyond them, but because they could not decipher the cursive script. Having established where the reading difficulty lay, I downloaded a freeware French handwriting computer font designed by a primary school teacher in France. The font was installed on the school network and worksheets prepared to teach the class explicitly how French handwritten characters were shaped and joined so that the cursive forms would present fewer recognition difficulties. This action research project was written up as a book chapter (Wilson, 2001b).

Such small-scale investigations, driven by a blend of irritation and curiosity, have the potential not only to enhance individual MFL teachers' professional development in general, and performance management objectives in particular, but also to inform good practice across the subject department and the whole school. A disincentive to becoming a teacher–researcher is the common misconception that the role always necessitates time-consuming, intensive and supervised study leading to a dissertation-length publication. The reality is that a more senior colleague within the department or school can function as a mentor or 'critical friend', offering advice and support as necessary during the project, and that often a 'one side of A4' research note with conclusions and recommendations will suffice when reporting back to other members of staff. Wherever teaching and research form a 'seamless garment' within the MFL classroom, both MFL teachers and their students with SEN are likely to reap immense benefits. No hurdle must be placed in the way of this symbiosis.

Teacher–researchers in the field of technology-enhanced MFL learning for students with SEN should also 'work smart', looking out for curriculum development and materials production opportunities as they proceed. In the case of my own MFL handwriting recognition project, I used the French cursive font not only to devise keyboarding activities, but also to word process reading comprehension tasks based on letters simulating authentic French handwriting. Many hands can make lighter work too. In the early 1990s, several projects successfully piloted MFL teaching to students with

SEN using technology, creating in the process both teaching materials and good practice. They included the CILT/National Curriculum Council (NCC) and National Foundation for Educational Research (NFER) Projects investigating the extension of MFL teaching to students with SEN in a range of mainstream and special schools within a number of local education authorities; the Suffolk/Norfolk Project, which focused on MFL teaching in special schools; and the National Flexible Learning Project North East – Modern Languages, which targeted foreign languages for all at key stage 4. In 2001, the British Educational Communications and Technology Agency (BECTA) followed suit with a Special Needs and MFL workshop convened to produce SEN-specific ICT resources that subsequently appeared online. Although such initiatives raise awareness, trial new ideas and test feasibility, their project materials also have a short shelf life, going out of print or offline after a year or two.

In a world where methodology always lags behind technology in classroom practice, the MFL teaching community is fortunate to have a precious online continuous professional development resource in the form of the ICT4LT website, which is regularly updated by its founder (Davies, 2011). For more SEN-specific issues, there are online discussion groups, several like the SENCO Forum and Linguanet Forum of some longevity, others like the Yahoo group MFL Resources and the TES (Times Educational Supplement) MFL and SEN Forums of more recent vintage with teaching resource databases. If a critical mass of MFL teachers moves to the likes of Facebook and Twitter to discuss classroom practice, then the new social media will play their part too. What ultimately matters, though, is the content, quality and trustworthiness of members' contributions and their versatility in moving between the roles of master and apprentice pedagogue for the benefit of the anonymous student with learning difficulties. Message threads initiated by a young MFL teacher with what is perceived as a struggling student with a rare impairment often end with the same teacher confident and ready to apply the advice received from more senior colleagues. Sadly, such teachers seldom report back on the success or otherwise of the strategies suggested. No matter how spectacular technology can be, it is the passion for learning of students with SEN and their teachers that counts when the new technology eventually loses its lustre.

References

Bongaerts, T., de Haan, P., Lobbe, S. and Wekker, H. (eds) (1988) *Computer Applications in Language Teaching*. Dordrecht: Foris Publications.

Böss, A., Koldkjær, J. and Obel, H. (1988) *EDB-programmer i Folkeskolen – et forsøgsprojekt* [electronic data processing programs in primary schools – a pilot project]. Holstebro, Denmark: Holstebro Kommunale Skolevæsen.

Collett, J. (1980) *Computers in Language Teaching.* Canterbury, New Zealand: Canterbury Monographs for Teachers of French.

Council for Educational Technology (1986) *CALL for the Computer: Computer Assisted Language Learning for the Modern Language Teacher.* London: Council for Educational Technology.

Couper, H. (1996) Teaching modern languages to visually impaired children. *Language Learning Journal* 13, 6–9.

Davies, G. (1982) *Computers, Language and Language Learning.* London: Centre for Information on Language Teaching and Research.

Davies G. (ed.) (2011) *Information and Communications Technology for Language Teachers (ICT4LT),* Slough, Thames Valley University, accessed 28 August 2011. http://www.ict4lt.org/

Department for Education and Skills (2001) *Special Educational Needs Code of Practice.* London, DFES, accessed 28 August 2008. http://media.education.gov.uk/assets/files/pdf/s/sen%20code%20of%20practice.pdf

Hilger, E. (2000) *E-Mail-Austausch zwischen dem Bildungs- und Beratungszentrum für Hörgeschädigte in Stegen und der Freedom High School in Morganton/North Carolina: Ein interkulturelles Kooperationsprojekt zwischen hörgeschädigten und guthörenden Schülern [Email exchange between the educational and advisory centre for the hearing impaired in Stegen and Freedom High School in Morganton, North Carolina: An intercultural cooperation project between hearing-impaired and hearing students].* http://www.bbzstegen.de/zusatz/projekte/hilger/projektbericht.pdf. No longer online.

Janitza, J. (1985) *Enseignement Assisté par Ordinateur des langues étrangères [Computer-assisted teaching of foreign languages].* Paris: Hatier.

Kecskés, I. (1987) *Mikroszámítógépek használata az idegennyelv-oktatásban [Using microcomputers for foreign language education].* Budapest: Tankönyvkiadó.

Joint Council for Qualifications (2010) *Access Arrangements, Reasonable Adjustments and Special Consideration General and Vocational Qualifications, 2010–2011.* Online at http://www.jcq.org.uk/attachments/published/538/22.%20AARASC%201011.pdf

Költzsch, J. (2002) Förderung der Schriftsprachkompetenz im Englischunterricht mit gehörlosen Schülern durch Schreiben von E-Mails [Promoting written language competence in English lessons with deaf students through email writing]. *Hörgeschädigte Kinder* 39 (4), 14–24.

Langenscheidt-Redaktion (ed.) (1985) *Computergestützter Fremdsprachenunterricht: Ein Handbuch [Computer-supported foreign language teaching: a handbook].* Berlin: Langenscheidt.

Licklider, J. (1962) Preliminary experiments in computer-aided teaching. In J.E. Coulson (ed.) *Programmed Learning and Computer-Based Instruction* (pp. 217–239). New York: Wiley.

Mazzotti, G. (ed.) (1987) *Lingue, Tecnologie e Unione Europea [Languages, Technologies and European Union].* Milan: Marzorati Editore.

Pennington, M.C. (ed.) (1996) *The Power of CALL.* Houston, TX: Athelstan.

Wiązowski, J. (2002) Computer assisted language learning as a bridge to social inclusion of blind learners in mainstream schooling. In *Proceedings of the 11th World Conference of the International Council for Education of People with Visual Impairment,* Noordwijkerhout, the Netherlands, 27 July–2 August 2002, accessed 11 August 2011. Online at http://www.icevi.org/publications/ICEVI-WC2002/papers/01-topic/01-wiazowski.htm

Wilson, D.R. (2001a) Building bridges to inclusive foreign language education through appropriately applied technologies. In J. White (ed.) *Fourth Conference on Foreign*

Language Education and Technology (FLEAT IV Proceedings), Japan Association for Language Education and Technology (pp. 84–90), accessed 28 August 2011. Online at http://www.specialeducationalneeds.com/mfl/fleat4/paper.doc

Wilson, D.R. (2001b) Applying new technologies appropriately to foreign handwriting recognition difficulties. In T. Atkinson (ed.) *Reflections on ICT* (pp. 41–52). London: Centre for Information on Language Teaching and Research, accessed 28 August 2011. http://www.specialeducationalneeds.com/mfl/handwriting.doc

Wilson, D.R. (2007) *References to Support Inclusion in Modern Foreign Languages with Information and Communications Technologies*, accessed 28 August 2011. http://www.specialeducationalneeds.com/mfl/mflsenictbiblio.doc

Part 2

Case Studies

4 The 21st Century Languages Classroom – The Teacher Perspective

Elina Vilar Beltrán and
Auxiliadora Sales Ciges

Introduction

Since the Salamanca Statement of 1994, European countries have sought to make inclusive education possible for all. There are, arguably, according to Belanger (2006) five successful factors that favour inclusion: collaboration (with parents/carers, in the classroom and with the teaching team), agreement on support among the professionals involved in change, leadership by school heads, planned scheduling of changes and adjustments in accordance with the professionals' needs, attitudes and values.

In 2005, the European Commission published a report on the provision of language teaching in Europe to pupils with special educational needs (SEN). The report *'Special Educational Needs in Europe: The Teaching and Learning of Languages: Insights and Innovation'* emphasises the need for training at the core of research devoted to making language learning accessible for all (European Commission, 2005). Teachers who are new to inclusive practices need to develop expertise and find alternative ways of teaching languages and resources that would include, for example, a range of digital technologies to enhance more traditional approaches in the language classroom. According to Stevens and Marsh (2005: 109) *'it appears that there are significant numbers of pupils whose needs are not being recognized'*.

Taking into account the fact that we are all citizens of a multicultural world, with a trend towards pluralingualism, where knowledge of languages can be effectively used to communicate in different circumstances (Common European Framework of Reference for Languages, 2001), we all have the right of, and can benefit from, learning languages. An inclusive model is therefore needed to encourage citizens' cultural enrichment, by acknowledging and respecting diversity, through exchange, dialogue and critical active participation in society (Sales & García, 1997).

As stated in the introduction to the book, according to McColl (2000: 5) *'foreign language learning, far from interfering with language development as was once thought, stimulates its development, and gains can be detected right across the curriculum'*. However, in order for these benefits to be available equitably to all, there is a clear need for well-trained and interdisciplinary teams of professionals to work together in schools and to craft strategies for improving student achievement. It is usually the case that teachers in inclusive environments are specialists either in special needs education, information technology or modern languages but they are rarely trained in all areas, as Pearson and Chambers (2005) report in a study on language students' experiences during initial teacher training.

It is the aim of this chapter to consider whether all children are included in the foreign language classroom, and if so, how? In order to have two different European perspectives, we conducted a small-scale study in both England and Spain on the basis of: (a) familiarity with the systems and their similarities and differences as pointed out in the next two sections, (b) the institutional links between King's College London and Universitat Jaume I and the participating schools and (c) the collaborative research undertaken by the authors of this chapter. We were interested to explore the situation in primary and secondary schools by interviewing language teachers, and also to assess their knowledge and training in two main areas: inclusive education and technology. Data from our empirical study are presented after a general introduction to the languages and information and communication technology (ICT) policies of the two contexts where the investigation was carried out.

English and Spanish School Systems and the Teaching of Languages

Mainstream schooling in England can be divided in two broad sectors, that of independent education, on the one hand, and state education on the other. Independent schools do not necessarily have to follow the National Curriculum (NC); however, they must offer an option of sufficient range and depth to be appropriate for the age, aptitude, ability and SEN of the pupils placed there. State schools follow the NC although some variations are permitted. Another category is that of special schools, which can be independent or state maintained. The number of students in these institutions, however, has slowly diminished since the *Salamanca Declaration*, in 1994, a strategy in which UNESCO (1994) persuaded most countries to move towards a unified education for all and generated a movement towards a more inclusive system. These days, more children identified with SEN participate in the same classes as children who are not deemed to have a special need. Some children might be attending a mainstream school with a special unit and spend part of their time in it as these units cater for children who are experiencing difficulties.

Languages provision varies not only from sector to sector but according to the type of school and even within individual schools in spite of the imposition of a NC that was designed to provide equality of opportunity *inter alia*. Currently, as already mentioned in Chapter 1, Languages are only compulsory in Key Stage 3, that is, for students aged 11–14 and there is an entitlement for all pupils at Key Stage 2. The situation is in continuous flux as the present government has expressed its commitment to an early start and to strengthen the study of languages at Key Stage 4.

In Spain, the study of languages has experienced a different turn. Learning a language, other than Spanish and the co-official language (Catalan, Basque and Galician) in the bilingual communities, is now required in primary and compulsory secondary education (6–16 years old) and, where possible, it is offered in nursery stages (3–6 years old). English is the most common option, although some schools might offer French, German or Italian instead or as an optional subject from age nine.

Spain's equivalent NC is called LOE (*Ley Orgánica de Educación* (2006)), which was established in 2006. There are state schools, privately run schools funded by the State and purely private schools. Some of these are bilingual and multilingual schools, where subjects other than the foreign language are taught in a language that is not Spanish or the co-official language (Basque, Catalan or Galician). Although this used to be the case for privately run institutions exclusively, it is being implemented in public schools since the LOE was passed. Performance, however, is hampered so long as there is a mismatch in the pretensions of the Law and the training the teachers have received to work in a language that is not their mother tongue.

Although there are special schools in Spain, the practice is that all children should be integrated into the regular school system. Here, again, controversies arise over the training received by the teachers in subjects of special education and the support they receive so that, where possible, all children follow the same curriculum (Moliner *et al.*, 2010).

Until recent years, both in Spain and other European countries, pupils with SEN were exempt from studying a foreign language. In the case of English, the most common taught foreign language in Europe, this translated into a higher degree of difficulty for some alumni at the time to face the world in the 21st century. Today, with the policies of education for all, languages are more accessible, but it is necessary to consider under what conditions they are best taught. Although, as already mentioned, according to the LOE (Real Decreto 1630/2006) it would be advisable for children to begin learning a foreign language at nursery level (3–6 year olds), it is sometimes impossible owing to the shortage of trained teachers and the uncertainty of provision. The global spread of English has resulted in its use as the international lingua franca (Burns, 2005; Seidlhofer, 2004). More than two decades ago, Beneke (1991) already estimated that in 80% of verbal exchanges between foreign or second language users of English there were no native speakers involved. Considering this remarkable evolution of the English language into one that is now widely mastered by non-native speakers, it is both timely and appropriate to establish a research agenda in an attempt to make the learning of English, and in our opinion, of languages in general, accessible to everyone. Crombie's contribution to the European Commission report (2005: 184) stresses that '*young people whatever their disability or ability have a right to learn a language of their choice at whatever level they can*'.

There is still a need for further research into the specific features of English as a lingua franca (ELF); however, the findings so far seem to suggest that ELF functions as a tool to facilitate communication and to show one's identity within different linguistic or cultural background groups (Ife, 2007). ELF researchers argue that there is a need for a '*pluricentric rather than a monocentric approach to the teaching and use of English*' (Jenkins, 2006: 173) and that it is necessary for both teachers and learners to develop intercultural as well as purely linguistic skills. Thus, rather than setting the students' academic target in attaining native-speaker or near-native-speaker competence, the stress should be placed in helping the learners develop an intercultural personality (Alcón Soler & Safont Jordà, 2007; McKay, 2002; Snow *et al.*, 2006; Velasco-Martin, 2004). According to McColl, '*a successful language programme is one that provides learners with progressive challenges* that can be met, *so that, at whatever level they are working, students can experience success as learners*' (2005: 107).

Bearing these considerations in mind, learning a language should not only result in the acquisition of a new linguistic and cultural system, but it would also enhance the knowledge of the learners' own systems. For that reason, everyone should be able to benefit from this two-fold enriching experience, and, with the help of digital technologies, physical barriers (such as distance) can be removed and at the same time other mental activities might be improved.

Technology Enhanced Language Teaching – From Theory to Practice

Regarding ICT knowledge, the NC in England has set statutory requirements to use ICT in all subjects, except for physical education, at Key Stages 2, 3 and 4, and investment in training has been provided accordingly. At Key Stage 1 teachers decide where it is appropriate to teach the use of ICT to support their learning in all subjects. Digital technologies have come to play an important role in the English school curriculum and we believe they can contribute to making the learning of a language more immediate and relevant. Fitzpatrick and Davies (2003) point out the potential of tools such as the internet for easy contact with other countries and authentic written and spoken materials. McColl (2005: 107) states that:

We must take any and all opportunities to get the foreign language out of the classroom. This doesn't just mean making use of ICT to facilitate virtual communication with people abroad, but exploiting the local communities as well – the community of the school itself, the neighborhood, local businesses – anything that will demonstrate the fact that languages are relevant no matter where you happen to be, and that differences are interesting, not threatening.

According to the LOE, in Spain, technology also features strongly in the school curriculum. The autonomous communities have invested, in their own ways, both in software and hardware. For example, in 2009, the Andalusian Regional Government (*Junta de Andalucía*), in the south of Spain, decided to provide all 10–12 year olds in state schools with free laptops that were to be returned upon finishing their studies. Similar initiatives include the provision of interactive whiteboards (IWBs) for schools in all the country, the development of educational software and training of teachers.

As with all tools and resources, if these are not used properly and devoid of an appropriate pedagogy, their purpose is defeated. At two major conferences focusing on languages and technology, IALLT and

EUROCALL 2011, there were impressive accounts of projects showing how technology could encourage language learners. Although most showed that the students, not matter how young, were able to work with the given technology almost instantly, they all had a common factor: motivated and enthusiastic teachers, practitioners who had devoted time to learn to use the tool and had the ability to equip their class with skills that will be useful in their future.

As much as it is easy for many generations to pick up a book and read it, annotate it, and, in short, use it in many different ways, that is also the case with newer generations and technology. Of course, as it happens with books, this would vary depending on social, economical and geographical factors. In 2001, Prensky published his paper *Digital Natives/Digital Immigrants*, which attracted a great deal of controversy. First, he defined the former as '"native speakers" *of the digital language of computers, video games and the Internet'* (Prensky, 2001: 1) then described those of us who were not born into that world, that he calls the 'digital world', as the digital immigrants '*who would speak of digital technologies with a different* "accent"' (Prensky, 2011: 15). If understood as a metaphor, we wholeheartedly relate to that distinction, although it seems rather contradictory that the creators of the so-called digital world are in fact, the digital immigrants. Generally speaking, however, there seems to be a component of naturalness in the way 'digital natives' use technology. This does not mean that it is used in the right way, but it should be seen as a strength to bring into the language class.

Considering that the language learners' reality is the context described above, we believe that technology, in any shape or form, should feature in the classroom; again, as long as the teacher has received training, is confident and sees a need for it. Most of our students will probably use Facebook and Twitter (and may even think that emails are old-fashioned), will have a mobile phone and a computer or, at least, access to one. They will have played with video-consoles and, depending on their age, might keep or follow a blog. Most of the things they like will be digitally stored and they will not be afraid to handle a device or a new software package. Teachers would still be the ones who, for the main part, would decide what tools to use to meet learning objectives but it could usefully be a combined process of learning together.

Teachers' Perceptions/Perspectives in England and Spain

This section provides an outline of the participants' that took part in the interviews for this study and an analysis of their perceptions with regards to the teaching of languages and the use of technology in inclusive settings. We were interested in examining the practices in the UK and Spain given their seeming similarities in their commitment to ICT education and differences with regards to language provision.

In order to identify potential interviewees for our research, we sent out paper questionnaires to several mainstream and special schools asking about their language provision and practices and enquiring about their interest in our project: in England we sent 47 questionnaires out to schools in London and the south east, and in Spain we sent 60 questionnaires to the city of Castelló de la Plana on the east coast. The areas and schools were determined by the teacher-training agreements of the researchers' universities. Among other things, the returns that approximated to 39% in England and 18% in Spain, provided us with the details of those participants who were willing to meet for an interview in their schools. We conducted our interviews with the help of an *aide-mémoire* for which we identified three main broad areas to be discussed with the participants: context, pedagogical approach, and differentiation and modification in response to difference. Within these three areas, we also explored issues related to training and the use of technology.

We visited seven schools in England and interviewed eight language staff: seven teachers and one Language Support Assistant (LSA). They all had ability sets according to school policy. Our sample of secondary schools provide a taste of the varied educational provision in England: one academic selective boys' independent school, one comprehensive sports specialist boys' school, one Catholic girls' school, one mainstream school with a special unit, one Church of England school and one specialist school for arts and technology.

In Spain, we visited seven schools (all bilingual (Catalan/Spanish) mainstream state schools, one of them with a high ratio of traveller pupils and students with physical disabilities) and interviewed nine language teachers. The job of language support assistant does not exist in the Spanish educational system.

Table 4.1 provides a summary of the schools we visited and the teachers we interviewed. Note that the first year of secondary education in England, i.e. when languages are compulsory subjects, is the final year of primary

Table 4.1 Summary of the interviews

England				*Spain*			
Teachers		*Schools*		*Teachers*		*Schools*	
LT	*LSA*	*Secondary*	*Primary*	*LT*	*LSA*	*Secondary*	*Primary*
7	1	6	1	9	0	2	5

education in Spain. We therefore believe that the distribution of our participating schools represents similar school populations.

Summary of the Interviews in England

The teachers interviewed taught from two to three languages, except for
the primary school teacher for whom French was part of several other subjects. They were all part of large languages departments and used varied
methods in their practice, combining both traditional and innovative
approaches. Our interviewees mentioned differentiating in the class and
having support from LSAs and (Special Educational Needs Coordinators)
SENCOs. One of the teachers suggested that what she did in the class was
'good practice for anyone really' (TE4). The one primary school teacher said he
used 'an interactive whiteboard, pictures, music and props to allow children to access
a variety of learning styles: auditory, kinaesthetic and visual' (TE8) and there was
also one-to-one support in his class. Most participants had learnt about SEN
either in specialised programmes or from the school's SENCO, and they mentioned teaching children with dyslexia, dyspraxia, autism, hearing impairments and other speech and behavioural difficulties. The SENCOs in all the
schools were very active, in some cases organising weekly meetings with the
staff to talk about issues that ranged from general terminology to specific
cases. The teachers were well informed about the individuals in their class
and had the SENCOs support for their subject. Some schools also had language teaching assistants (LTAs) and native speakers in their classes.

With regards to training in technology, all our participants had received
some sort of in-house tuition and/or PGCE (Postgraduate Certificate in
Education) instruction. They all seemed to be comfortable using it in their
schools; all had IWBs in their classroom, and made use of these. At least once
a week, they all taught in the computer room, which was equipped with
language learning resources, or in the language lab or media suite. The interviewees created their own digital materials and adapted them, when necessary, to their students' needs and also made use of the virtual environments
in their schools to set homework or share their work with other colleagues
(usually word documents and presentations). No one mentioned using any
authoring package to create their materials, preferring to use ready-made
ones, such as images, videos, songs or newspapers. Some used websites that
required a subscription such as *linguascope* (http://www.linguascope.com/)
for elementary, beginner and intermediate online exercises on various languages and *A tantôt* (http://www.atantot.com/) with modern foreign language (MFL) resources for IWBs; they also mentioned other free resources

such as *languages online* (http://www.languagesonline.org.uk/) a website with language exercises created using the *freeware* package *Hotpotatoes*, the BBC languages website (http://www.bbc.co.uk/languages/) with interactive courses and further resources and Voki.com (see Connor, Chapter 8 in this volume for a case study on this tool).

One interviewee explained that '*children who are dyslexic or dyspraxic will do most of the work on their laptops*' (TE1) but, notably, unless they had dispensation from the support department, the other children in that school were not allowed to take their laptops in the class. In another school where it was 'not school policy' (TE4) to use individual laptops, the teacher and the LSA provided adapted materials instead. The remaining schools were more flexible about the use of computers in class, although one of the teachers thought '*it would be a disaster if all the students brought their laptops*' (TE2).

Even though the context, the pedagogical approach, the training, resources and facilities seemed to be ideal for an inclusive teaching scenario, there was a recurrent and worrying issue that had to do with 'disapplication' of children from the language and there were comments such as 'quite often the first subject to go is languages' (TE3) in support of other subjects like English or Maths.

Summary of the Interviews in Spain

All our interviewees taught one foreign language and, when possible, also used varied teaching approaches, which included the incorporation of technology, IWB mainly, in their practice. The scenarios in the schools we visited were quite different to those described in the previous section. There was a maximum of two language teachers in the primary schools and there were slightly larger groups in the secondary ones. The situation of staff shortage was one of the main concerns:

In schools where there is only a class per year group, it is possible to meet the needs of all primary and most nursery students with a single teacher, resulting in a workload of about 25 contact hours per week and care for approximately 200 children. In schools where there is more than one group, a single teacher cannot manage to teach the years prior to primary stages (TS6).

All the language teachers we interviewed reported communication with the 'educational therapist', the SENCO's equivalent in Spain, was non-existent and all thought that '*the continuous changes in the languages and SEN specialists staff stop us from doing all that could be done*' (TS8). Teachers in this study were faced with little or no help. One of the interviewees mentioned having a child with autism in her classroom:

> ... he has been in my class for a couple of years now, he is very good at telling the date and the time, and knows most songs by heart, but does not understand what he is saying. He can take part in some activities but otherwise he is just there. It is very hard but no one comes to talk to me about it. The class tutors get the students' reports and no one communicates with me. I could actually be an interesting source of information as I teach every child in the school, but there are just no exchanges between us. Furthermore we get new specialists almost every year and sometimes we share them between schools (TS7).

Only the secondary schools that took part in the study had LTAs regularly and one of the primary schools had managed to have one for the first time, but they were unsure as to whether they would still have them the following year: *'We seemed to have shown the authorities that we are interested in languages in the school, all the teachers are very keen in learning English so I organised a course for them and, as a consequence, this year they offered us the possibility to have one LTA'* (TS6). None of the other primary schools had them.

One of the teachers we interviewed illustrated basic needs with respect to the training received with regards support:

> There is a lot of theory about inclusion and integration, but in reality it is all about problem solving. In one of my lessons, I had to work with a child on my lap, and thus, it is a trial and error experience, sometimes it works sometimes it doesn't. In order to be able to teach my class, sometimes I just have to provide that student with toys so that he's quiet. There is a lot of pressure from the authorities, parents etc. I have to buy things in 'bargain' shops, try to find other appropriate materials on my own, there is absolutely no training for this (TS2).

The general feeling was that the things they managed to do in the class were the result of self-teaching.

There is the added difficulty of, what we call 'nomadism' (or 'peripatetic') that seems to characterise language teachers, where, except in the rare case in which the school has outgrown its students or in which the unused Science lab has become the languages classroom: *'there never seems to be an allocated space for foreign languages, even in cases of newly built schools like ours'* (TS4). It is not uncommon for the teacher to have to move from classroom to classroom with a suitcase full of materials and any available technology, usually not more than a CD player, which probably makes it difficult for at least half of the class to do the listening exercises properly. *'Our resources, computers for example, are very limited, and we have to book them in advance if we want to use them. I believe it is a real shame because I think that students could benefit from being in multimedia environments'* (TS3). They also had the possibility of booking the multi-purpose room, which has a large screen, one computer and a projector, but the usual environments were traditional classrooms with a TV and DVD in them occasionally. Although from analogue to multimedia, languages have been a pioneer in technology, in five of the seven schools we visited, IWBs and computers were locked away and unused:

> I waited for two months since the start of the academic year for the IWB to be installed, the children are looking forward for me to use it in class, and I have now been waiting two more months for someone to install the projector. I don't know if I will still remember how to use it when they finally install it (TS7).

Only the secondary schools had virtual environments, however the two teachers we interviewed did not use them and there seemed to be limited resources available for the language students. Two of the primary schools were using Dropbox (www.dropbox.com) as a repository space for staff to share schools' official and related documents and in one of those schools a teacher had created a language blog for all her students and the school community in general. Her blog holds a bank of digital materials; anyone interested in keeping up to date with events related to the English modules can access it freely. Interestingly, she mentioned that 'the fact that students know that they are being recorded and that what they produce will be posted on the blog makes them want to pronounce it perfectly, and they also practise it many more times than usual' (TS4), something that has been reported in the literature by other language and technology researchers. According to Godwin-Jones (2003: 13) 'self-publishing encourages ownership and responsibility on the part of students, who may be more thoughtful (in content and structure) if they know they are writing for a real audience'.

Discussion and Conclusions

McColl (2005: 103) has referred to statements from parents and educators about language learning and children with SEN such as 'there are more important things for her to learn' or 'Why make them do a subject that is too difficult for them?' She suggests that a case for learning a foreign language had still to be made in some instances, even if, when talking about inclusive education, it was generally felt that no children should be denied access to the full curriculum. It seems that schools in the present study provide foreign language teaching for all, but in the case of some schools in England, only until the point when learners start to struggle, and not necessarily with the foreign language. The simple question 'Are you enjoying learning a foreign language?' is rarely asked and it is readily assumed by many, that languages are too difficult and even unnecessary. A great many strategies were employed to support learners and with considerable success. Increasingly, solutions to difficulty with language learning were cited as the following illustrative anecdote from an Inclusion Consultant from the North West of England reported during this research:

> A girl with a cochlear implant attending a local high school was being considered for disapplication from German. This was to allow her some lesson time for catch up time in other subjects, such as Maths and English, which were felt to be more important in her acquisition of her native tongue. However, discussions concerning this were forestalled when it was reported back that the girl in question was one of the better students of German! A decision was quickly made, NOT to withdraw her from German lessons.

In the case of Spain, children are all together in language classrooms, but the training and support for teachers is either insufficient or non-existent. For inclusion to be effective, proper preparation is crucial as is the importance of ensuring accessible curricula. This means having course materials that are 'barrier-free' and where they are 'accessible for students with disabilities, the more "usable" it is to all students' (Doyle & Robson, 2002: 1). In general, the rhetoric of inclusion was not generally in evidence in practice in languages classrooms although there were notable efforts from some individuals. There were issues such as the ones indicated that were really troubling the teachers, and the lack of communication and readiness of technology being imple-mented was proving to be a major obstacle to these efforts. Theories of inclu-sive and universal design advocate adapted environments for any given need. For this, we believe that both the micro-elements (materials and resources) and the macro-elements (classrooms and spaces) must be accessible. According to Abbott (2007: 6) integration 'was the process by which schools and other institutions made small changes in order to enable particular learn-ers to share a lesson or a subject, or get access to a building' inclusion however 'is a much more fundamental concept by which the needs of potential users with learning difficulties are considered at an earlier stage and learning environments are set up to be inclusive, whether or not the need for such changes appears to be present'.

Both interaction and collaboration are key to learning a language, as is finding a need to use it. In Spain, dubbing in film and television hinders active learning outside the classroom, and considering that most of the movies and series are usually in English, it would definitely be to their advantage if they were subtitled instead. As the classroom is often the only contact with the foreign language for mainstream school students, the use of Web 2.0 and both virtual and real exchanges need further promotion. In addition to providing opportunities never possible before, technology can also bring new inclusive experiences by offering a variety of access channels to information. A potential virtual learning environment that could be implemented in these schools would be Edmodo.com, specifically designed for educational settings.

As other authors in this volume show, Crombie, in Chapter 7 for example, there are tools that are easy to set up, easy to use and students seem to enjoy their features. The use of social media in teaching and learning is sometimes banned for security reasons, but there are countless alternatives; the following website (http://c4lpt.co.uk/top-100-tools-for-learning-2011/) provides the top 100 tools for learning in 2011, which could serve as a useful guide for language teachers, it is put together every year by the Centre for Learning and Performance Technology (C4LPT). These days, most of the websites provide self-explanatory videos for the teachers to initially assess the potential, or lack of it, to use it in class.

Although the results in this chapter only report on those interviews conducted in the south of England and a city of Spain, we also spoke to and visited other schools in the UK and Spain to provide 'evidence of success'. We found the response of one Depute Head Teacher in a special school in Scotland who gave a full account of how they taught languages to their pupils and the role played by technology in their context very enlightening:

ICT provides a vehicle for pupils with additional support needs to participate in the subject of Modern Foreign Languages. This is especially so when pupils have no functional speech or have dysarthric speech. Using high tech voice output communication aids (VOCAs) helps to 'level the playing field' for pupils and allows them to demonstrate their understanding of a foreign language and enables pupils to participate in discussions and class lessons. Symbols are used on the VOCAs to represent words to ensure that pupils who have difficulty with reading can still communicate in a Foreign Language. Use of VOCAs also allows pupils to participate in role play. Role play is a very important part of teaching a Modern Foreign Language and it can be difficult to replicate role play by use of symbol boards and flashcards. Pupils in Capability Scotland's Corseford School who use high tech VOCAs all have French vocabulary programmed into them so that they can call up this vocabulary as and when they need it during class lessons or whenever they need it. Pupils are taught where to find this on their VOCAs just as they would be taught to find any other new vocabulary or Topic. Teachers' forward planning ensures that vocabulary is programmed in advance so that it is there, ready for use when it is needed. This then opens up the wider curriculum and educational opportunities for pupils as it helps ensure that there is breadth, depth and progression across all aspects of Language and Literacy. (Fiona Catterson, Deputy Head Teacher, Capability Scotland, Corseford School)

There are also examples of inclusive schools in Spain that carry out commendable work in this regard. The language staff at *Colegio Padre Jerónimo,* Madrid, explained how they had learned to adapt their own materials from teaming up with the inclusion experts in the school. By working together with the specialists, they had developed a bank of materials for their English classrooms to enable all the children to participate.

There are cases of good practice in both countries, language teachers and other specialists working together with the same purpose. There are good solutions throughout, however, it seems that most of these stay within the schools' doors (Stevens & Marsh, 2005) and are not being publicised or disseminated as they could be, a missed opportunity to children's disadvantage and the whole teaching community in general.

Our data indicate that digital technologies assist in the creation of materials, in the presentation of contents and in making learning accessible for everyone, and in general, there was considerable agreement that attention to SEN benefits all learners (Jones & McLachlan, 2009). It is important to ensure that students with SEN are not just physically present but included, with support, in the learning taking place. The introduction of new learning materials in a multi-modal way, that is, through sound, sight, touch, smell and so on, where possible, is essential, for instance, for students with dyslexia (Crombie & McColl, 2001) or those within the autistic spectrum disorder (Wire, 2005), and we would argue it is a way to cater for all the different learning styles in the classroom.

One of the obvious benefits of using digital technology for language teaching and learning would be its potential for virtual communication, be this synchronous or asynchronous, at the user's own pace, time and ability; thus, removing many barriers present in face-to-face communication. This advantage provides language learners with an excellent opportunity to practise their language skills with other speakers, hence the importance of training in the use of, for example, Web 2.0 technologies to be able to apply these to enhance not only language learning, but a more general 'digital learning'. According to Pegrum (2011): '*Students can be encouraged to experiment with self-presentation on blogs or in digital stories, in the process developing the digital public voices that will be essential to their professional and social futures*' (2011: 18). With regards to digital stories, a useful tool for language teachers would be creating comics with Makebeliefscomix.com, especially interesting is the section devoted to using the tool with children with SEN.

We believe it would be fruitful for teachers with specialisms in languages, technology and inclusion to work together as a team, in order to provide accounts of more examples of successful stories and practical solutions such as the ones we have tried to provide here. Knowledge can be further shared in international communities in international exchange programmes or online networks, collaborating with other practitioners in a variety of ways that can promote an inclusive teacher learning community. Such collaborative experiences have potential consequences for teachers' skills and expectations in enabling them to feel more confident and appreciated, more capable of teaching and leading, and more sensitive to diversity (Sales *et al.*, 2011).

References

Abbott, C. (2007) *e-Inclusion: Learning Difficulties and Digital Technology*. Bristol: Futurelab.

Alcón Soler, E. and Safont Jordà, M.P. (eds) (2007) *Intercultural Language Use and Language Learning*. Dordrecht, The Netherlands: Springer.

Belanger, S. (2006) Conditions favorisant l'inclusion scolaire: Attitudes des enseignantes du primarie [Conditions for inclusive schools: Teacher's attitudes]. In C. Dans, C. Dionne and N. Rousseau (eds) *Transformation des pratiques éducatives: La recherche sur l'inclusion scolaire* (pp. 63–88). Québec: Presse de l'Université du Québec.

Beneke, J. (1991) Englisch als *lingua franca* oder als Medium interkultureller Kommunikation. In Grebing, R. (ed.) *Grenzenloses Sprachenlernen* (pp. 54–66). Berlin: Cornelsen.

Burns, A. (ed.) (2005) Interrogating new worlds of English language teaching. *Teaching English From a Global Perspective* (pp. 1–15). Alexandria, VA: Teachers of English to Speakers of Other Languages.

Crombie, M. and McColl, H. (2001) Dyslexia and the teaching of modern foreign languages. In L. Peer and G. Reid (eds) *Dyslexia – Successful Inclusion in the Secondary School* (pp. 211–217). London: David Fulton.

Common European Framework of Reference for Languages (2001) accessed June 2012. http://www.coe.int/t/dg4/linguistic/Source/Framework_en.pdf

Doyle, C. and Robson, K. (2002) *Accessible Curricula. Good Practice for All.* Cardiff: UWIC Press.

European Commission (2005) *Special Educational Needs in Europe. The Teaching and Learning of Languages: Insights and Innovation.* Brussels: European Commission DG EAC, accessed June 2012. http://ec.europa.eu/languages/documents/doc449_en.pdf

Fitzpatrick, A. and Davies, G. (eds) (2003) *The Impact of Information and Communications Technologies on the Teaching of Foreign Languages and on the Role of Teachers of Foreign Languages,* EC Directorate General of Education and Culture, accessed June 2012. http://www.camsoftpartners.co.uk/docs/Futurelab_CALL_Article.htm

Godwin-Jones, R. (2003) Emerging Technologies. Blogs and Wikis: Environments for On-line Collaboration. *Language Learning and Technology* 7 (2), 12–16.

Ife, A. (2007) A role for english as lingua franca in the foreign language classroom. In Alcón, E. & Safont, M.P. (eds) *Intercultural Language Use and Language Learning* (pp. 79–100). The Netherlands: Springer.

Jenkins, J. (2006) Current perspectives on teaching World Englishes and English as a Lingua Franca. *TESOL Quarterly* 40 (1), 157–181.

Jones, J. and McLachlan, A. (2009) *Primary Languages in Practice. A Guide to Teaching and Learning.* Maidenhead: OUP.

Ley Orgánica de Educación (2006) accessed June 2012. http://www.boe.es/aeboe/consultas/bases_datos/doc.php?id=BOE-A-2006-7899

McColl, H. (2000) *Modern Languages for all.* London: Routledge.

McColl, H. (2005) Foreign language learning and inclusion: Who? Why? What? – and How. *Support for Learning* 20 (3), 103–108.

McKay, S.L. (2002) *Teaching English as an International Language: Rethinking Goals and Approaches.* Oxford: Oxford University Press.

Moliner, O., Sales, A., Ferrández, R. and Traver, J. (2010) Inclusive cultures, policies and practices in Spanish compulsory secondary education schools: Teachers' perceptions in ordinary and specific teaching contexts. *International Journal of Inclusive Education.* Epub ahead of print 22 December 2010. DOI: 10.1080/13603110903165158.

Pearson, S. and Chambers, G. (2005) A successful recipe? Aspects of the initial training of secondary teachers of foreign languages. *Support for Learning* 20, 115–122.

Pegrum, M. (2011) Modified, Multiplied, and (re-)mixed: Social media and digital literacies. In M. Thomas (ed.) *Digital Education. Opportunities for Social Collaboration* (pp. 9–35). New York: Palgrave Macmillan.

Prensky, M. (2001) Digital natives, digital immigrants. *On the Horizon* 9 (5), 1–6.

Prensky, M. (2011) Digital wisdom and homo sapiens digital. In M. Thomas (ed.) *Deconstructing Digital Natives. Young People, Technology and The New Literacies* (pp. 15–29). London and New York: Routledge.

Sales, A. and García, R. (1997) *Programas de Educación Intercultural* [Intercultural Education Programmes]. Bilbao: Desclée De Brouwer.

Sales, A., Traver, J. and García, R. (2011) Action research as a school-based strategy in intercultural professional development for teachers. *Teaching and Teacher Education* 27, 911–919.

Seidlhofer, B. (2004) Research perspectives on teaching English as a lingua franca. *Annual Review of Applied Linguistics* 24, 200–239.

Snow, M.A., Kamhi-Stein, L.D. and Brinton, D.M. (2006) Teacher training for English as a lingua franca. *Annual Review of Applied Linguistics* 26, 261–281.

Stevens, A. and Marsh, D. (2005) Foreign language teaching within special needs education: Learning from Europe-wide experience. *Support for Learning* 20 (3), 109–114.

UNESCO (1994) *The salamanca statement and framework for action on special needs education*, accessed January 2012. http://www.unesco.org/education/pdf/SALAMA_E.PDF

Velasco-Martin, C. (2004) The non-native English-speaking teacher as an intercultural speaker. In L.D. Kamhi-Stein (ed.) *Learning and Teaching from Experience: Perspectives on Non-native English Speaking Professionals* (pp. 277–293). Ann Arbor, MI: University of Michigan Press.

Wire, V. (2005) Autistic spectrum disorders and learning foreign languages. *Support for Learning* 20 (3), 123–128.

5 Using Technology to Teach English as a Foreign Language to the Deaf and Hard of Hearing

Ewa Domagała-Zyśk

Introduction

Information and communication technology has created a new reality: people can study, make friends, do shopping, play, learn and discuss different topics through the use of it. Some people might feel afraid of this de-personalization of human contacts, but on the other hand it creates new opportunities for many. In this chapter, the word *deaf* is written in two forms, *Deaf* and *deaf*, written most often as *D/deaf*. The capitalized Deaf reflects Woodward's (1972) idea and denotes these individuals who view their deaf-ness not as a biological or audiological state, but as a symbol of their cultural identity. The word deaf is used to denote the medical aspects of hearing loss, but it also describes the part of the population with hearing loss, who do not declare their belonging to the Deaf Culture, but want to think about their deafness as an audiological state. Taking into account these differences the author uses most often the term D/deaf to denote these two groups of people with hearing loss, as this chapter addresses the needs of both groups.

For D/deaf and hard of hearing people, the internet plays an immensely important role: it creates an opportunity for alternative communication, makes the education process more interesting and enables them to com-municate with different persons and institutions by the use of writing or online signing, without using speech (Barak & Sadovsky, 2008). Internet communications have replaced previous communication devices for deaf people, like letters, faxes or text telephones (TTY/TDD) (Agboola & Lee, 2000; Power *et al.*, 2007).

Using computer technology goes on a par with using English. Students from non-English speaking countries have to make up for this drawback and learn English as a foreign language in order to update their knowledge and skills. In these countries, English has become a must also for disabled students, among them D/deaf and hard of hearing persons. As the core of deafness is language disability, and D/deaf persons have problems using their national languages, this creates a new challenge both for the D/deaf students and their teachers. The aim of this chapter is to present the ways in which ICT can support the process of learning English as a foreign language by groups of D/deaf and hard of hearing students. The author plans to achieve this aim by the analysis of the literature on using the internet and other technological equipment in education of the D/deaf, and through a presentation of her own use of ICT during her English classes with Polish D/deaf students.

Educational Challenges for D/deaf and Hard of Hearing Students

D/deaf and hard of hearing students do not constitute a homogenous group: taking into account the time of this disability onset (prelingual, interlingual or postlingual), the level of hearing loss (mild, moderate, severe, profound) and environmental factors such as family make-up (for example, the student may have hearing parents and siblings or D/deaf parents and siblings) and type, time and results of therapy undertaken, we can name several dozens of types of hearing disorders (Krakowiak, 2003, 2006). Even today it is hard to discover the causes of hearing loss: it might be genetic in its character or may appear as a result of illnesses, toxins or drug usage, or mechanical or acoustic injury. It is important to know that almost every deaf or hard of hearing person possesses some level of hearing sensitivity that might be diagnosed, assessed and used as a basis for electro-acoustic hearing aids that amplify the sounds, or cochlear implants that convert acoustic waves into electric waves. These technological devices, together with some others (such as Frequency Modulation (FM) systems or acoustic loops) may significantly improve the D/deaf and hard of hearing person's ability to gain access to spoken language, and to magnify their educational and social opportunities.

The main educational problem for students with hearing loss is the lack of the possibility of direct access to the ethnic language and any other spoken language. The most important choice to be made by the parents of a D/deaf child is the choice of the communication method: in general it might be speech, sign-supported speech, writing, sign language or cued speech. This choice, in consequence, often implies the choice of educational path, such that the student might be educated in special schools for the D/deaf, or in integrated or inclusive environments.

Deafness, when not accompanied by other serious biological or psychological impairments, does not by itself lower the person's cognitive development (Domagała-Zyśk, 2001, 2003, 2005, 2006, 2010b; Marschark et al., 2002). However, a D/deaf or hard of hearing student experiences significant barriers both in language perception and in expression: hearing loss creates an obstacle in communication, and a barrier between a D/deaf person and the hearing community. It obstructs social learning and the possibility of discovering reality by language (Krakowiak, 2006). Deaf and hard of hearing students do not acquire language by simple participation in everyday conversations with their family members, peers or strangers; they do not listen to the radio or non-captioned TV programmes, and they are not able to catch other people's speech if they do not see their lips perfectly. It is extremely difficult for a D/deaf student to learn language spontaneously: s/he has to be taught it. This shows the necessity of individual treatment for each D/deaf or hard of hearing child and the need for access to individually chosen services and technological devices.

Education of D/deaf and hard of hearing students has changed much in recent times. At the beginning of the 20th century, such students were most often placed in segregated special centres for the D/deaf and ended their education at the vocational school level, working later in institutions where they did simple, menial jobs. Nowadays, in most cases, hearing impaired students are taught in integrated or inclusive schools together with their hearing peers, and have the possibility to access universities and work in different job positions, including white-collar positions.

However, school integration of D/deaf and hard of hearing students with the wider group is not an automatic and taken for granted process. There are several conditions to make it effective: they are connected with the pupil's biological and psychological characteristics, the teacher's conduct of behaviour and educational methods used, the school environment characteristics, and the social and demographical features of the class community (Borders et al., 2010; Korzon, 2006). Taking this into account we can not always speak about a fully functional integration of D/deaf and hard of hearing students within their classroom: sometimes the integration is only organizational in its character: the pupils spend time together in the school environment, but there are no real social and emotional relationships between the disabled and non-disabled class members (Hulek, 1992; Stinson & Antia, 1999). In order to avoid such a situation, different measures can be taken to improve communication between the hearing and D/deaf or hard of hearing class members, and technological support is a powerful tool here. Technology enables students to participate more vividly in class communication, to contact peers by text messages or emails, and even to participate in class discussions, as the D/deaf student can prepare a text message quickly and comfortably and send it in real time to other members of the group, thus participating fully in the class activities.

However, even before considering the technological support of the D/deaf pupils it is essential for the teacher and the D/deaf student's peers to remember the basic rules of effective classroom communication. For the D/deaf or hard of hearing child it is important to see the interlocutor's face, and it is important that this person is located in a well-lighted place, speaks at a normal pace (not too fast but without slowing the tempo) and with normal levels of loudness (hearing aids and cochlear implants make the sounds loud enough, so the speaker does not have to shout).

It is generally accepted that more than 95% of D/deaf and hard of hearing students have hearing parents. When they receive implants at a very early age, or use properly fitted hearing aids, they usually study from a very early age in mainstream pre-schools and schools. That means that they have restricted contacts with D/deaf communities and with proficient sign language users. As a consequence, they do not always know sign language and do not treat it as a primary tool of instruction and communication. On the other hand, their speech is not always easily intelligible and in order to hear their interlocutor's voice the conversation has to be conducted in a carefully controlled environment (no background noises, interlocutors face easily visible, appropriate tempo, rhythm and style of speaking). As it is normally difficult to create such conditions, technology may serve as a means of securing a satisfying communication environment. Using liquid-crystal display (LCD) or overhead projectors, text messages and emails, devices such as captioned telephones offer secure effective communication between D/deaf or hard of hearing and hearing people.

Technology Serving the D/deaf and Hard of Hearing

Most technology for the D/deaf and hard of hearing can be considered under the heading assistive technology (AT), although the more usually term within the community is simply technology. Assistive technology is understood as *'any item, piece of equipment or product system, whether acquired commercially or off the shelf, modified or customized that is used to increase, maintain or improve functional capabilities of individuals with disabilities'* (20 U.S.C.1401par.602(1)). It might be a complicated speech-to-text reporter system, but could also be a presentation prepared for the class in general that significantly increases the capability of a deaf student to participate in a class, or a text messaging service that improves the D/deaf student's functional capability of communication and enables communication with teacher and peers without using speech that might be hard to comprehend or even unintelligible for the D/deaf student's interlocutors (Lartz *et al.*, 2008).

There are many types of technological devices and services that can be used by D/deaf students (Lartz *et al.*, 2008; Power & Power, 2010). Some of them are the devices and techniques that are also commonly used by the hearing population, like computers, TVs, cell phones or pagers, internet and email, instant messaging, overhead projectors or LCD projectors, videos, videophones, videoconferencing software with remote sign language interpretation services, presentation programs, interactive whiteboards, captioning (including real-time captions of ongoing conversations) (Lartz *et al.*, 2008) and vlogs (video logs – a visual blog that allows deaf students to communicate online in sign language).

Other services have been produced exclusively for deaf users, like hearing aids, cochlear implants, FM systems (devices that transmit the speaker's voice directly into the system used by a D/deaf person, so that the speaker's voice is heard above the background noise), text relay service (a service where text characters are changed into speech), teletype-writer TTY (Power *et al.*, 2007) (an electro-mechanical typewriter used to communicate typed messages), video relay (a telecommunication service that allows communication over the phone in real time, using a sign language interpreter) and voice recognition software (that converts a speech signal to a sequence of words).

There are numerous benefits that come from the use of AT in the education of D/deaf and hard of hearing students. When D/deaf students are provided with visual information, for example by the use of on-screen presentations, overhead or LCD projectors or interactive whiteboards, they were able to obtain more concrete information. Even more importantly, this can be stored and reused at home to serve as a point of reference during homework. This increases the students' ability to remember information and gives them more time to process it. As a consequence, students feel more independent and secure in their learning process and highly motivated to continue with education of this type.

Technology serves as a tool to enhance education and to promote socialization of D/deaf and hard of hearing students. This is very important, as much research has shown that D/deaf and hard of hearing students have severe problems regarding socializing within hearing communities. AT greatly increases the communication opportunities between teachers and students: older students do not have to ask a hearing parent or a custodian to make a phone call in case of their absence, as the student can contact a teacher or a tutor without assistance: this simple fact increases their independence and self-esteem. D/deaf and hard of hearing persons who do not use sign language also have serious problems with communication within their group: as their speech is sometimes hard to understood, not only hearing people, but also their D/deaf or hard of hearing peers have serious difficulties with lip reading it. Technology is also supportive in this case; devices such as mobile phones, and some smartphones in particular, may help to exchange social information through the use of short written messages, as text or email. Also, as with hearing people, D/deaf and hard of hearing persons willingly use social networking technologies for socialization purposes: they are avid users of different forums and services such as MySpace, Nasza Klasa (in Poland) or Facebook.

There are individual differences among deaf students as to the choice of AT. Each D/deaf student has their own preferences and a discussion about this is crucial at the beginning of a course. Even if an interactive whiteboard, for example, is a miraculous device, a particular student may prefer to work with a traditional paper handbook or a classical computer screen and this should be recognized and respected by the teacher.

Using AT also has some drawbacks, but when analysing the possible barriers that impede the use of AT, they seem to have little to do with the functioning of the technology. Rather, they arise from difficulties in coordinating information from different sources of input (instructor, visual presentation, interpreter) or the personal problems of teachers or students who are learning how to use different technological devices. The situation of a D/deaf student participating in a technologically supported class together with hearing peers is a challenging feat: a D/deaf student, for example, is not able to listen to the instructor and look at the presentation at the same time. If a sign language interpreter is also present in a classroom, the situation starts to be even more complicated. The student has to coordinate information coming at once from three sources. In practice, s/he has to choose whether to try to lip-read or to use the presentation as a main means of information, very often feeling frustrated at not being able to access all the information provided during a class. It may create a situation where AT actually causes more distractions than benefits for the D/deaf student.

Another important problem is that of cyberbullying (Bauman & Pero, 2010), as pupils with disabilities are frequently targeted by bullies, and those with severe disability (like deafness) are twice as likely to be bullied as children with disabilities that are not readily apparent (Sullivan, 2006). D/deaf and hard of hearing children quite often lack some social skills, such as the ability to decipher social information or social maturity, and this makes them easier targets for victimization. Further research is necessary to explore these topics, but a teacher should not neglect the potential risk connected with virtual contacts between D/deaf and hard of hearing students and other users of the internet. Before starting to be independent web users, D/deaf pupils should be prepared and informed about possible ways to cope with difficult situations.

To sum up, technological support for the D/deaf should be used very early and should last all their life – in accordance with the philosophy of life-long learning. More and more studies have addressed this area of interest (Mackowiak, 1989; Stinson *et al.*, 1988; Zazove *et al.*, 2004) and they conclude that the use of technology is increasing among disabled people and greatly improving their education outcomes: technology makes education more individual, scientific, powerful, immediate and equal. Technology helps create a learning environment that is supportive to everybody, not only to disabled persons. This idea, usually termed *Universal Learning Design,* describes a visible tendency to support such products and environments that may be used by all people, without the need for adaptation or specialized design (Mace, 2001). The task of educators is to work actively so as to provide multiple and flexible methods of presentation suitable for students with different learning styles, talents and challenges, to assess their knowledge with the use of flexible techniques of assessment and to provide diversified means of engagement to challenge and motivate each student.

English as a Foreign Language for the D/deaf – Challenges for English as a Foreign Language (EFL) Methodology

English is often claimed to be the language of knowledge, economy and interpersonal relationships, a key component of success on the job market and a tool enabling access to civilization goods. According to research conducted by the British Council, it is used by about 2 billion people worldwide, it serves as an official language or a language with a special status in at least 75 countries on different continents and as a *lingua franca* in many others. About 25% of the world's population speak English to some level of competence. Fluent usage of English is a synonym of good education, and that is why in many non-English speaking countries pupils learn English as an obligatory school subject. As a consequence, English is commonly spoken in many European countries: 89% of Swedes declare they speak English, and this is also true for 59% of Germans, 87% of the Dutch, 57% of Slovenians, 46% of Croats and 29% of Poles (Eurobarometer, 2010). Lack of knowledge of English means inaccessibility to high quality cultural goods (internet, media, travelling), restricted social opportunities (entertainment, social networks) and a lowly job position.

D/deaf and hard of hearing students in Poland and other non-English speaking countries are thoroughly aware of these phenomena and are motivated to learn English as a foreign language so as to not ignore contemporary social trends and in order to be competitive on the job market. It was not so previously: for example, in Poland till 2001 students with hearing impairment were not included in foreign language classes in primary and secondary schools. That meant they did not receive a full comprehensive education before entering University. According to the 2001 regulations, D/deaf students are obliged to participate in foreign language classes from their first grade, as are hearing pupils. When it comes to learning a second foreign language, D/deaf students – if it is their wish – can be waived from this course, giving more time and possibilities to master their ethnic and first foreign language. Foreign language classes have been available for D/deaf university students in Poland since the late 1990s (Domagała-Zyśk, 2001, 2003). It was at that time that the first students with hearing impairment, often educated in integrated schools, entered universities. This situation demanded from Higher Education institutions a thorough change of their education system so that it became accessible to students with different disabilities.

Taking into consideration both contemporary psycholinguistic knowledge and the accounts of successful attempts of teaching foreign language to the D/deaf, it must be stressed that there are no psychological or methodological obstructions to teaching a foreign language to the D/deaf. To show this, much psychological research may be cited, for example Krakowiak (2003), MacSweeney (1998), Parasnis (1998) and Marschark et al. (2002), in which D/deaf students present intellectual abilities similar to those of hearing students, in some areas reaching even better results (Bavelier, 2006; Parasnis et al., 1996; Rettenbach et al., 1999), although the danger of overgeneralization of these results needs to be avoided. In pedagogical literature there are also descriptions of some successful experiments involving teaching a foreign language to the D/deaf (Domagała-Zyśk, 2001, 2003, 2005, 2006, 2008, 2010a, 2010b, 2010c, 2010d; Harań, 2005; Janakova, 2004; Kellett Bidoli & Ochse, 2008; Kontra & Bartha, 2010; Ochse, 2008). It is worth noticing that the students presented different degrees of hearing loss and different methods of teaching were used. Taking this into consideration it may be pointed out that EFL for the D/deaf and hard of hearing methodology, known as surdoglottodidactics in Poland, in general does not differ from a classical foreign language learning methodology, neither as far as the approach nor as far as the methods of teaching are concerned. Moreover, the author's view is that creating a special methodology would mean creating a special language ghetto. Because of this, it is advisable to try to do the opposite: foreign language learning should be treated as a tool to open D/deaf students' minds, to give them a tool to communicate with others and to provide access to different sources of information such as the internet in order to help them feel integrated into society.

While teaching the D/deaf, a teacher can use the approach to foreign language learning that he or she thinks most suitable: be it a communicative approach, humanistic approach, self-directed learning approach or total physical response, just to name a few of the most common ones (Harmer, 2001). The methods of teaching (understood as a way of selection and portioning the material to be taught into didactic units and individual lessons), are also not different from those used in a regular classroom. They depend on a teacher's intuition or teaching style, and are usually based on the approach chosen by a teacher. The only things that are different are the techniques of teaching, understood as the teacher and the students' activities during a lesson. Generally the techniques used in a classroom should be modified according to the abilities and disabilities of a particular D/deaf student, that is why the ideal solution seems to be to work with the students individually or in small groups of 3–4 people. Teaching the D/deaf, a teacher must know a special way of communicating with his or her D/deaf students (be it an oral method, sign language or cued speech), bring special visual prompts to make the clues for learning visible, use writing as a way of communication much more often, be careful about his or her position in a classroom and speak more clearly than usual (Domagała-Zyśk, 2003, 2005, 2006, 2008, 2009a, 2009b, 2011a, 2011b, 2011c; Krakowiak, 2003).

D/deaf students in non-English speaking countries usually show high motivation to learn English as a foreign language (Kellett Bidoli & Ochse, 2008; Kontra & Bartha, 2010; Ochse, 2008). This was addressed, among other topics, in research presented in Domagała-Zyśk (2011d). Eleven deaf subjects (nine female and two male), all but one of whom experienced a hearing loss of 90 dB or more, completed a paper and pen questionnaire concerning their motivation to learn a foreign language. The results show that D/deaf students present mature and integrated motivation for this activity. They are aware that knowing a foreign language gives them additional knowledge about other countries and makes it possible for them to travel abroad and have contact with foreigners. On the other hand, the students treat English as a useful tool that enables them to proceed in their chosen career more rapidly. When asked about the factor that motivates them most to undergo the effort of learning a foreign language, the vast majority of them chose a teacher as the person who supports and encourages their learning. Commenting on these results, Domagała-Zyśk (2011d) concludes that the D/deaf participants of the study present mature motivation for foreign language learning in all three dimensions as proposed by: they formulate and know the reasons for learning a foreign language, estimate adequately their abilities and challenges in this process and experience positive emotions during this process. However, it is the teacher's responsibility to acknowledge this motivation and create such an educational environment as to support the child to the utmost. Communication and internet technology serves as a valuable tool in this process.

However, the D/deaf and hard of hearing students experience many difficulties in the process of foreign language learning. These difficulties are connected not only directly with their deafness, but also with some characteristics of the students' family and school environment that may either stimulate or inhibit the child's language development. The most important of these factors is the quality of language that is used in the students' natural environments: when limited and poor language is used, there are not enough occasions for conversations in the native language and parents and teachers do not make a conscious effort to work systematically on expanding the child's vocabulary, resulting in their having poor command of a native language. This factor will disrupt foreign language vocabulary acquisition. A second source of difficulties in foreign vocabulary learning can be connected with the lack of practice in using some of the words in the native language: D/deaf and hard of hearing people rarely participate in spontaneous, incidental dialogues. It means that they did not acquire the language naturally, but they were taught almost all the language they have and some words may create a difficulty for them – for example words like 'conclusion', 'immature', 'decisive', 'self-centred', 'determined', 'reserved', 'down-to-earth person', 'countryside', 'genetically engineered food', 'genes' (Domagała-Zyśk, 2009).

Deaf and hard of hearing students also have a limited ability to hear their own voice and this impedes their ability to learn the proper pronunciation, stress and intonation of words. Even if they know the phonetic transcription of a word, without the support of a teacher and a speech therapist they are not able to produce proper sounds. While mastering the pronunciation, they have limited abilities to correct their own voice production and thus learning the pronunciation of the words is much more difficult for them than for hearing students. However, our experience is that if deaf students speak their native language and want to speak a foreign one, they should be provided with the possibility of trying it – and technology may serve as a great facilitator here as it is shown in the next part of the chapter.

ICT as a Tool Enhancing Teaching and Learning English as a Foreign Language to the D/deaf and Hard of Hearing

Information and communication technology is immensely important for students with hearing impairment: it is commonly accessible and based mostly on visual input and text. It is an invaluable source of support in the process of learning English as a second language, both for the hearing and non-hearing subjects.

As during each school class, an English teacher working with the D/deaf and hard of hearing should first of all check the possibility to employ every possible specific and non-specific technological device and service that might improve teaching quality. With younger children it is important to check whether they have switched on their hearing aids or cochlear implants as only then will they benefit from it. Any problems connected with the use of these devices should be discussed with the child's parents as they might be unaware of the difficulties. If a classroom is equipped with FM systems or induction loop, the teacher should check the rules of its usage and take care to switch it on properly each time that a D/deaf child attends the class. Apart from the technological support the teacher should be aware of the regular rules of effective communication: talk with his/her face directed towards the child, check the light, take care of the child's position in the class and make sure the child is able to lip-read both the teacher's and other students' words (the students' desks should be ideally placed in a classroom in a shape of a crescent moon).

Different non-specific technological devices, like cell phones, computers with internet access, smartphones, Tablets and others can improve the teaching process during English as a foreign language class. The most important benefit of all of them is the possibility to communicate in a foreign language freely with the D/deaf students' hearing and hearing impaired peers thanks to emails, text messages, forums and chats. Virtual reality where this takes place is a sphere of equal chances: using it, the D/deaf persons can, but do not have to reveal their disability, and more than 40% of D/deaf internet users like this last option (Power & Power, 2004). They feel really independent, as they do not need an interpreter or any special communication environment and may communicate from any place where they are: a bus, a park or a school playground. Using mails and short messages in English makes their disability invisible and helps them fight the stereotypes connected with hearing impairment. On the other hand, mobile phones and other equipment can be used even during the class and improve face to face communication.

Written communication via internet and mobile phones might serve as a tool to improve the teacher–student formal communication (for example, they can communicate in English about changes in the schedule, or the deadlines for homework), but it can also improve the teaching process in itself. Before the class starts the student can get an email with the course syllabus, handouts for the particular classes, additional texts to be read and any kind of material the teacher thinks might be useful. Having these materials, a D/deaf student could get prepared for the class in advance: by knowing the topics of discussion beforehand it will be less difficult to follow the class discussion. A mobile phone is a favourite AT for me and my D/deaf students. It makes it possible for me to be in contact practically all the time. As the groups are small (2–3 people) I ask them to inform me (in English, of course) about each smallest change in our timetable. If they feel like they are going to be some minutes late I expect them to send me an SMS (*'I am sorry there's a traffic jam in the centre, I will be late'*). Using this way of communication they can also cancel or postpone a class (*'so see you on Tuesday at 5 pm'*), inform me about their sudden illness or unexpected success during exams, or check whether I am all right after my flu (*'Will I meet with you on English today at 4 o'clock in afternoon?'*), not to mentioning Christmas or Easter greetings. Employing this type of communication in English as part of the EFL curriculum makes the teaching process very practical, and makes up for any lack of speaking exercises during the teaching process. The hearing students spend a lot of time conversing in a foreign language: the D/deaf student can do almost the same using text messages, emails or chats.

There are plenty of other sophisticated technological devices that might support the foreign language learning process in itself, but the most effective of them seems to be an interactive whiteboard. Both the D/deaf students who learn in integrated settings and in special schools for the D/deaf can benefit from its use. In a mainstream class the D/deaf student can follow the class simultaneously with the hearing students more easily, as all the exercises proposed for the students might be visible for him/her (and also for other class members) on the board. This solves the everlasting problem of D/deaf students: they are not able to look at the book lying on the table and lip-read the teachers' words at the same time (for example, when the teacher says: *'Look at page 51 and listen to my comments'*). So far it was an insoluble task, but thanks to the interactive white board a D/deaf student can look at the page from the book provided on the whiteboard and lip-read the teacher's words if the teacher stays next to the board.

The interactive white board and free access to manifold internet sites creates even more possibilities for use by D/deaf students, as it makes it possible to involve a varied language input tailored exactly for the students. One problem with D/deaf students' foreign language education is that there are no special books for this group of clients in any country – the group is not big enough and so diversified that it is impossible to match their needs with a common coursebook. This implies the situation that the teacher has to search for plenty of extra reading and grammar material for D/deaf students. The internet is a valuable source of such materials and very often they are accompanied by interactive exercises, that might be freely used, as on the web sites of the publishing houses. For my students the most interesting topics were those connected with living conditions, the interests and problems of D/deaf students in other countries, travelling, fashion and sport, and we found plenty of interesting materials about these topics.

Literacy should be treated as the most important goal for D/deaf students' education and the strongest predicator for success in education. Today not only literacy in the child's native language, but also in English seems to be an important educational aim in many countries. It is not easy to achieve, as even the newest research demonstrates that the level of reading comprehension among D/deaf students is still significantly lower than among their hearing peers (Reitsma, 2008). Once again AT can help here: the internet provides an excellent opportunity for improving reading and writing skills, and the students can read books, journals and magazines online, both in their ethnic and foreign languages. Some students systematically do this and one of mine, Luke, was lucky enough to publish his life story (in English) in an online magazine, *On Cue*. It is also worth noticing that new types of internet technology, devices and programs have been invented and implemented to increase the D/deaf students' literacy skills (Debevc & Peljhan, 2004; Mueller & Hurtig, 2009; Reitsma, 2008).

It should also be remembered that a reasonable group of hard of hearing and sometimes even D/deaf students communicate with speech in their ethnic language. This group should also be taught English pronunciation and the research shows it can be done successfully: in Domagała-Zyśk and Podlewska's research (2012) native speakers understood as much as 62% of the D/deaf and hard of hearing students' speech production in English as a foreign language. This research implies that the teacher's effort should be directed towards teaching pronunciation and technology: there are many digital pronunciation exercises on the market and as the deaf students have to repeat these exercises much more often than the hearing students, this creates an opportunity for diversified practice. A meaningful enterprise in this field was proposed by Podlewska (2012) in their program *DoctorCue*, where new technologies, together with cued speech, are employed to create interesting materials for teaching D/deaf students English pronunciation.

Television still appears to be the most common media used by a majority of D/deaf students, almost all of them admit they spend a lot of time watching TV and it is definitely their favourite pastime. Consequently, captioning is the next service that has to be discussed here. Watching films or news in a target language is a well known strategy to improve foreign language mastery; unfortunately, deaf students cannot benefit from it without subtitles, as it is very difficult or almost impossible to lip-read from the screen. The only possibility is to provide subtitles and this service is very popular and financed by the state in many countries, although unfortunately not in Poland. The solution is to fight for new legislation (and Polish Deaf and hard of hearing people have started to do that), use the sites with the subtitles provided (fortunately, there are many films and materials with English subtitles) or prepare subtitles on one's own, as this is not a very complicated technique. Watching films and programmes with subtitles, including those stored in YouTube, immensely widens the accessibility of different teaching materials for the D/deaf population.

English teachers, however, should be strongly aware of the fact that D/deaf students can face serious obstacles while using electronic media. We should remember first of all, that deafness means that the students have problems not only with listening and speaking, but with using language. This means that the words usually known by their peers may be unknown to them, and sentence structures of the real language might appear too difficult to access meaning. That is why English teachers of the D/deaf should remember the following things:

- D/deaf students cannot be left alone with un-prepared English texts, as they are usually not able to cope with real English materials from the internet on their own. As it seems too difficult for them, they quickly become disappointed with English on the internet in general and do not like using it. We must remember that D/deaf students usually do not pick up information spontaneously, listening to the radio programmes, watching TV, using computer games, freely sharing information with their peers – they usually have to be taught each piece of knowledge we want them to possess. Because of this, it is advisable to help them by deciphering instructions, manuals and other introductory information. My students were very surprised after reading one text specially prepared for them that the internet was invented in the late eighties (and they definitely could not understand how it was possible for people like me to study and graduate without using it). Before working with such material, a teacher has to explain all the unknown historical, geographical or language issues.

- The teaching material has to be carefully chosen and analysed by a teacher beforehand. It is difficult to employ commonly used computer programs for learning English with the D/deaf as the majority of them use sounds to communicate with the user, and melodies and songs are inevitable parts of almost every teaching program. When such software is used by a D/deaf student, it usually makes him or her frustrated as it reminds them constantly about their disability, so the teacher's task would be to find programs based more on visual than audio signals.

- We should not feel disappointed or frustrated if deaf students reluctantly use email communication in looking for English-speaking friends. As they have greater problems than others in expressing their thoughts by the use of words and expressions, their messages are sometimes rather clumsy. If they try to communicate with a person who is also a Deaf or a hard of hearing one, this impedes and hinders communication, which is a source of frustration and discourages students from trying again. Teachers should also remember that D/deaf students are usually aware of the low level of their writing skills and are rather reluctant to present them in a new situation; that is why they prefer to make new friends by speaking with them face to face. Only when they feel safe enough (perhaps in contact with their teacher or students from their group), will they be ready to use written English freely and will not be too ashamed of mistakes and basic survival structures used in their letters.

- Using AT also requires active participation from the D/deaf people themselves, teamwork among teachers, facilitators, learning support assistants and interpreters and constant updating of the teachers' knowledge about new technologies, so as to avoid the situation of being a digital immigrant.

Conclusion

I wonder why is it so difficult to discuss the issues connected with hearing aids, mainly from the technological point of view. For example: I went to the agency where a hearing care professional worked on my hearing aids. His task was to accommodate it to the kind of my hearing loss. If only I had started asking about the technical details (e.g. what is the name of the computer software used), I got a very general answer (e.g. 'This is the software suggested by the producer of the hearing aids'). I was a stubborn client and I asked about the interface of it and I got to know that this is confidential information! I asked if the hearing aid they proposed me is operated by HI-PRO or NoahLink, so they told me to contact the producer. Finally I wanted to know if the hearing aid had the option to cooperate with HiFi, a computer or a Smartphone. In this situation I got an answer that there are no such hearing aids available.

I cannot understand this: why the specialists are so little interested in new technologies for the deaf ?

Tom

This statement by one of the Polish D/deaf students shows perfectly two things: the D/deaf people themselves are very much interested in using new technologies and see them as potentially immensely supporting their functioning. On the other hand, they are sometimes still treated as not very knowledgeable users of it, and specialists working with the D/deaf and hard of hearing students seem not to understand fully the significance of new technologies for education and everyday functioning of D/deaf and hard of hearing people. Nevertheless, the use of AT is increasing among the D/deaf population, it is beginning at an early age and holds potential to equalize the student's experience at a mainstream school (Michaels & McDermott, 2003). AT can be fruitful not only in educational situations but also in social participation, especially when a D/deaf person communicates with a hearing counterpart (Vincent *et al.*, 2007). Technology can be named as a powerful '*equalizing force*' (Michaels & McDermott, 2003: 29) in D/deaf education, and can foster the D/deaf students' meaningful inclusion into general classrooms and support them in presenting their knowledge, thus promoting their e-inclusion into the society in general.

References

20 U.S.C.1401par.602(1). Individuals with Disabilities Education Act, accessed 16 January 2013, http://idea.ed.gov/
Agboola, I.O. and Lee, A.C. (2000) Computer and information technology access for deaf individuals in developed and developing countries. *Journal of Deaf Studies and Deaf Education* 5 (3), 286–289.
Barak, A. and Sadovsky, Y. (2008) Internet use and personal empowerment of hearing-impaired adolescents. *Computers in Human Behavior* 24, 1802–1815.
Bauman, S. and Pero, H. (2010) Bullying and cyberbullying among deaf students and their hearing peers: An exploratory study. *Journal of Deaf Studies and Deaf Education* 16 (2), 236–253.

Bavelier, D. (2006) Do deaf individuals see better? *Trends in Cognitive Sciences* 10 (11), 512–518.

Borders, C.M., Barnett, D. and Bauer, A.M. (2010) How are they really doing? Observation on inclusionary classroom participation for children with mild-to-moderate deafness. *Journal of Deaf Studies and Deaf Education* 15 (4), 348–357.

Debevc, M. and Peljhan, Ž. (2004) The role of video technology in on-line lectures for the deaf. *Disability and Rehabilitation* 26 (17), 1048–1059.

Domagała-Zyśk, E. (2001) *Możliwości nauczania języków obcych uczniów z uszkodzonym słuchem*. In Z. Palak (ed.) *Pedagogika specjalna w reformowanym ustroju edukacyjnym* (pp. 235–242). Lublin: Wydawnictwo UMCS.

Domagała-Zyśk, E. (2003) Nauczanie języka angielskiego studentów z uszkodzonym narządem słuchu. In *Audiofonologia XXIII*, 127–136.

Domagała-Zyśk, E. (2005) *Specjalne potrzeby edukacyjne niesłyszących studentów uczących się języka angielskiego*. In K. Ciepiela (ed.) *Procesy poznawcze i język. Klasyczna problematyka - współczesne rozwiązania. Cognition and Language. Classical problems - contemporary solutions* (pp. 159–168). Piotrków Trybunalski: Naukowe Wydawnictwo Piotrowskie.

Domagała-Zyśk, E. (2006) *Edukacyjne i terapeutyczne wartości lektoratu języka angielskiego dla studentów niesłyszących*. In K. Krakowiak and A. Dziurda-Multan (eds) *Przekraczanie barier w wychowaniu osób z uszkodzeniami słuchu* (pp. 423–432). Lublin: Wydawnictwo KUL.

Domagała-Zyśk, E. (2008) Specific features of the deaf persons' memory and foreign language learning. In Z. Telnarová (ed.) *Vidim, co Neslyším. Proceedings of international conference on the problem of assistance to aurally-handicapped students in their preparation and study at universities* (pp. 98–102). Ostrava: Ostravska univerzita v Ostravé.

Domagała-Zyśk, E. (2009) Poziom motywacji niesłyszących studentów do uczenia się języków obcych. Lublin: Chair of Special Pedagogy Library KUL.

Domagała-Zyśk, E. (2009a) *Trudności osób niesłyszących w nabywaniu słownictwa w języku obcym i sposoby przezwyciężania tych trudności*. In M. Dycht and L. Marszałek (eds) *Dylematy (niepełno)sprawności – rozważania na marginesie studiów kulturowo – społecznych* (pp. 223–236). Warszawa: Wydawnictwo Salezjańskie.

Domagała-Zyśk, E. (2009b) *Lekcje i zajęcia języka obcego dla uczniów niepełnosprawnych*. In H. Komorowska (ed.) *Skuteczna nauka języka obcego. Struktura i przebieg zajęć językowych* (pp. 232–246). Warszawa: Wydawnictwo CODN.

Domagała-Zyśk, E. (2010a) *Procesy pamięciowe u osób z uszkodzeniami słuchu a nauczanie ich języka obcego*. In M. Wójcik (ed.) *Edukacja i rehabilitacji osób z wadą słuchu – wyzwania współczesności.* (pp. 119–130). Toruń: Wydawnictwo Edukacyjne "AKAPIT".

Domagała-Zyśk, E. (2010b) *Uwarunkowania rozumienia tekstu w języku obcym przez osoby z uszkodzeniami słuchu*. In Z. Palak, A. Bujnowska and A. Pawlak (eds) *Aktualne problemy edukacji i rehabilitacji osób niepełnosprawnych w biegu życia* (pp. 163–173). Lublin: Wydawnictwo UMCS.

Domagała-Zyśk, E. (2010c) *Idea integracji a potrzeby niesłyszących studentów w zakresie uczenia się języków obcych w szkołach wyższych*. In S. Byra and M. Parchomiuk (eds) *Student niepełnosprawny. Wybrane konteksty* (pp. 155–165). Lublin: Wydawnictwo UMCS.

Domagała-Zyśk, E. (2010d) *Kształcenie studentów z uszkodzeniami słuchu w Stanach Zjednoczonych. W*. In S. Byra and M. Parchomiuk (red.) *Student niepełnosprawny. Wybrane konteksty* (pp. 169–180). Lublin: Wydawnictwo UMCS.

Domagała-Zyśk, E. (2011a) *Style uczenie preferowane przez niesłyszących uczestników lektoratu języka obcego*. In M. Białas (ed.) *Specjalne potrzeby niepełnosprawnych* (pp. 243–260). Kraków: Arson.

Domagała-Zyśk, E. (2011b) El uso de las tecnologías de la información y de la comunicación en el aprendizaje de lenguas extranjeras en los estudiantes sordos. *Escuola Albierta* 13, 137–153.

Domagała-Zyśk, E. (2011c) Kompetencje uczniów niesłyszących i słabo słyszących w zakresie posługiwania się językiem angielskim w szkołach podstawowych, gimnazjach i szkołach ponadgimnazjalnych. In K. Karpińska-Szaj (ed.) *Neofilolog* 36 (pp. 91–111).

Domagała-Zyśk, E. (2011d) *Wspieranie osób z uszkodzeniami słuchu w edukacji uniwersyteckiej w Polsce i na Świecie.* W. In J. Baran, T. Cierpiałowska and A. Mikrut (eds) *Teoria i praktyka oddziaływań profilaktyczno-wspierających rozwój osób z niepełnosprawnością* (pp. 212–218). Kraków: Wydawnictwo Naukowe Uniwersytetu Pedagogicznego.

Domagała-Zyśk, E. and Podlewska, A. (2012) *Umiejętności polskich studentów z uszkodzeniami słuchu w zakresie posługiwania się mówioną formą języka angielskiego.* W. In K. Kutek-Sładek, G. Godawa and Ł. Ryszka (red.) *Student z niepełnosprawnością w środowisku akademickim* (pp. 134–157). Kraków: Wydawnictwo św Stanisława BM.

Eurobarometer (2010) accessed 15 January 2013, http://ec.europa.eu/public_opinion/index_en.htm

Harań, B. (ed.) (2005) *Kształcenie studentów niepełnosprawnych w zakresie języków obcych. Teaching foreign languages to disabled people.* Siedlce: Wydawnictwo Akademii Podlaskiej.

Harmer, J. (2001) *The Practice of English Language Teaching.* London: Longman.

Hulek, A. (red.) (1992) *Uczeń niepełnosprawny w szkole masowej.* Kraków: WSP.

Janakova, D. (ed.) (2004) *Methodology Guide to Learning and Teaching English for the Deaf, Hard of Hearing and Vision Impaired Students and Their Teachers.* Prague: Charles University.

Kellett Bidoli, C.J. and Ochse, E. (eds) (2008) *English in International Deaf Communication.* Bern: Peter Lang.

Kontra, E.H. and Bartha, Cs. (2010) Foreign language education in Hungary: Concerns and controversies. *Sociolinguistica* 24, 61–84.

Korzon, A. (2006) *Wsparcie studentów niesłyszących na drodze ku wyższym szczeblom edukacji.* In J. Baran, T. Cierpiałowska and A. Mikrut (eds) *Teoria i praktyka oddziaływań profilaktyczno-wspierających rozwój osób z niepełnosprawnością* (pp. 206–211). Kraków: Wydawnictwo Naukowe Uniwersytetu Pedagogicznego.

Krakowiak, K. (2003) *Szkice o wychowaniu dzieci z uszkodzeniami słuchu.* Stalowa Wola Katolicki Uniwersytet Lubelski, Wydział Nauk Społecznych, Filia w Stalowej Woli. Stalowa Wola.

Krakowiak, K. (2006) *Pedagogiczna typologia uszkodzeń słuchu i osób nimi dotkniętych.* In: K. Krakowiak and A. Multan *Nie głos, ale słowo… Przekraczanie barier w wychowaniu osób z uszkodzeniami słuchu* (pp. 255–289). Lublin: Wydawnictwo KUL.

Lartz, M.N., Stoner, J.B. and Stout, L.J. (2008) Perspectives of assistive technology from deaf students at a hearing university. *Assistive Technology Outcomes and Benefits* 5 (1), 72–91.

Mace, R. (2001) accessed 15 January 2013, http://www.ncsu.edu/project/design-projects/udi/

Mackowiak, K. (1989) Deaf college students and computers: The beneficial effect of experience on attitudes. *Journal of Educational Technology Systems* 17, 219–229.

MacSweeney, M. (1998) Cognition and deafness. In S. Gregory, P. Knight, W. McCraken, S. Powers and L. Watson (eds) *Issues in Deaf Education.* London: David Fulton Publishers.

Marschark, M., Lang, H.G. and Albertini, J.A. (2002) *Educating Deaf Students: From Research to Practice.* New York: Oxford University Press.

Michaels, C.A. and McDermott, J. (2003) Assistive technology integration in special educationteacher preparation: Program coordinators' perceptions of current attainment and importance. *Journal of Special Education Technology* 18 (3), 29–44.

Mueller, V. and Hurtig, R. (2009) Technology-enhanced shared reading with deaf and hard-of-hearing children: The role of a fluent signing narrator. *Journal of Deaf Studies and Deaf Education* 15 (1), 72–101.

Ochse, E. (2008) Access through EFL to multimodal non-fictional discourse. In C.J. Kellett Bidoli and E. Ochse (eds) *English in International Deaf Communication* (pp. 251–275). Bern: Peter Lang.

Parasnis, I. (1998) Cognitive diversity in deaf people: Implications for communication and education. *Scandinavian Audiology* 27 (49), 109–115.

Parasnis, I., Samar, V.J., Bettger, J.G. and Sathe, K. (1996) Does deafness lead to enhancement of visual-spatial cognition in children? Negative evidence from deaf non-signers. *Journal of Deaf Studies and Deaf Education* 1, 145–152.

Podlewska, A. (2012) Adaptacja materiłów dydaktycznych w nauce języka angielskeigo studentów z dysfunkcja słuchu. In Z. Palak, D. Chimicz and A. Pawlak (red.) *Wielość obszarów we współczesnej pedagogice specjalnej* (pp. 383–390). Lublin: Wydawnictwo UMCS.

Power, D., Power, M.R. and Rehling, B. (2007) German deaf people using text communication: Short message service, TTY, relay services, fax, and e-mails. *American Annals of the Deaf* 152 (3).

Power, M.R. and Power, D. (2004) Everyone here speaks TXT: Deaf people using SMS in Australia and the rest of the world. *Journal of Deaf Studies and Deaf Education* 9 (3), 350–360.

Power, M.R. and Power, D. (2010) Communicating with Australian deaf people about communication technology. *The Australian and New Zealand Journal of Audiology* 32 (1), 31–40.

Reitsma, P. (2008) Computer-based exercises for learning to read and spell by deaf children. *Journal of Deaf Studies and Deaf Education* 14 (2), 178–189.

Rettenbach, R., Diller, G. and Sireteanu, R. (1999) Do deaf people see better? Texture segmentation and visual search compensate in adult but not in juvenile subjects. *Journal of Cognitive Neuroscience* 11, 560–583.

Stinson, M., Stuckless, E.R., Henderson, J. and Miller, L. (1988) Perceptions of hearing impaired college students toward real-time speech to print: RTGD and other educational support services. *The Volta Review* 90, 339–348.

Stinson, M.S. and Antia, S.D. (1999) Considerations in educating deaf and hard-of-hearing students in inclusive settings. *Journal of Deaf Studies and Deaf Education* 4, 163–175.

Sullivan, P. (2006) Children with disabilities expose to violence: Legal and public policy issues. In M. Feerick and G. Silverman (eds) *Children exposed to violence* (pp. 213–237). Baltimore: Paul Brookes.

Vincent, C., Deaudelin, I. and Hotton M. (2007) Pilot on evaluating social participation following the use of an assistive technology designed to facilitate face-to-face communication between deaf and hearing persons. *Technology and Disability* 19, 153–167.

Woodward, J.C. (1972) Some observations on sociolinguistic variation and American sign language. *Kansas Journal of Sociology* 9, 191–200.

Zazove, P., Meador, H.E., Derry, H.A., Gorenflo D.W., Burdick S.W. and Sanders, E.W. (2004) Deaf persons and computer use. *American Annals of the Deaf* 148, 376–384.

6 Information and Communication Technology – An Instrument for Developing Inclusive Practice in the Training of Modern Languages Teachers

Lynne Meiring and Nigel Norman

Introduction

> ... those with special educational needs must have access to regular schools which should accommodate them within a child-centred pedagogy capable of meeting these needs. (UNESCO, 1994: viii)

This robust statement of intent from 1994 set a clear international agenda of inclusion, to which all countries must aspire. Clearly it will be interpreted differently by individual countries, and the implementation of the ideal will remain contentious, even nationally. What remains paramount, however, is that the rights of special educational needs (SEN) pupils to the most effective and suitable education must remain a priority. Clearly such a priority has resource implications, particularly where provision is in mainstream settings. Moreover, and even more significantly than in 1994, this will include resource issues of a technological nature.

Resources must also be allocated to support services for the training of mainstream teachers ... Appropriate technical aids to ensure the successful operation of an integrated education system must also be provided. (UNESCO, 1994: 42)

The UK Context

Provision for SEN over the last decade has, in many respects, remained largely unchanged in the UK. This is demonstrated by the statutory procedural guidance of the Code of Practice for England (DFES, 2001), Wales (WAG, 2002), Scotland (Scottish Parliament, 2004) and Northern Ireland (DENI, 1998; DENI, 2005: Supplement), which remain the current Frameworks for provision. It does appear, however, that change is imminent in England. The 2011 Green Paper (DfE, 2011b) sets out a vision for reform, including wide ranging proposals to improve outcomes for children and young people who are disabled or have SEN. Based on these proposals there does seem to be an emphasis on disability and SEN, whereas in Wales the agenda has broadened to include a wider range of educational needs, such that SEN forms a part, albeit a significant one, of the broader term additional learning needs (ALN) (WAG, 2010). Whichever term is considered in the context of teaching and learning, the implications for an inclusive classroom are considerable, in that both ALN and SEN encompass a wide range of needs. This is manifested by the widening of the agenda of inclusion, and the increased and broadened emphasis on Human Rights, given particular prominence in the Salamanca Agreement (UNESCO, 1994), and subsequently in UK legislation (Equality Act (Home Office, 2010), Every Child Matters (DfE, 2003), and Rights to Action (WAG, 2004)). These factors clearly impinge upon initial teacher training and continuing professional development of teachers. This emphasis emerges strongly in UNESCO 1994:

Universities have a major advisory role to play in the process of developing special needs education, especially as regards research, evaluation, preparation of teacher trainers, and designing training programmes and materials. (UNESCO, 1994: 28)

One of the major issues is whether there may be a case for a distinctive pedagogy for particular learning needs within modern foreign language (MFL) lessons. This clearly has relevance for the selection and use of resources, and in particular the role and benefit of information and communication technology (ICT) in an inclusive curriculum. It is equally important that student teachers, during their initial training, gain the appropriate knowledge, understanding and experience in this area if they are to meet the needs of all learners in the classroom. This is acknowledged by the UK government's response to the commissioned Ofsted review of SEN in England (Ofsted, 2010), which expresses the need to:

> ... overhaul teacher training and professional development to better help pupils with special educational needs and to raise their attainment. (DfE, 2011a)

It is further endorsed by the government consultation (DfE, 2011b), which highlights the fact that teachers state that they do not always have adequate training to identify needs and provide the right help, and that special needs pupils feel frustrated at the lack of the right help at school. Of greater concern perhaps is the fact that the life chances of pupils with special needs remain disproportionately poor. Clearly therefore, it is vital that such issues are identified and addressed during initial teacher training.

Legislation – Implications

In identifying pupils with SEN it is significant that the first standard for the Award of Qualified Teacher Status in England and Wales states that student teachers need to:

> ... understand the diverse learning needs of pupils and endeavour to provide the best possible education for them to maximise their potential, whatever their individual aspirations, personal circumstances or cultural, linguistic, religious and ethnic backgrounds. (WAG, 2009: S1.1)

Further references include the need for student teachers 'to understand their responsibilities under the SEN Code of Practice for Wales', and to 'differentiate their teaching to meet the needs for those with Special Educational Needs'. Both these references identify the fact that this will be difficult to achieve unaided, and refer to seeking specialist advice on 'less common types of Special Educational Needs' (WAG, 2009: S2.6, S3.3.4). Another distinctive feature of the Code of Practice is the references to the contribution of ICT as a tool to support inclusive practice. Furthermore the rapid rate of advance of technology has significantly increased the options available for pupils with SEN to access the curriculum in the inclusive classroom. In terms of the training of student teachers, it is clear that the current generations have very well developed technical ICT skills, but what is lacking is both the pedagogy and a knowledge of the specialised technology available to meet the needs of individual learners.

Other challenges facing student teachers stem from the time restrictions of the initial teacher training course, which prevent them gaining in-depth understanding and experience of the different types of need they will encounter in school. Also they have to negotiate the requirements of an inclusive curriculum, which demand that the pupil no longer has the responsibility of adapting to the curriculum, but that the curriculum has to adapt to the pupil. This situation has been further exacerbated in England and Wales by the fact that SEN is now considered within the broader concept of ALN, which embraces a wider range of needs (WAG, 2010). The Welsh Assembly Government have indicated that ALN includes a wide range of needs (see Table 6.1).

Although it could be argued that the needs highlighted in Table 6.1 have always existed, the challenge has increased in that inclusive practices mean that student teachers are far more likely than in the past to encounter these pupils in their classes on a regular basis. In addition, the increased awareness that comes with the repositioning and redefining of the term SEN within a broader range of needs (ALN) has necessitated the development of student teachers acquiring a more specialised pedagogy. The rationale for this wider term has emanated from a recognition of the diversity and complexity of

Table 6.1 Diagram illustrating the categories of ALN defined by WAG (2010: 58–59)

Additional learning needs

Asylum seeking refugee children	Pupils with a disability	Pupils with medical needs	Bullied, e.g. lesbian, gay, bisexual, transgender	Children in families with difficult circumstances
Gypsies and travellers	Certain minority ethnic pupils including English as an Additional Language (EAL)	Pupils who perform or who have employment	Young carers	School refusers and school phobics
Young offenders	Children of migrant workers	Young parents and pregnant youths	Pupils with SEN	Looked after by local authority

the needs of learners in schools (e.g. WAG, 2010: 58). It is interesting to note that the more able and talented (MAT) are not considered in this broader category in Wales, unless they also demonstrate an additional learning need (see Table 6.1); but clearly in an inclusive classroom their particular individual needs are as valid as those of all pupils. The definition of ALN refers to learning needs that are greater than those of pupils' peers of the same age, but it falls short of the full definition of SEN in the Education Act (1996) used in the SEN Code of Practice (DfES, 2001; WAG, 2002):

A child has special educational needs … if he has a learning difficulty which calls for special educational provision to be made for him. (Education Act, 1996: Section 312 (2))

and:

He has a significantly greater difficulty than the majority of pupils of his age. He has a disability which prevents or hinders him from making use of educational facilities of a kind generally provided for children of his age. (Education Act, 1996)

The Codes of Practice have identified four broad categories of types of SEN:

(a) communication and interaction; (b) cognition and learning; (c) behaviour, emotional and social development and (d) sensory and/or physical. Although each category includes a wide range of pupils these do have limitations in the context of the inclusive classroom in that, for example, many children have 'inter-related needs' (WAG, 2002), and also in that many individuals with ALN do not fall into these categories. The Code of Practice does, however, offer to student teachers some very useful guidelines in terms of identifying specific needs within the classroom 'triggers' and suggesting intervention strategies to meet the needs of individual learners. It should be noted that many of these intervention strategies are general in nature, such as the recommendation for 'flexible teaching arrangements' (e.g. WAG, 2002: 7.62, p. 87), where student teachers would need significant guidance. One of the possibilities for flexible teaching arrangements exemplified in WAG (2002) is the use of ICT. Although over a decade since the publication of the Code of Practice, there is a significant number of references to the role of ICT and technological aids in supporting inclusive practice and meeting the needs of individual pupils. Again these would not be specific enough to instruct the beginning student teacher adequately, for example *'access to alternative or augmented forms of communication'* (WAG, 2002: 7.62, p. 87). It would appear therefore that for student teachers to become effective teachers of ALN there are two major challenges, which constitute two significant areas of pedagogy: meeting the needs of all learners, and the role of ICT in improving/enabling the learning experience. Figure 6.1 summarises the challenges faced by student teachers in the inclusive classroom. First, on a conceptual level, students need to know and understand the legislative framework, within which they are operating, such as, for example, in the case of special needs, the Code of Practice, which gives information on the roles and responsibilities of relevant parties, as well as the identification and assessment of special needs. In particular they will also need to understand their individual role in identifying pupils for intervention at school action level (e.g. WAG, 2002: 68). They also need a knowledge and understanding of different types of need, which can be gained from other professionals, the internet or literature (e.g. Buttriss & Callander (2008), which covers a range of need, indicating key characteristics for identification and key support strategies).

Once the knowledge and framework are secure, perhaps a more difficult task is grasping a realistic way to differentiate learning. Often this is an area covered later in initial teacher education programmes, but is arguably one that should be addressed and applied earlier. Thus, they will be able to avoid

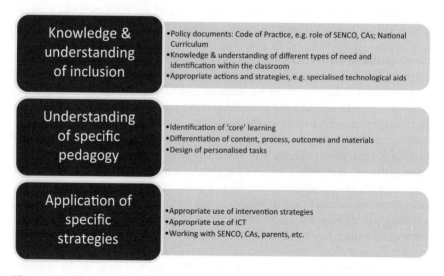

Figure 6.1 Summary of challenges facing student teachers in the inclusive classroom

the classic pitfalls of 'teaching to the middle' and thereby marginalising pupils whose needs render them more difficult to include. Third, student teachers will be very much at the forefront of implementing intervention strategies, particularly under the UK assessment category of 'school action', with the expectation that an appropriate strategy will have addressed the pupil's need and will enable the pupil to make progress in his/her learning. Clearly one significant intervention strategy is the use of technology, and although it is certainly not the only strategy to improve the learning experience of children with ALN, it is clear that it does have a substantial role to play. Chambers (1999: 202) recognises the importance of knowledge and expertise in the area of ICT, if pupils' needs are to be met, and in particular the need for *'in-service training (for example in ICT and autonomous, flexible approaches to learning), the necessary resources (e.g. hard- and software, time to plan, and support'*.

As Comfort and Tierney (2007: 82) suggest: *'The technology is increasingly user-friendly and has opened up a whole new world of possibilities for the teaching and learning of languages'*. This use of technology needs to be linked to both the learning objectives of the pupils and their individual needs.

Role and Benefit of ICT in the Curriculum

The importance of ICT for pupils with SEN was signalled in 1993 by Sir Ron Dearing in his review of the National Curriculum. This was translated into an Access Statement (Common Requirements) in the National Curriculum ((DfE/WO, 1995; ACCAC, 2000), which included significant references to the inclusion of technology and technological aids to enable pupils with SEN to access the curriculum and progress. The DfEE Action Programme (DfEE, 1998b: 26) states: *'There will be more effective and widespread use of Information and Communications Technology to support the education with Special Educational Needs, in both mainstream and special schools'*. This was further emphasised by numerous references in the Code of Practice (DfeS, 2001: 5:58, 6:66, 7:49, 10:7). These references to the importance of ICT to special needs in the policy documents clearly raise the question of how ICT can improve the learning experience of pupils with ALN. From the perspective of student teachers it is useful to consider this improvement from the point of view of ICT as:

- a motivator;
- a pedagogical tool;
- a tool for administration and resourcing.

ICT and motivation

Perhaps one of the primary considerations for student teachers of MFL is how to motivate pupils by capturing their interest and attention. ICT offers an obvious immediacy and visual impact, mainly on account of its multi-media and multi-sensory features. In an inclusive classroom these features are essential in order to include a wide range of pupils with a wide range of needs. An interactive whiteboard, for example, represents a medium that is both familiar (screen) and associated with enjoyment (games, TV, DVD). This exploits the potential of a pre-existing receptivity, which in turn often leads to a more positive predisposition towards learning. This engagement of the learners afforded by the medium is particularly significant because of the well-established relationship between motivation and discipline. Once engaged, many issues of behaviour and control assume secondary importance, because of the altered working environment. As Kennewell states:

> When you observe pupils using ICT, rather than traditional methods, you usually notice a higher level of motivation, a more intense engagement with the activity, and a greater willingness to explore ideas and to persevere in the face of challenge. (Kennewell, 2004: 23)

In addition Cox (1999) in Kennewell (2004) proposes that this use of ICT, if correctly channelled, leads to significant improvements in learning. She suggests that the reason might be that ICT gives pupils more control over their learning, producing greater efforts and improved personal outcomes for all learners. Although this control over their learning may be more to do with learner perception of autonomy than the reality, in that the teacher gives pedagogical direction and a framework to the learning, the element of learner control stems from the ability to manage the pace of the learning personally. In addition to this, the learner can determine the frequency of repetition that he/she individually needs, without the pressure and stress of either the teacher or peers.

Kennewell links three of TTA's (1998) distinct features of ICT: speed, provisionality and interactivity, specifically to motivation (Kennewell, 2004: 23). Although these will be discussed in detail below, it is useful to note Kennewell's emphasis on immediate response (speed and interactivity), and self-correction (provisionality) in relation to motivation. Provisionality removes much of the stigma attached to traditional forms of error correction, facilitates improvement and engenders more pride and ownership of work. The interactivity similarly affords a more private and personal response to learning, removing self-consciousness, embarrassment and low self-esteem, and enhancing wellbeing. A computer is non-judgemental!

ICT as a pedagogical tool

Although an understanding of motivation is an essential component in the development of student teachers' skills, it appears to present fewer problems than the development of pedagogy, with its very precise and structured set of skills. This requires knowledge, planning and preparation, teaching techniques, use of resources, and task design. Cox and Webb (2004: 6–7) advise: *'Teachers need to understand the relationship between a range of ICT resources, and the concepts, processes and skills in their subjects'*.

Clearly to establish discrete pedagogies for all learners is impractical, and research by Norwich and Lewis (2001) suggests that this might not be the most effective way of meeting the needs of all learners in the inclusive classroom. Student teachers would certainly benefit more from initially establishing what Norwich and Lewis describe as a pedagogy that is common to all learners, rather than pedagogies for specific groups of learners. This would, however, require significant adaptation of the pedagogy, sometimes for specific groups of learners, and, where necessary, individual learners. The pedagogy would be established as a continuum of teaching approaches, rather than a continuum of types of special needs. This gives recognition to the fact that the needs of learners cannot necessarily be linked to the sub-group of learning difficulties to which they belong, but that these needs change over the course of time. Also there are shared characteristics common to different groups of learning need, making it more appropriate to establish common approaches, rather than specific pedagogies.

Hence a continuum of teaching approaches, suggested by Norwich and Lewis (2001), might provide a useful way forward for student teachers attempting to meet the needs of all learners in their classes. In terms of language learning, the core pedagogy might be as general as all learners needing to encounter language, practise language and have opportunities to apply and use language related to specific topics. The challenge therefore for student teachers for each of these language-learning processes is how they can be organised and managed for all learners, that is, how the core pedagogy can be adapted. It is clear that in considering adaptation of a core pedagogy, ICT will play a significant role in enabling, for example, individual pupils to have more examples of a particularly difficult concept, more practice in a difficult area or more specialised equipment. Thus, for instance, the visual representation of flowcharts and timelines will greatly benefit learners struggling to sequence ideas and processes, and writing frames will enable learners with literacy difficulties, including dyslexia. Although this could arguably be achieved in other ways, the distinctive features of ICT, which will be discussed later, provide a unique medium for the learner in terms of individual progress, and for the teacher in terms of management of the learning environment.

Thus ICT becomes a considered and integrated part of a wider pedagogy, rather than a discrete and random add-on to everyday teaching and learning. Perhaps as a starting point student teachers need to understand the significant role of ICT for particular groups of learners, or manifestations of learning difficulty. Blamires (1999) makes a useful distinction in this context between two groups of learners; the first being those who require technology to gain any access to the curriculum at all, and a second group that could arguably include all learners, but in particular pupils with ALN, whose learning is enhanced through the use of ICT. Pupils such as travellers, who experience a 'broken' or interrupted curriculum, could potentially remediate gaps in their learning. Modules of work can be stored electronically and accessed remotely, at any time and in any location. Work can also be submitted electronically, marked and returned electronically, together with the potential for a professional dialogue between teacher and learner. The importance of this for these pupils in sustaining a teacher–pupil relationship, in addition to remediating the learning, is self-evident.

Another useful model is the taxonomy of e-inclusion (Abbott, 2007), which proposes three categories. First there is the use of technology to train or rehearse, which is linked primarily to a behaviourist model of learning. Second there is the use of technology to assist learning, which can, for example, compensate for a disability or difficulty, in order to enhance learning. The technology, therefore, becomes the key through which learning takes place for pupils at all levels. The third category in the taxonomy, technology to enable learning, gives technology a far more crucial and active role in that it renders learning possible, that is, without technology the learning would be impossible.

Categorising the use of technology in these ways provides student teachers with a useful and essential platform and access point in managing a vast bank of potential strategies and resources. Based upon the categories of Blamires (1999) and Abbott (2007), and to accommodate the needs of the increased demands of the inclusive classroom with a wider spectrum of needs, it may be useful for student teachers to consider the use of technology under the headings of: enablement, enrichment, and extension.

ICT as an instrument for 'enablement' provides a unique entry to the curriculum for pupils who otherwise would be excluded. This physical access is described by Day (cited in Blamires, 1999: 5) as '*technology at its most dramatic, liberating the pupil from the physical barriers to learning.'* A visually impaired pupil, for example, might require facilities such as screen magnifiers, whereas a physically impaired pupil without the use of their hands would need speech to writing facilities. If such pupils are to access the curriculum, ICT represents a veritable lifeline. Buttriss and Callander (2008: 171–174) have a useful A–Z of resources, linked to the Code of Practice, and illustrating a range of ICT applications, which can support enablement. Organising and orchestrating ICT for these pupils will clearly be beyond the brief of student teachers, but their role would be one of negotiation with relevant colleagues, and an understanding of the potential of the technology to enable access.

'Enrichment' allows most pupils, and especially pupils with SEN, to improve the quality of the learning, which impacts positively on progress, described by Day (cited in Blamires, 1999: 5) as *'the power of technology to support the pupil in particular areas of difficulty.'* A pupil with a very low reading age can be severely hindered in all areas of the curriculum, and although targeting the improvement of this particular need will remain paramount, pupils need to be allowed to progress within the curriculum and not be held back by one area of difficulty. Hence, for example, the use of Clicker 5, (Crick Software), which adds sound to words and images, and the use of animation to visualise more difficult concepts such as verb tenses. The challenge for the student teacher of this particular group lies in understanding the particular needs of pupils in their class, their potential to improve and the ICT applications that can contribute to such improvement. Arguably this represents the largest group of learners within their classes.

'Extension' moves towards personalised learning, which allows pupils to develop their skills and understanding within and beyond the curriculum. Hence, for example, more able and talented pupils will have the possibility of realising their full potential by working in a more autonomous way, determining the direction of learning beyond teacher-directed content. This particular group of learners represents an additional challenge to student teachers who tend to prefer remaining in control of the learners and the learning in their classes. Once more able and talented pupils are identified, however, student teachers need to recognise that their role should not only be that of teacher/instructor, but also one of manager/ facilitator. As Page (1992: 84) suggests, if pupils are to become independent thinkers, able and confident learners: *'Teachers have to learn to let go, and learners have to learn to take hold'.*

Figure 6.2 provides a summary of the potential of ICT to contribute to including all learners.

From the perspective of student teachers, such a framework of provision will demand a high level of knowledge of ICT, and of the availability of

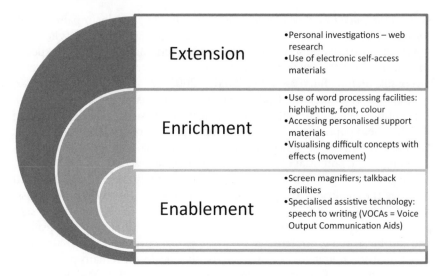

Extension
- Personal investigations – web research
- Use of electronic self-access materials

Enrichment
- Use of word processing facilities: highlighting, font, colour
- Accessing personalised support materials
- Visualising difficult concepts with effects (movement)

Enablement
- Screen magnifiers; talkback facilities
- Specialised assistive technology: speech to writing (VOCAs = Voice Output Communication Aids)

Figure 6.2 Summary of the potential of ICT within the inclusive classroom

hardware and software. Such knowledge needs to be harnessed to a relevant pedagogy that will meet the needs of individual learners. Whereas the specific knowledge of technology may require specialist advice and instruction, its application to an appropriate pedagogy (often a secondary consideration) should be a fundamental element in initial teacher education.

Administration and resourcing

In addition to the language-specific applications, ICT can also assist in the management of learning and resourcing. This can broadly be divided into two parts: record-keeping and target-setting, and selection and adaptation of resources. Franklin with Litchfield (Leask & Pachler, 1999: 110) describe this dual role of computers as *'an extra tool for teachers, dealing with both administrative burdens, and the necessity to create accurately designed, effective teaching materials'*. The student teacher will be confronted with a considerable amount of data, much of which will be generated from the requirements of the Code of Practice. Many schools have dedicated packages to manage such data, and although these will be very beneficial, student teachers will still need to familiarise themselves with the individual applications. Two of the main benefits of technology with regard to this data are security and backup (Leask & Pachler, 1999: 120). In addition to this there is the time-saving element, whereby templates can be used and forms readily adapted, and also the confidential dissemination of information between colleagues within and beyond the teaching institution. Perhaps the most relevant example of this for student teachers is the individual education plan (IEP). Few student teachers are directly involved in the creation of these documents, but they are required to use them on a daily basis, and often apply them to the context in which they are teaching. At times this requires adding supplementary information relating to their subject. Example 6 below illustrates the work done by one student teacher.

Distinctive Characteristics of ICT for all Learners

It is useful for student teachers, in developing a pedagogy for all learners, to consider the distinctive characteristics of ICT for teaching and learning, and to transfer these to an appropriate application for the inclusion of all learners in the MFL classroom. TTA (1998: 4, 14–15) suggests the features of speed and automation, capacity and range, provisionality and interactivity. Kennewell (2004: 21) also includes clarity, authenticity, focusability and multi-modality.

These complex ICT concepts represent additional challenges that need to be incorporated into the already developing pedagogy of student teachers. Each feature needs to be considered in terms of its application to ICT, appropriacy for different types of learners and application to the MFL classroom. Based on Meiring and Norman (2005) the Table 6.2 has been adapted to include all learners, and to provide an accessible guide for student teachers.

Practical classroom examples

The following examples illustrate how some student teachers have applied some of the distinctive features of ICT practically in the classroom, to include different types of need.

Example 1 – SEN

In the area of capacity and range, one student teacher, who was very keen for her SEN pupils to interact with pupils in France, prepared, in conjunction with a French school, a series of simple questions for her pupils to ask pupils in France. These were rehearsed during lessons, to refine accuracy and pronunciation, and a video-conference was organised to allow each pupil to ask one question. French pupils responded and although the SEN pupils found this difficult to understand, it was recorded to be used in subsequent lessons. Pupils anticipated this exchange of language with considerable enthusiasm, it added status to the practice that took place prior to the video-conference, and provided an authentic application of language skills

Table 6.2 Application of the features of ICT to include all learners in the MFL classroom

Contribution of ICT	Features of ICT	Examples of types of ALN including MAT	Examples of activities adaptable for MFL
Speed and automation (TTA, 1998)	Produce text more quickly; perform mundane operations quickly; reduces unnecessary tasks; immediacy and visual impact	Literacy; dyslexia; learning difficulties	Word processing in Foreign Language (FL); matching picture and text; gap-filling; PowerPoint and interactive whiteboard presentations of language, including sound stimulus
Capacity and range (TTA, 1998)	Organising and categorising of vast bank of information/ material; removing geographical barriers of learning environment; retrieve info. at own pace; multi-media	Physically impaired; Emotional and Behavioural Difficulties (EBD); pupils with limited concentration spans; Attention Deficit Hyperactivity Disorder (ADHD); MAT	Authentic visuals and material; video; range of media (text, visual, sound, motion); communication with native speakers; research 'live' contexts- simulations, games
Provisionality (TTA, 1998)	Trying out ideas to modify learning; improving own learning; immediate feedback	Pupils lacking self-esteem and confidence; MAT	Word processing: draft/redraft; matching activities; pronunciation; assessment, Assessment for Learning (AfL).
Interactivity (TTA, 1998)	Non-threatening interaction; rapid, dynamic feedback	Autistic; EBD; MAT; pupils with prolonged absence	Word processing; games; CD-ROM simulations; hyperlinks; communication with native speakers

(continued)

Table 6.2 (*continued*)

Contribution of ICT	Features of ICT	Examples of types of ALN including MAT	Examples of activities adaptable for MFL
Clarity (Kennewell, 2004)	Appropriate font, layout and colour schemes; use of pictures; removal of extraneous material; animation; three-dimensional presentation	Literacy; dyslexia; visually impaired; learning difficulties; cognitive difficulties	Display work using word processing, Desktop Publishing (DTP), Publisher, etc. Wordle; PowerPoint and interactive whiteboard presentations of language
Authenticity (Kennewell, 2004)	Genuine tasks and materials; processing text to numeric data	All learners	Websites; email; project work; databases; spreadsheets, bar charts, graphs
Focusability (Kennewell, 2004)	Allows learning to be refined to essentials; enlargement and emphasis, according to pupil need; within-text glossing; spotlight and blind 'reveal' features (interactive white board)	All learners	Word-processing; interactive whiteboard: use of search engines, incl. online dictionaries
Multi-modality (Kennewell, 2004)	Appeals to different learning styles: sight, hearing; interlinking of senses; kinaesthetic (drag and drop)	Physically impaired; EBD; pupils with limited concentration spans; ADHD	Interactive whiteboard and PowerPoint presentations; text, visuals, sound, animation

with real individuals in real time, while breaking down geographical and distance barriers.

Example 2 – Literacy

In the area of provisionality, one student teacher used word processing and graphics to enable pupils with writing difficulties to produce wall displays on their home town. The student teacher provided a bank of useful words and phrases, from which pupils selected, used the 'copy and paste' facility, and were challenged to personalise some of the phrases. They worked in pairs to produce the first draft, which was then checked by the student teacher, and subsequently re-drafted. The final version, which included the graphics, was displayed in the classroom, as an accurate and well-presented display. The benefits of this feature of ICT enabled pupils with writing difficulties to produce a piece of work, of which they were proud, and in an inclusive classroom, one which was comparable with those produced by their mainstream peers. It also enabled pupils to work collaboratively and to improve their own learning, without having to completely rewrite their original draft. It also enabled pupils to experiment with design and layout, and improve their final product. Again, the public display of a high-quality product lent the activity additional status and meaning, and contributed to raising self-esteem and improving wellbeing.

Example 3 – Speech and language difficulties

With regard to interactivity, one student teacher designed an activity to allow pupils with communication difficulties, and who were reluctant to use oral skills, to create 'vokis' (digital representations of oneself, or talking avatars). They selected their avatar from a bank of characters, and either recorded or transcribed text for the 'voki' to communicate. In the case of recorded speech, a degree of anonymity was provided and with transcribed text authentic French accents were produced by the pupils. In both cases pupils were able to gain confidence in speaking, in a non-threatening and motivating context, teachers were able to monitor the work outside the classroom and other pupils enjoyed the creativity and impact of the 'vokis'. Manifestly this could also be used to share information and language in a more dynamic way with pupils from other countries.

Example 4 – Most able and talented/gifted and talented

In the area of multimodality, one student teacher asked two pupils to prepare a weather report, using hand-held camcorders, to present to the rest of the class. The role of one pupil was to operate the camcorder, and a more able and talented pupil was chosen to present the report. This enabled the latter to refine and extend their range of language with an authentic purpose, providing classmates with listening and viewing opportunities, as well as opportunities for peer-assessment. It transformed an otherwise routine task of comprehension into a more meaningful and realistic practice activity for both presenter and audience. Individual pupils subsequently came to the interactive whiteboard to 'drag and drop' different weather symbols to different locations in France for specific days and times, in conjunction with the 'recorded' weather report, which could be repeated for pupils who struggled to understand. A particular advantage of this example is enabling more able pupils to use their skills for the benefit of other pupils, and in the process to develop their own autonomy and extend their language production.

Example 5 – Visual impairment and learning difficulties

With regard to focusability, one student teacher teaching a mixed-ability class during the presentation stage on the subject of classroom objects, was able to colour-code the gender of the words, and using the 'blind–reveal' facility of the interactive whiteboard software, motivate the class by revealing a partial image and allowing others to guess the word. In addition, as the board was densely packed with words, making it difficult for some learners to identify individual words, the student used the 'spotlight' feature to highlight individual words and labels for less able pupils. Also, for pupils who had visual impairment, the words could instantly be enlarged so that they could read them and participate in the whole-class interaction. Initially pupils were also able to 'drag and drop' labels, and then categorise the words through 'drag and drop' into masculine, feminine and plural. All this could be achieved through one flipchart containing a series of words and images. The outcome of this resource was to include learners of different abilities, 'embed' the vocabulary and to begin the process of grammatical awareness. The results of the movements of the words and images on the screen, based on pupil participation, could then be saved, and printed as a record for pupils of the work covered in the lesson. In addition, during this presentation, pupils could add to the set vocabulary through access to an online dictionary, thus enabling some pupils to move beyond the core learning, to both 'enrich and extend'.

Example 6 – Administration and resourcing of SEN

One student teacher was asked to discuss the precise targets of Individual Education Plans (IEPs) with some special needs pupils in the classroom. The student quickly became aware that the pupils were struggling to understand the IEPs, so decided to reconfigure them to make them more accessible and include the language-specific targets. This was done primarily through removing text and replacing with graphics, and allowing pupils to respond to the targets through the use of the same graphics. In this process the technological medium made a significant difference both to pupils' understanding and to their ability to convey their perceptions to the teacher.

Resourcing

One of the challenges in initial teacher training, given the plethora of ICT resources available, is to channel student teachers into appropriate selection and relevant use. In order to do this they must be able to articulate a pedagogical rationale, influenced by the needs of the learners. In spite of the numerous multimedia resources, student teachers still need to address perhaps some of the more fundamental applications of ICT, such as word processing, which enable them to 'differentiate materials easily for specific pupils/classes' and 'edit [resources] after a lesson for improvements and corrections' (Dugard & Hewer, 2003: 16). Further features of word processing, which enable student teachers to adapt materials easily to include a wide range of learners are, for example:

- font (size, type), e.g. Comic Sans for facilitating reading for special needs pupils;
- use of tools, such as bold, italics, highlighter, to emphasise important points, for pupils with learning difficulties;
- use of graphics to clarify instructions and convey meaning, for pupils with literacy problems;
- use of colour for making text more readable, for pupils with reading difficulties, such as dyslexia;
- use of animation, for pupils who have difficulties with cognitive understanding;
- use of drop-down menus, for pupils who have literacy problems, e.g. spelling.

Linked to the use of technology in motivating pupils is the place of games in including all learners. Games have the capacity to transform relatively mundane practice activities into more dynamic, enjoyable opportunities for learning. They can be linked to vocabulary learning, understanding of grammar and development of skills. Technology can provide immediacy of feedback and competition, and also encourage working at speed and to deadlines. The attention of the learner is focused on the medium, rather than the linguistic content, which is rendered more accessible by the properties of the medium. The advance of new technologies, including the potential of mobile phones, also enables this access to learning beyond the classroom. From the perspective of the student teacher, many of these games can be authored to target precise learning goals, for example the many and varied possibilities offered by the software 'Task Magic' (text match, picture match, sound match, pic-sound, grid match, dialogues, multi choice.)

A further resourcing possibility is the use of specific software and websites. Most of the recent course books have accompanying software, which have the advantage of being linked specifically to the particular unit of work. The use of such software by student teachers is arguably less time-consuming in terms of preparation, although again they will need a precise rationale for how the software moves the learning forward. One advantage of these packages when networked in a computer room is that all pupils can access them at different levels and work on them at their own pace.

One of the disadvantages of using software is that, like course books, it can become quickly outdated. Internet sites therefore, do have a significant role to play in offering up-to-date, authentic material. They have a particular significance for including all learners, in that they can provide a virtual experience of the foreign language and culture, from which some pupils with certain types of social background, and types of learning difficulty, might otherwise be excluded. This facility can be extended to include networking with foreign nationals through video-conferencing and email contact, in both real time and delayed time. The potential of electronic communication to create links can be channelled to enable all learners to participate. Hence, wikis and blogs can become a shared platform with learners from other countries. Galloway (2009: 35) describes this inclusion through social networking as 'richer socially constructed learning', which in the case of modern languages was only previously possible through visits, exchanges and contact with language assistants, all of which only included a relatively small number of pupils. Student teachers need to be aware of the obvious dangers of such networking, but Pachler et al. (2007: 307) also highlight that communications can lack substance on account of the familiarity of the medium to learners. For the student teacher therefore, the challenge is to harness the possibilities of the medium to meaningful learning opportunities and outcomes.

Conclusion

Clearly the inclusive classroom with its range of needs represents multiple challenges to the student teacher – challenges which, if they are not met, will have significant implications for individual learners. The knowledge, understanding, expertise and experience required will demand the development of a distinctive and adapted pedagogy with attendant appropriate resourcing. ICT clearly has a significant part to play in this resourcing, which makes further demands on pedagogy and technical ability. Manifestly the seeds sown in the initial teacher training programme should be nurtured in a continuum of early and continuing professional development throughout the teacher's career, if we are to achieve the following:

Every child, whether in mainstream or special setting, deserves a world-class education to ensure that they fulfil their potential. (DfE, 2011b)

A key role of teacher training programmes must, therefore, be to ensure that student teachers are able to identify sufficiently early areas of need, set appropriately high expectations for pupils and develop relevant skills to meet the needs of every child in the inclusive classroom.

References

Abbott, C. (2007) *E-Inclusion: Learning Difficulties and Digital Technologies.* Bristol: FutureLabs.

ACCAC (2000) *Modern Foreign Languages in the National Curriculum in Wales.* Cardiff: National Assembly for Wales.

Blamires, M. (ed.) (1999) *Enabling Technology for Inclusion.* London: Paul Chapman Publishing Ltd.

Buttriss, J. and Callander, A. (2008) *A–Z of Special Needs for Every Teacher.* London: Optimus Education.

Chambers, G.N. (1999) *Motivating Language Learners.* Clevedon: Multilingual Matters Ltd.

Clicker 5, Crick Software, accessed 23 August 2011. http://www.cricksoft.com/uk/products/tools/clicker/home.aspx

Comfort, T. and Tierney, D. (2007) *We Have the Technology! Using ICT to Enhance Primary Languages.* London: CILT Young Pathfinder 14.

Cox, M. and Webb, M. (eds) (2004) *An Investigation of the Research Evidence relating to ICT Pedagogy. Version 1.* Coventry: Becta.

DENI (1998) *Code of Practice on the Identification and Assessment of Special Educational Needs.* Bangor: Department of Education Northern Ireland.

DENI (2005) *Supplement to the Code of Practice on the Identification and Assessment of Special Educational Needs.* Bangor: Department of Education Northern Ireland.

DfE (2011a) *Government proposes biggest reforms to Special Educational Needs in 30 Years.* Press release, accessed 15 August 2011. http://www.education.gov.uk/inthenews/inthenews/a0075344/government-proposes-biggest reforms to-special-educational -needs-in-30-years

DfE (2011b) *Support and Aspiration: A New Approach to Special Educational Needs and Disability.* A consultation. London: HMSO.

DfE (2003) *Every Child Matters.* London: HMSO.

DfE/WO (1995) *Modern Foreign Languages in the National Curriculum.* London: HMSO.

DfEE (1998b) *Excellence For All: Meeting Special Educational Needs: A Programme of Action.* London: DfEE.

DfES (2001) *Special Educational Needs Code of Practice.* Annesley, Notts: Department for Education and Skills.

Dugard, C. and Hewer, S. (2003) *Impact on Learning. What ICT Can Bring to MFL in KS3.* London: CILT New Pathfinder 3.

Education Act (1996). London: HMSO.

Galloway, J. (2009) *Harnessing Technology for Every Child Matters and Personalised Learning.* Abingdon: Routledge.

Home Office (2010) *Equality Act.* London: HMSO.

Kennewell, S. (2004) *Meeting the Standards in Using ICT for Secondary Teaching.* London: Routledge Falmer.

Leask, M. and Pachler, N. (eds) (1999) *Learning to Teach Using ICT in the Secondary School.* London: Routledge.

Meiring, L. and Norman, N. (2005) How can ICT contribute to the learning of foreign languages by pupils with SEN? NASEN. *Support for Learning* 20 (3), 129–134.

Norwich, B. and Lewis, A. (2001) Mapping a pedagogy for special educational needs. *British Educational Research Journal* 27 (3), 313–326.

Pachler, N., Barnes, A. and Field, K. (2007, 3rd edn) *Learning to Teach Modern Foreign Languages in the Secondary School: A Companion to School Experience.* London: Routledge.

Page, B. (ed.) (1992) *Letting Go, Taking Hold. A Guide to Independent Language Learning by Teachers For Teachers.* London: CILT.

Ofsted (2010) *The Special Educational Needs and Disability Review,* accessed 15 August 2011. http://www.ofsted.gov.uk/resources/special-educational-needs-and-disability-review

Scottish Parliament (2004) *Education (Additional Support for Learning) (Scotland) Act, 2004.* Edinburgh: Scottish Government. http://www.scotland.gov.uk/Publications/2005/05/11112347/23484

Task Magic, accessed 23 August 2011. http://www.mdlsoft.co.uk/

TTA (1998) *The Use of ICT in Subject Teaching: Expected Outcomes for Teachers.* London: Teacher Training Agency and the Department of Education.

UNESCO (1994) *The Salamanca Statement and Framework for Action on Special Needs Education.* Salamanca, Spain: Ministry of Education and Science.

WAG (2002) *Code of Practice for Wales.* Cardiff: Welsh Assembly Government.

WAG (2004) *Children and Young People: Rights to Action, Circular No. 5/2/04.* Cardiff: Welsh Assembly Government.

WAG (2009) *The Qualified Teacher Status Standards Wales 2009 (2009 No.25).* Cardiff: Welsh Assembly Government.

WAG (2010) *A Curriculum For All Learners. Guidance to Support Teachers of Learners With Additional Learning Needs.* Cardiff: Welsh Assembly Government.

7 Foreign Languages for Learners with Dyslexia – Inclusive Practice and Technology

Margaret Crombie

Introduction

'Should K be learning a language at school?' That was the question that first stimulated my interest in foreign language learning and dyslexia. It turned out that this particular child was being asked to study three foreign languages simultaneously and I knew her to be severely dyslexic. Though I answered the question, I had no research on which to base my answer at this time, some twenty-odd years ago, and felt the need to investigate further to ensure that any answers I offered in this domain were based on a well-informed view of the field. Even though the situation has changed in the intervening time, dyslexia and language learning are subjects that some feel uncomfortable about mentioning in the same breath. For some people the term dyslexia means that language learning is problematic – dyslexia is about what learners cannot do and not what they can (Csizér *et al.*, 2010; Eisenstein, 2010). However, from my own research and that of others, this need not be the case. With appropriate help, teaching and encouragement, dyslexia need not disenfranchise any learner who is seriously motivated to learn another language. It may not be easy for those whose dyslexia is severe and where there are complex phonological problems, but there is much that can be done to ensure that those with dyslexia maximise their abilities and gain a useful knowledge and expertise in the use of a language other than their own (Marsh, 2005; McColl, 2000;

Nijakowska, 2010; Schneider & Crombie, 2003). This chapter aims to highlight the areas that many with dyslexia find difficult and how these difficulties can be tackled or circumvented through the use of appropriate support and technologies to achieve an acceptable standard of communication in another language. I begin by considering the terminology, clarifying what is meant, and propose methods of using assistive technologies and information communication technology (ICT) alongside traditional methods to improve learning opportunities and promote learning of foreign languages among those who do not find learning another language easy.

Information and Communications Technology (ICT)

The term 'ICT' is used to cover all kinds of technologies that assist users to produce, access and use information. According to the Scottish Government (2011), it includes *'e-learning (electronic learning), m-learning (mobile learning)'* and encompasses areas such as telephony and broadcast media that are constantly changing, as well as the audio and video technologies that are well established in the minds of most language teachers and learners. Assistive technology, when applied to ICT, involves the adaptation, alteration or inclusion of equipment or systems so that those with difficulties can be involved alongside others.

Inclusion

In a book and a chapter that has 'inclusive' in their titles, it may seem to be a fatuous and irrelevant task to try to define such terminology. However from experience and research, I have had to conclude that the meaning of 'inclusion' and 'inclusive education' is not obvious to all – hence the decision to make this my starting point towards consideration of how technology may be able to help. I therefore open this chapter with a discussion of inclusive practice and consider how the term inclusive education might be applied to language learning. Perhaps the best example I can think of to explain what inclusion is, is to start from what it is not. During previous research into language learning in a school classroom (Crombie, 1997), I visited a mixed ability classroom of middle-class teenagers, some of whom were keen to learn and others who, though well behaved and tolerant, were less interested and would rather have been elsewhere. The teacher was standing amid the class firing questions at the young people, most of whom were responding well and participating fully in the proceedings. The language used was mainly French, with intermittent reversal into English when explanation was required, and most of the children understood the communication well. 'A typical and very ordinary situation!', you may think. However, there was one small group of children who did not seem to be participating and had their own work to do. This did not seem to be related to the work of the others. When at a convenient break in the class activity, I asked the teacher about the group, I was told that this group was the 'remedial' group, and they had their own work to do. As the class settled to do some written work relating to the previous activities, I took myself over to the 'remedial' group. The group looked settled and intent on a listening activity. I indicated to one boy, Robert by name, that I wanted to speak to him. He, like the others in the group, was wearing a set of headphones attached to a listening centre. He removed the headphones. 'What are you doing?' I asked. This might have seemed like an injudicious question, but Robert's answer was totally unexpected: 'Nothing!' said the young man honestly, 'But if I just keep quiet, she (the teacher) won't know, and we'll get peace!' Later, conversation with the teacher revealed that this young man had dyslexia, and the others in the group had similar difficulties with literacy and access to language learning in its true sense.

The notion that if you sit learners in a mixed ability classroom and they are quiet and well behaved, you achieve inclusion is sadly misguided, though I am sure that particular teacher had no idea of what the young man had said to me nor of how he was feeling that day. The use of technology was ill-judged and inappropriate and served only to give the youngsters a smoke-screen behind which they could rest, secure in the knowledge that they would not be found out if they could just keep quiet. The rest of the small group were similarly disenfranchised from the learning that was taking place in the classroom, but had realised how to survive life in the language learning classroom without embarrassment, and without the teacher requiring to do anything more than arrange the classroom in a way that separated those who found language learning difficult.

Compare that scenario with one the following day when I arranged to visit the support for learning teacher in the same school. The same small group were there, but this time on their own, working with the support teacher who was herself learning French, having mastered the language to a reasonable level when a school pupil herself. The communication was lively and interactive with the lesson clearly paced at the students' level, much repetition using a range of techniques and approaches designed to provide reinforcement of the language skills that had just been taught in a multisensory way to maximise the learning that was taking place.

It is not hard to see from this example where the inclusive practice lay, and how opportunities for inclusion and inclusive education were being missed by the first teacher. How many more Roberts are there who are in mainstream classes but are not included, but whose teachers are unaware of their students' lack of engagement with language learning? The majority of teachers would wish to know how to help those with literacy difficulties, but with the whole range of difficulties and talents in a class of mainstream learners, the time to research the best methods is often in short supply. Knowledge of appropriate technology, well considered, judiciously selected and adapted where necessary can help enormously (Crombie, 1999; Crombie & Crombie, 2001; Smythe, 2010).

Perspectives on Dyslexia

Adopting one particular perspective or level of analysis with regard to dyslexia is unlikely to be helpful. All perspectives have a contribution to make to our overall knowledge about language learning and literacy difficulties (Rassool, 2009). Whether we consider the psychological and emphasise for example phonemic awareness, or consider the linguistic/psycholinguistic looking at meaning and understanding, or socio-cultural with a focus on cultural issues such as the role parents may play, educational with schools as the focus or whatever, no one perspective has all the answers, but all have a part to play. An interdisciplinary perspective is, therefore, adopted to maximise the insight available to help us assist learners.

Difficulties Associated with Dyslexia

From a cognitive dyslexia perspective, auditory and visual processing and sequencing problems will affect speaking, listening, reading and writing in the target language (Goswami, 2002, 2010; Nijakowska, 2010; Schneider & Crombie, 2003; Thomson & Goswami, 2008). Dyslexia also affects the ability to easily come to terms with the phonology or sound system of any language (Crombie, 2000; Thomson, 2009). This impacts on learning to read, write and spell in home language, and in learning a new language also affects speaking. In the early years, rhyming and rhythm are usually areas of difficulty. Sometimes oral language and pronunciation or enunciation are problem areas, but this may not be the case generally as many children outgrow early speech and language difficulties (Crombie, 1997; Crombie, 2000; Scarborough, 1990). Organisational skills are often affected and sometimes numeracy and motor skills (Kay & Yeo, 2003; Levin, 1990; Nicolson & Fawcett, 1994). Dyslexic learners are therefore sometimes considered to be lazy (Shaywitz, 2005), and unwilling to try owing to not handing in their homework on time when this is really a problem over sequencing and ordering the days, and planning ahead to meet deadlines.

Poor short-term and working memory will influence the ability to learn and remember vocabulary, grammar, word order and syntax. Poor memory for what has been said will impact on understanding and ability to respond in the new language, and this is likely to be exacerbated by stress (Rai et al., 2011; Sparks & Ganschow, 1991). It will affect word finding abilities for both home and foreign language (Goswami, 2000; Jeffries & Everatt, 2004; Sparks et al., 2000). Additionally, sequencing and organisation difficulties impact on a students' ability to get their work in on time and affect the ordering of their letters, words and sentences that are necessary for successful language learning (Crombie, 1997). Bearing in mind that automaticity is necessary for processing information in another language and is an area of difficulty for dyslexic students in their home language (Reid, 2009), gaining automaticity in a new language will be difficult to achieve.

If considered only from a cognitive dyslexia perspective, we may largely ignore why it is that we want children to learn another language. Individuals do not exist in a vacuum, and for language to be useful, social factors must be taken into account. We do not just want children to learn a language to prove they are academically able to do it, though that is the way it is sometimes seen by dyslexic students and on occasions also by their teachers (Schneider, 2009). I have often been asked, 'What language is the easiest one for dyslexic children to learn?', my answer is generally 'What language will the young person be likely to use?', 'What are the options?'. If language learning is seen as just another school activity in which it is particularly hard to achieve, then students generally, and dyslexic students in particular, are likely to doom themselves to failure. For too long, too many teachers have seen language teaching as 'preparing children for language learning' in the belief that teaching one language will prepare children for learning any language they choose at a later point. Though there is an element of truth in this, children are unlikely to appreciate this at the time. Being able to see the purpose in language learning from a communicative socio-cultural perspective is important (Schneider, 2009). We must transcend the disciplines to adopt an approach that takes account of all perspectives and involves language learners in determining what works best for them. This is important for all learners who find language learning hard, not just those who have dyslexia. It has to be said also that the approaches that suit dyslexic learners will be likely to benefit many non-dyslexic students too.

Classroom Learning Versus Learning in a Multilingual Environment

At this point it is worth mentioning the difference between learning a language in the language learning classroom, and learning in an immersion environment as a young child. Considering this cognitively, children who are brought up bilingually or multilingually learn one language very much like they learn their mother-tongue, they may mix languages for a time, but will sort out which words are appropriate over the course of time. If they are dyslexic, it is likely they will be dyslexic in all the languages they are learning, and phonology, reading, writing and spelling are likely to be affected in all languages (Downey *et al.*, 2000). However, language learning in the classroom involves a process of learning vocabulary (words and phrases), translating the vocabulary into home language, and then responding – a very different process from thinking and actually living in more than one language. In this chapter I consider mainly classroom-type learning, and view technology as a classroom essential for 21st century learning. Technology is:

> if not the solution, at least a part of the process to minimize the impact of dyslexia on individuals, to promote social inclusion assisting with the difficulties, the anxieties and the problems that dyslexics have to face in everyday situations. (Torrisi & Piangerelli, 2010: 6)

Because dyslexia affects reading and writing in the home language, and often does not seem to be influencing abilities in speaking and listening, it has been believed that the avoidance of reading and writing and concentration on speaking and listening would be the way forward for foreign language learning. However, this has not been the case. Research (Schneider & Crombie, 2003; Sparks *et al.*, 2000) tells us that to cut out reading and writing is to take away useful channels of learning, so it is important to acknowledge this and ensure that accessibility to all four skills are included in any programme of teaching, whether by humans or with the assistance of ICT.

So what are the principles of learning that apply and how can the technologies help?

Principles for Teaching Dyslexic Learners

Principles of teaching and learning are well researched and involve:

- multisensory learning and teaching – hear it, see it, say it, do it (write it, draw it, act it out, dance it);

- overlearning (without boredom!);
- teaching the phonology of the new language (introduce phonics from the start);
- the inclusion of visual and kinaesthetic material whenever possible (picture cues, photographs, video, real materials (food, classroom objects)). Present material visually and aurally simultaneously (video with subtitles, avatars with speech bubbles, cartoons with auditory output).

(Crombie, 2000; Nijakowska, 2010; Schneider, 1999; Schneider & Crombie, 2003; Schneider & Ganschow, 2000).

The adoption of a metacognitive approach will help learners to decide how they learn best and this can then be taken into account in the teaching programme, and will help teachers and learners to determine what is likely to work best with regard to technology (Vilar Bertrán, 2007).

The reason for learning a language is mainly for communication, so consideration should be given to how communication can be achieved with success and lack of embarrassment to those who exhibit considerable difficulties in much of their learning. Technology in the 21st century has an important role to play in all our lives, but that role is particularly important for those with dyslexia as it can give them a level of accessibility to language learning that would have been impossible a few decades ago.

The increased use of ICT over recent years with the accompanying relative lowering of prices has made appropriate technologies more accessible and affordable for learners from different backgrounds. *'Any function in the child's cultural development appears twice, or on two planes. First it appears on the social plane, and then on the psychological plane'* (Vygotsky, 1966: 44). The social plane is what makes learning meaningful and therefore must not be neglected; today's technologies must take account of social aspects if they are to be successful. We must not assume that they will solve all our dilemmas as we saw in the example of Robert and his group. Technology however, when used judiciously taking account of the most important principles of teaching and learning for dyslexic learners, and with appropriate planning and forethought, can be an enormous asset to the learning of all students with literacy difficulties.

Digital Technology

The range of hardware and software over the last decade has vastly increased and improved with the introduction of digital recorders, digital cameras, MP3 players and iPods (with and without video facility), scanner pens, tablets, smartphones, androids, iPads and netbooks; with touchscreens and apps, and ready access to the internet and worldwide web. Technology is currently moving fast and it can be difficult for teachers and parents to keep up with the pace. However, for most young people this is not a great problem. While there are many 'techno-phobes' who are 'techno-timid' among the teaching profession, there are very many fewer young people who fear technology, and most are 'techno-curious'. In the next few paragraphs I will mention a selection of tools for use in the language classroom – some old, some new. However these are offered as suggestions only. By the time the book is published, some of my suggestions may already be obsolete. These are only examples of the kinds of technology that might help dyslexic learners, and how these might be used (Keates, 2002). There is not space to go into precise detail here of how each works, but there is much information available on the web that will guide those interested in following up, and using or developing tools that will benefit students' learning. The main disadvantages of technology for the language-learning classroom is that the hardware is generally quite expensive, so may not be within the reach of all schools. However, with decreasing costs relatively, it seems likely that, over time, the costs of assistive technology as it applies to dyslexic learners may well match the equivalent costs of books.

If one relates the technology to the individual, one can see how ICT can be applied to make learning easier for those who find access to languages difficult. Technology has the potential to provide a motivating learning tool that can offer appropriate support – for example giving multisensory learning to the point of automaticity with opportunities for overlearning without boredom. With the help of teachers who can discuss errors (learning points) and help students select and customise the technology appropriately, we can have a recipe for success.

The combination of appropriate hardware and software, the use of computer with or without an interactive whiteboard, and appropriate tools, gives one the facility to produce learning materials in another language with speech, visual images (still and video) and the ability for repetition until the pupil gains the confidence to use specific phrases with comfort. Text-to-speech technology has much to offer in home language for those with weak reading skills being able to highlight difficult text and hear the words spoken. It has probably even more to offer to those learning a foreign language. With added features, such as being able to insert pictures, video or maps, it becomes a tool, not just to help with the language, but also to help with cultural aspects that make the language meaningful and contextual. With a tool such as the Textease suite of programs, or similar software tools, teachers can tailor the materials to the learning needs of students giving learners the opportunity to see, hear, repeat (to match the teacher's example), write (type) and play-back to ensure accuracy. Such a tool can provide additional support to teaching and learning and present opportunities for making learning multisensory with the overlearning much needed by dyslexic pupils. Vocabulary practice can be gained using concept diagrams with pictures and matching words.

Mobile (m-)learning, in the form of mobile devices such as phones, tablets and MP3 players for example, offers opportunities and challenges to teachers and students alike. It has the potential to level the playing field through giving access anywhere the dyslexic student wishes it, but it also has the potential to separate those who can afford the latest technology from those who can not.

Scanning pens have the potential through scanning lines of text, to translate material and words that are not immediately recognised, and read them out. The screen is small as one would expect in such a portable device, but if the student finds it helpful it is certainly worth pursuing as it does give the student immediate feedback. The IRISPen Translator will scan text into a computer and give immediate translation. It can read text aloud to aid listening and learning of language.

Tools such as Balabolka which is free multilingual text-to-speech software (TSS) have the power to read text from the computer screen out loud using voices built in to your computer or others that you can select for yourself and install. The onscreen text can be saved in various formats to be played back later. Font and background colour can be altered to suit the learner. When an audio file is played on a computer or on modern digital audio players, the text is displayed synchronously, which is a great advantage for dyslexic students promoting visual input and making learning more multisensory.

Audacity is a free, open source, multilingual audio editor and recorder that can be used to record and edit live and previously recorded audio material. It can be used to produce speech at a speed that dyslexic students can cope with, then speed up to the speed of natural speech once the young person can follow. Both the above tools are available as Access Apps (JISC, 2011a), a suite of free utilities that can be carried on a memory stick by anyone with dyslexia to aid their access to technology. Balabolka is also on My StudyBar (JISC, 2011b), a very useful tool that enables dyslexic students to readily access support through being able to change font size, background colour, as well as giving free support material for planning, reading and writing, by way of a readily accessible toolbar.

Slideshare enables teachers to produce and share PowerPoint presentations. Teachers can produce quality material that language learners enjoy and which takes account of cultural aspects of learning about another country, as well as introducing and reinforcing language – with opportunities for the overlearning that dyslexic learners may require. YouTube videos can be embedded to give added effect and interest and, using an interactive whiteboard, can be shared with a group or whole class.

ReadTheWords can speak back any text either typed or uploaded. ReadTheWords brings the text to life in the form of an avatar that stimulates language learners in a dynamic way. Material can be downloaded onto MP3 players so students can repeat what they have heard as often as they like or need to master the vocabulary. The service is currently only available in English, French and Spanish.

Dyslexic students often have trouble learning left and right in their own language and are often confused. Google Earth can be used to show street plans of a target country and can be used to take students on a virtual field trip. Directions can be given in the target language and the student invited to take a tour and find out where they end up. Being at the correct destination will depend on following the directions accurately. The quality of the photographic material available on Google Maps will give the pupils a good sense of what the area is like and introduce all the pupils to the area and geography of the country linking subjects across the curriculum. A number of different routes can be planned allowing for differentiation within the classroom.

Lingoes Portable is a portable dictionary and text translation software that can be carried on a pen drive. It contains a dictionary and can translate text and offer the pronunciation of words in over 80 different languages. For those with short-term and working memory difficulties there is the security of being able to gain a reminder of any words forgotten, or never known, but needed to gain comprehension of the document or file being dealt with.

Writing is difficult for most dyslexic learners in their home language and very much more difficult in a foreign language. Accessing the right words with the correct pronunciation is particularly difficult for dyslexic students learning other languages (Torrisi & Tartari, 2010). Besides being available to aid English-language writing, Penfriend can also aid writing in a number of foreign languages by helping predict the words the young person is about to use. For dyslexic students, recognition of words on screen is easier than trying to produce the word correctly in the first instance. Penfriend can also read back what has been written, either a block of text or an entire document, so students can check they have written what they meant to write. This not only allows dyslexic learners to understand the contents of a document they may not be able to read, but also helps them to associate the sound of words with how they look on the page. The program has an onscreen keyboard, which means that those who are unable to touch type do not have to constantly switch between screen and conventional keyboard, thus losing their train of thought.

Wordle is a useful tool for both teachers and learners to enable the production of word clouds from any given text (Figure 7.1). Wordle offers a means to promote visualisation of text, a skill that, when mastered by dyslexic students, can promote much faster learning of vocabulary, words and phrases. Wordle is not only useful for producing material for teaching purposes, but it can also enhance students' writing in the language classroom. A screenshot can be made of Wordle, and they can then be embedded in other documents and files. Speech can be added to produce the multisensory learning likely to be required.

Podcasting offers students a convenient and portable means of accessing languages. Teachers have the option of making their own material or downloading existing podcasts, many of which are free to download, presenting teachers with useful additional activities to give support and offer overlearning opportunities for dyslexic learners. Podcasts have proved extremely successful with learners generally, and with dyslexic learners in particular as they offer a means of learning through mobile devices and computers that have 'street-cred' for the learners. Examples of useful podcasts are Coffee Break Spanish and Coffee Break French, available through the Radio Lingua Network which produces a range of material in a variety of languages.

Lochaber High School (LHS), in Highland, Scotland has been experimenting with podcasting for students with dyslexia. The project was initially intended to provide additional support to learners with dyslexia across the curriculum, but is now available to all Lochaber High School students to use. Learners can download material to their USB pens, mp3 players or burn

Figure 7.1 A Wordle for this chapter

to CDs for listening to anywhere they choose (Figure 7.2) (Lochaber High School, 2011).

The opportunities provided by podcasting could be further developed using video in addition to speech, thus the student can hear, repeat and see (contextualise). The writing aspect can be supported in class by the addition of activities involving actual writing to give kinaesthetic learning or through the production of digital work that will make their learning even more meaningful.

This is, however, not a substitute for actually speaking the language in a meaningful context. Activities such as role play are useful and do not require the use of technology. However, meaningful conversations can be engaged in at the students' own level through web conferencing using tools such as Blackboard Collaborate 11. Though such interactive tools are not substitutes for engaging in face-to-face conversation, they can offer the self-conscious student some anonymity if the video element is not used. Together with the facility to make recordings of interactions, such tools can be used for revision, for teacher training, for practising conversations and for the students to question the teacher. PowerPoints and presentations with appropriate

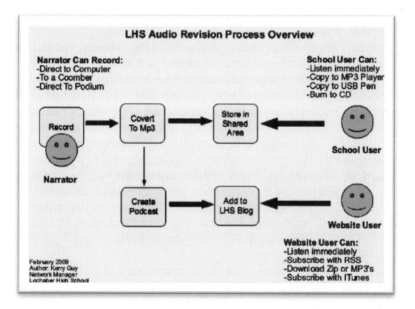

Figure 7.2 Podcasting at Lochaber High School (*reprinted with permission from Lochaber High School*)

vocabulary and pictures can be uploaded on to a whiteboard in advance to facilitate the teaching aspect and give the learner visual support. Where face-to-face contact is easy, there is probably no advantage, but where pupils are out of school for any reason, need extra tuition over and above what is available in class, or wish to practise some additional conversations, then they are useful tools. There is also the possibility of bringing in a teacher or student from the countries where the language is spoken to make a more meaningful situation where the learners can ask questions without fear of getting a wrong answer and promoting peer ridicule.

The use of Skype has made a huge impact on the world of communications generally and offers yet another means of support to the dyslexic student and to learners more generally (Dudley, 2009). Skype is already popular with many learners and is easy to use. E-pals are the equivalent of pen-pals of former years and with careful teacher-to-teacher contact ahead of pupil-to-pupil contact, arrangements can be made to ensure that pupils are well matched, thus ensuring the dyslexic student is not embarrassed by a lack of competence or confidence in the target language. Skype therefore offers opportunities for 'real-time authentic communication with speakers of students' target language' (ibid) and through instant messaging gives students the opportunity not just to use the language, but also to practise writing skills without the fear of the 'red ink' of former times.

Social networking sites, such as Facebook, offer students possibilities for being further engaged in communicative learning. Though students may begin by lurking and only participating on the periphery, generally they will go on to engage with others and become more skilled in the type of communication involved (Ryberg & Christiansen, 2008). The possibilities as an education environment for language learning are largely untapped as far as dyslexia is concerned, but the possibilities are there and there is much potential to develop the social communicative elements in a way that is non-threatening.

Email, on the other hand, may appeal more to those whose command of the target language is weak. Using some of the previously mentioned tools (e.g. Penfriend) to generate email, dyslexic students may feel less anxiety and produce more writing through the informal nature of the contact, thus benefiting from the 'rich context for language development to occur' (González-Bueno, 1998: 56).

Vokis are talking avatars that all students can customise to look like themselves or what they might like to look like. They can then utilise their Voki to speak in their target language. Vokis can be created free and the Voki website contains sample lesson plans and material, for example for learning the alphabet in the target language with Voki. The teacher can produce the model avatar, and the student can emulate the pronunciation of the language. This gives further opportunities to dyslexic learners for overlearning and gaining automaticity in language before using the language. The virtual learning environment is less threatening than the real classroom world.

There are a number of websites that offer material to teachers to use. The Languages online website (State of Victoria Department of Education and Early Childhood Development, 2007) for example offers much useful material for teachers to use and/or model including programs such as Cartoon Story Maker. This website has song downloads to help teach repetitive songs, has a Cartoon Story Maker program and interactive games, all useful in giving repetition and overlearning to learners with difficulties as well as those who have none. However, information on copyright should be observed and permission obtained whenever required.

Miscositas.com (Langer de Ramirez, 1996) is another example of a website that offers a range of languages and materials suited to language learners of all levels and abilities with opportunities for teaching vocabulary through repetition, audio and video, using virtual illustrated picture books as well as links to other material that teachers and learners might find useful in promoting learning. Since it was created in 1996, the site has been expanded greatly and now offers illustrated picture books, downloadable activities, manipulatives, mini-posters, thematic units with lesson plans, student worksheets. From the site, teachers can link into Facebook and/or Twitter to share ideas and materials, and offer suggestions. From the main site teachers can link into the Miscositas blog or wiki and contribute.

The above suggestions are only a few possibilities, and these will quickly be overtaken by newer uses of technology that can be applied to learning in general and the teaching and inclusion of dyslexic learners in particular. While not everyone will agree with Richardson (2010: x) that *'Learning the tools is easy, learning with the tools is more nuanced'*, there is immense scope for the enthusiastic teacher to develop and apply appropriate and useful learning tools that will meet the needs of pupils wherever their difficulties and strengths may lie.

Firewalls can be problematic in barring material from being downloaded, and often schools require to find a route around the firewall as it is clearly there for the safety of the children and young people, and security of the computer systems. If this is a problem, it may be possible for teachers to download resources onto their home computer first.

Many of the technologies have not yet been well researched so we cannot yet be sure of their benefits. More research is needed to ensure the most effective means of language learning through the use of technology. The cost of some software can be high, and the number of languages on some sites is limited and may not include those desired. Some programs and applications will only work on specific operating systems so this needs to be checked carefully before installation.

Safety on the internet must be considered as a priority and it is the teacher's job to ensure that all material is suitable for the age and stage of the child or young person. Copyright should always be observed, and there are sometimes notes about this on the various websites. However, observing copyright may simply mean giving due acknowledgement to the writer and owner of the materials.

All resources need to be thoroughly checked for their suitability and ease of use. If a tool is difficult to use, this can exacerbate the existing difficulties that the dyslexic learner has. Teachers need time to familiarise themselves with the available technology to ensure their learners benefit appropriately, and that the tools are used in the best ways.

Conclusion

'Wherever we find an impossible challenge to inclusive educational provision, there is usually a way in which digital technology can make a significant difference' (Laurillard, 2007: xvi). However, it is important to constantly evaluate the tools to ensure they are doing what is intended. Otherwise we risk alienating learners like Robert who struggle to learn languages owing to his difficulties with literacy.

We need also to consider the impact of technologies on organisational structures such as schools and colleges (Conole & Oliver, 2007: 15) and now need to evaluate if schools are 'fit for purpose'. Are they designed to accommodate the technologies of the 21st century appropriately? From the sociocultural perspective we must consider how legislation is impacting on learning and if the laws on accessibility and equality are truly effective in ensuring inclusion for all. Technology may not solve all our problems with regard to teaching and learning. Taking account of pedagogical issues is important and teachers must ensure that learners are taken into account and that what we do using technology is at least as good as what we do without technology. We must consider if the advantages of using '*x*' (technology) over '*y*' (more conventional tools and techniques of teaching and learning) yield benefits in terms of including dyslexic pupils in the life of the class and community, and if the tools under consideration are suited to the learning styles and learning needs of the students. We must ensure that we really do 'include' learners, and that we do not inadvertently exclude them in our passion to ensure we make use of the latest technologies that are available (Warschauer,

2003). The range of digital tools and techniques is increasing ever more rapidly as we progress through the 21st century. For the sake of Robert and the many who, like him, struggle to learn a foreign language, we need to stand back, take time and consider carefully the best ways to proceed.

References

Conole, G. and Oliver, M. (eds) (2007) Macro dimensions of e-learning: Introduction. In *Contemporary Perspectives in e-Learning Research: Themes, Methods and Impact on Practice* (pp. 3–20). Abingdon: Routledge.

Crombie, M. (1997) The effects of specific learning difficulties (dyslexia) on the learning of a foreign language in school, *Dyslexia: An International Journal of Research and Practice* 3 (1), 27–47.

Crombie, M. (1999) It's all double Dutch! (Teaching foreign languages to dyslexic pupils). *Special Children*, 82, 9–12.

Crombie, M. (2000) Dyslexia and the learning of a foreign language in school: Where are we going? *Dyslexia: An International Journal of Research and Practice 6*, 112–123.

Crombie, A. and Crombie, M. (2001) ICT-based interactive learning. In M. Hunter-Carsch (ed.) *Dyslexia: A Psychosocial Perspective* (pp. 219–231). London: Whurr.

Csizér, K., Kormos, J. and Sarkadi, Á. (2010) The dynamics of language learning attitudes and motivation: Lessons from an interview study of dyslexic language learners. *Modern Language Journal 94*, 470–487.

Downey, D., Snyder, L. and Hill, B. (2000). College students with dyslexia: Persistent linguistic deficits and foreign language learning. *Dyslexia: An International Journal of Research and Practice 6*, 101–111.

Dudley, A. (2009) Skype in Foreign Language Classrooms. *Connexions*, 4 October 2009, accessed 28 August 2011. http://cnx.org/content/m32248/1.1/

Eisenstein, A. (2010) Dyslexia – a state of mind. Positions and Promotions. Online, accessed 21 August 2011. http://www.poandpo.com/in-sickness-and-health/dyslexia-a-state-of-mind-/

González-Bueno, M. (1998) The effects of electronic mail on Spanish L2 discourse. *Language Learning & Technology 2*, 55–70, accessed 28 August 2011. http://llt.msu.edu/vol1num2/article3/default.html

Goswami, U. (2000) Phonological representations, reading development and dyslexia: Towards a cross-linguistic theoretical framework. *Dyslexia: An International Journal of Research and Practice 6*, 133–151.

Goswami, U. (2002) Phonology, reading development and dyslexia: A cross-linguistic perspective. *Annals of Dyslexia 52*, 1–23.

Goswami, U. (2010) Phonology, reading and reading difficulty. In K. Hall, U. Goswami, C. Harrison, S. Ellis and J. Soler (eds) *Interdisciplinary Perspectives on Learning to Read: Culture, Cognition and Pedagogy* (pp. 103–116). Abingdon: Routledge.

Jeffries, S and Everatt, J. (2004) Working memory: Its role in dyslexia and other learning difficulties. *Dyslexia: An International Journal of Research and Practice 10*, 196–214.

Joint Information Systems Committee (JISC) (2011a) AccessApps, accessed 30 August 2011. http://www.rsc-ne-scotland.ac.uk/eduapps/accessapps.php

Joint Information Systems Committee (JISC) (2011b) AccessApps, accessed 30 August 2011. www.rsc-ne-scotland.ac.uk/eduapps/mystudybar.php

Kay, J. and Yeo, D. (2003) *Dyslexia and Maths*. London: David Fulton Publishers.

Keates, A. (2002) *Dyslexia and Information and Communications Technology: A Guide for Teachers and Parents* (2nd edn). London: David Fulton.

Langer de Ramirez, L. (1996) Miscositas.com, accessed 21 August 2011. miscositas.com

Laurillard, D. (2007) Foreword. In H. Beetham and R. Sharpe (eds) *Rethinking Pedagogy for a Digital Age: Designing and Delivering e-Learning* (pp. xv–xvii). Abingdon: Routledge.

Levin, B.E. (1990) Organizational deficits in dyslexia: Possible frontal love dysfunction. *Developmental Neuropsychology* 6 (2), 95–110.

Lochaber High School (2011) *The LHS Audio Revision Project*, accessed 1 November 2011. http://lhs.typepad.co.uk/weblog/about-this-audio-project.html

Marsh, D. (ed.) (2005) *Special Educational Needs in Europe – The Teaching and Learning of Languages: Insights and Innovation*. University of Jyväskylä, Finland: European Commission.

McColl, H. (2000) *Modern Languages For All*. London: David Fulton.

Nicolson, R. and Fawcett, A. (1994) Comparison of deficits in cognitive and motor skills among children with dyslexia. *Annals of Dyslexia* 44, 147–164.

Nijakowska, J. (2010) *Dyslexia in the Foreign Language Classroom*. Bristol: Multilingual Matters.

Rai, M.K., Loschky, L.C., Harris, R.J., Peck, N.R. and Cook, L.G. (2011) Effects of stress and working memory capacity on foreign language readers' inferential processing during comprehension. *Language Learning Journal* 61 (1), 187–218.

Rassool, N. (2009) Literacy: In search of a paradigm. In J. Soler, F. Fletcher-Campbell and G. Reid (eds) *Understanding Difficulties in Literacy Development* (pp. 7–31). London: Sage.

Reid, G. (2009) *Dyslexia: A practitioner's Handbook* (4th edn). Chichester: Wiley-Blackwell.

Richardson, W. (2010) *Blogs, Wikis, Podcasts and Other Powerful Web Tools for Classrooms* (3rd edn). London: Sage.

Ryberg, T. and Christiansen, E. (2008) Community and social network sites as technology enhanced learning environments. *Technology, Pedagogy and Education* 17 (3), 207–219.

Scarborough, H.S. (1990) Very early language deficits in dyslexic children. *Child Development* 61 (6), 1728–1743.

Schneider, E. (1999) *Multisensory Structured Metacognitive Instruction: An Approach to Teaching a Foreign Language to At-Risk Students*. New York: Peter Lang.

Schneider, E. (2009) Dyslexia and foreign language learning. In G. Reid (ed.) *The Routledge Companion to Dyslexia* (pp. 297–332). Abingdon: Routledge.

Schneider, E. and Crombie, M. (2003) *Dyslexia and Foreign Language Learning*. London: David Fulton Publishers.

Schneider, E. and Ganschow, L. (2000) Dynamic assessment and instructional strategies for learners who struggle to learn a foreign language. *Dyslexia: An International Journal of Research and Practice* 6, 72–82.

Scottish Government (2011) *Literacies Through Information and Communication Technology (ICT) and e-Learning*, accessed 1 November 2011. http://www.scotland.gov.uk/Topics/Education/Life-Long-Learning/17551/practice/ictandliteracies.

Shaywitz, S.E. (2005) *Overcoming Dyslexia*. New York: Vintage Books.

Smythe, I. (2010) *Dyslexia in The Digital Age: Making IT Work*. London: Continuum.

Sparks, R. and Ganschow, L. (1991) Foreign language learning differences: Affective or native language aptitude differences? *The Modern Language Journal* 75 (i), 3–16.

Sparks, R., Ganschow, L. and Javorsky, J. (2000) Déjà vu all over again: A response to Saito, Horwitz, and Garza. *The Modern Language Journal* 84 (ii), 251–259.

State of Victoria Department of Education and Early Childhood Development (2007) *Languages Online*. State of Victoria, Australia: Department of Education and Early Childhood Development, accessed 21 August 2011. http://www.education.vic.gov. au/languagesonline

Thomson, M. (2009) *The Psychology of Dyslexia: A Handbook for Teachers* (2nd edn). Chichester: Wiley-Blackwell.

Thomson, J. and Goswami, U. (2008) Rhythmic processing in children with developmental dyslexia: Auditory and motor rhythms link to reading and spelling. *Journal of Physiology Paris* 102, 120–129.

Torrisi, G. and Piangerelli, S. (2010) How new technologies can help with 'invisible disabilties'. *eLearning Papers,* No. 19, April 2010, accessed 27 August 2011. http://elearn ingpapers.eu/en/elearning_papers

Torrisi, G. and Tartari, T. (2010) ICTBell: A concrete contribution to combat social exclusion and the 'invisible' digital divide. *International Conference 'ICT for Language Learning' paper* (3rd edn), accessed 30 August 2011. www.pixel-online.net/ICT4LL2010/ common/.../IBL56-Torrisi,Tartari.pdf

Vilar Beltrán, E. (2007) Analysing EFL classroom transcripts: The codification of incidental focus on form episodes. *Porta Linguarum* 7, 119–134.

Vygotsky, L.S. (1966) Development of higher mental functions. In A.N. Leontyev, A.R. Luria and A. Smirnov (eds) *Psychological Research in the USSR.* Moscow: Progress Publishers.

Warschauer, M. (2003) *Technology and Social Inclusion: Rethinking the Digital Divide.* Cambridge, MA: MIT Press.

Useful Websites

http://lhs.typepad.co.uk/weblog/podcast/ (Lochaber High School podcast project)

http://radiolingua.com/ (Radio Lingua Network)

http://www.avatarlanguages.com/howweteach.php (Second life)

http://www.blackboard.com/ (Facilitates collaborative work)

http://www.callscotland.org.uk (Call Scotland)

http://www.education.vic.gov.au/languagesonline (Language learning resources from Victoria, Australia)

http://www.epals.com/ (For setting up epals arrangements)

http://www.facebook.com/ (Social networking)

http://www.google.co.uk/intl/en_uk/earth/index.html (Google Earth 6)

http://www.irislink.com/c2-1056-189/IRISPen-Express—the-smart-handheld-scanner–. aspx (The IRISPen)

http://www.jisctechdis.ac.uk/techdis/resources/detail/resources/resources_handy_ summary (A summary of online resources from JISC)

http://www.lingoes.net/en/index.html (Intuitive dictionary and text translation software)

http://www.ltscotland.org.uk/learningteachingandassessment/curriculumareas/ languages/modernlanguages/index.asp (Modern languages for Scottish teachers)

http://www.miscositas.com (A range of learning material for languages)

http://www.penfriend.biz/ (Predictive software in a range of languages)

http://www.readthewords.com (Text-to-speech)

http://www.rsc-ne-scotland.ac.uk/eduapps/accessapps.php (Access Apps)

http://www.rsc-ne-scotland.ac.uk/eduapps/mystudybar.php (My StudyBar)
http://www.rsc-ne-scotland.ac.uk/index.php (JISC Regional Support Centre Service in Scotland)
http://www.skype.com/intl/en-gb/home (Skype - video calls and instant messaging)
http://www.slideshare.net/ (Sharing presentation slides, videos etc.)
http://www.squidoo.com/voki (Speaking Avatar)
http://www.strath.ac.uk/scilt/ (Scotland's national centre for languages)
http://www.textease.com/ (Sophisticated text-to-speech)
http://www.thescottishvoice.org.uk/Home/ (Heather, the Scottish Voice) – free Scottish computer voice for schools and colleges in Scotland
http://www.voki.com/ (Speaking avatars)
http://www.wizcomtech.com (scanning pens)
http://www.wordle.net/

8 Creative Engagement and Inclusion in the Modern Foreign Language Classroom

John Connor

Introduction

Teaching foreign languages to pupils with learning difficulties can sometimes polarise opinion. 'Why are they doing French?' colleagues ask. 'Surely they'd be better off doing extra English.' Admittedly, on the face of it, this can be quite a persuasive and seductive argument, yet Ofsted subject survey reports, such as *The Changing Landscape of Languages* (Ofsted, 2008) suggest that: *'Pupils with learning difficulties and/or disabilities often participated very enthusiastically [in MFL], particularly with the strong focus on listening and speaking, advancing their oral and literacy skills'* (Ofsted, 2008: 35). Colleagues working with these pupils say that they have no history of failure in this subject, as it is often something novel and different for them. Perhaps it is time to move away from polarised arguments and move towards a consideration of a well thought out and appropriate pedagogy.

An Appropriate Pedagogy

Teaching languages to pupils with special educational needs is not without its challenges. Over time, however, there has been much debate and deliberation in the languages teaching community as to what might constitute a viable pedagogy for these pupils. Any consideration of interactive resources must take place in the context of such an appropriate pedagogy, as the resources alone will not deliver. The overriding question must always be 'How will this resource enhance learning?' There is no validity in using resources just because they are available, or because you can.

In terms of a viable pedagogy, a group of teachers working in special schools under the direction of Do Coyle (currently Professor of Learning Innovation at the University of Aberdeen) elaborated a seven step approach towards a framework for language learning for pupils with learning difficulties:

Step 1 – *Setting goals*: short term, constantly reinforced, limited use of target language in the interests of clarity.

Step 2 – *Meeting and understanding new language*: sound/spelling links, varied input strategies which are mainly kinaesthetic, a focus on listening and understanding.

Step 3 – *Imitation*: action, sign, symbol, verbal, written, or a combination. Based on immediate model with no undue reliance on memory. Varied, enjoyable and fun.

Step 4 – *Repetition*: rehearsing language many times over. Time lapse between model and repetition – an element of 'finding' the required language – learner makes minimal choice.

Step 5 – *Practising language*: no immediate models, prompted choices, recognition of pattern may occur, but no manipulation.

Step 6 – *Creative use of language*: realistic but not essential for all learners. Involves use of language already learned in non-rehearsed situations.

Step 7 – *Assessment, evaluation and recognition of achievement*: opportunities for praise and reward which will ultimately reinforce achievement. Impacts on students' sense of self-worth. Must also inform planning and monitor progress. (Coyle *et al.*, 1994: 34)

An Appropriate Methodology

Having thus established our framework, we must now consider an appropriate methodology to enable us to deliver it. Certain elements are key to a successful methodology:

- Catering for a range of learning styles.
- Engaging all the senses.
- Understanding the variety of cognition processes in play with pupils who find learning difficult.
- Empowering pupils to make their own meanings and be spontaneous, teaching language that can be useful to them.

Lesson planning could therefore incorporate methods that would encourage students to see, hear, re-verbalise, read, copy, write, discuss and touch what they were learning. Whenever possible, teachers should also give an example or demonstrate a skill. When teachers present information, they should appeal to all three modes of learning, multi-sensory approaches involve auditory, visual and tactile kinaesthetic elements in a mutually supportive way. Some examples might be:

- *Mirrors*: Using small compact make-up type mirrors so that pupils can compare the shape that their own mouth makes when saying a word with how the mouth is formed for the correct pronunciation.
- *Fernald method*: This method provides a kinaesthetic processing support to enable learners to process information more effectively and build up a store of words. The traditional method is to use a sand tray and the index finger to write a letter in the sand, saying it at the same time. This provides a tactile, kinaesthetic, visual and internal auditory linkage to reinforce the particular thing being taught. The method has been developed for whole class teaching languages in different ways: one example is for learners in pairs to write a letter at a time of a word on their partners back and for the partner to guess the letter.
- *Use of feet*: Sequencing can be a real problem for those with dyslexia (and many other pupils). Language teaching uses sequences – and language acquisition requires sequences. How can a teacher produce a kinaesthetic teaching resource for learners to practice a sequence? Using cut-outs of feet, laying them on the ground, and asking learners to walk through the sequence naming the parts of a sequence, is a kinaesthetic approach often used by teachers of pupils with specific learning difficulties (SpLD).
- *Multi-link bricks*: These are a common resource in many classrooms and are generally used to support the teaching of maths. If used in the same way as the walking exercise mentioned above, they can provide a good level of reinforcement for aspects of language, such as sentence structure, with the colour-coded bricks representing elements of syntax. This approach also affords pupils the opportunity to compare sentence structures, for example the fact that in English the adjective precedes the noun, whereas in the Romance languages the adjective tends to follow the noun. If colour is an issue, for example with pupils with colour vision problems, the same effect can be achieved by combining colour and shape, so that choosing the correct sequence of shapes ensures the production of an accurate phrase or sentence.
- *Film making and story boarding*: Sentence structure – grasping the concept/idea of a sentence and translating that, rather than word for

word, to convey the meaning instead of dealing with words individually.

- *Total physical response (TPR)*: Arising mainly from the work done in America by Dr James J. Asher, Professor Emeritus of Psychology at San José State University on second language acquisition. The method is based on the assumption that when learning a second language, that language is internalised through a process of code breaking similar to first language development. TPR requires no written or verbal response. Instead, students respond to spoken input from teachers by carrying out instructions correctly, or performing actions to help internalise the language. As Asher (1969) succinctly put it in a Cambridge University lecture, *'babies don't learn by memorising lists, so why should children or adults?'*. TPR is predicated on what Asher calls a 'language-body conversation', in which the child internalises the language map through physical responses, such as looking, smiling, laughing, turning, walking, reaching, grasping, holding, sitting, running and so forth.
- *Practice to the point of automatisation*: Automatisation means learning a skill to the point that the student can accomplish a task with ease, speed and little deliberate attention. Automatic reading occurs when a response to a letter, syllable or word becomes so established that the student does not have to consciously try to select an appropriate response.
- *Provide direct, systematic instruction*: Although some learners are able to intuit the structure of language and strategies for developing language arts skills, most need explicit, direct instruction in methods for reading, spelling, writing and study skills. Instruction should be systematic, starting with the most basic element of a skill, and progressing to more advanced elements.
- *Total positive encouragement*: One of the things that SpLD teachers are mindful of is the need to use positive encouragement all the time. Teachers are constantly assessing as well as teaching; we find it difficult not to show our disappointment when people get things wrong and this can be very de-motivating for learners, so the idea of total positive encouragement is that we are always being realistically positive.
- *Scaffolding*: With scaffolding, the aim is to ensure that the learners are supported appropriately so that there are not any barriers to learning.

These examples are cited only in order to give an indication of good practice for varied and alternative approaches to teaching:

Students with LDs face a diverse array of difficulties, depending on the cause of the disability and its severity. The possible solutions to help learners with disabilities succeed at learning an L2 are similarly diverse, and alternative teaching and assessment plans must be adapted to match the specific needs of individual students. (Abrams, 2008: 423)

For example, Arnold (1999) suggested that TPR activates one's mental capacities and stimulates their neural network, and similar and additional benefits can be achieved by using different techniques. According to Arnold and Fonseca (2004) *'universally considered vital for learning, motivation is a complex construct which depends to a great degree on the way we evaluate the multiple stimuli we receive in relation to a specific context'* (p. 122). Motivation has been central to language learning research for many years. Teachers in general, and linguists specifically, are constantly seeking innovative ways to engage students in active learning, and there is no doubt that digital technologies are the new focus of attention in this regard.

Interactive Resources to Enhance Levels of Engagement

So having established the basic principles of a viable pedagogy, the next step will be to examine where interactive resources might enhance the levels of engagement of students in the language learning process, and thus their progress. There has been an explosion in the availability of web-based tools, many of which can fulfil these broad aims. Web 2.0 tools, as they are known, are fully interactive and can be harnessed to provide vehicles for students' output. The role of the web as a repository of information for research is well enough documented, but language teachers lately have been experimenting with various of these tools to increase students' levels of engagement and motivation.

Websites, blogs and wikis

Many language departments have established a bespoke website, or a blog or wiki. The advantage of this is that the blog provides a platform for students' work, and if properly moderated can be an excellent vehicle for peer assessment, an important element of assessment for learning.

The blog, therefore, provides two of the key elements of engagement and motivation: audience and purpose. The audience, through the blog, is potentially global. There are many examples of blogs where students from other countries have commented on the work of students here in the UK. This is a powerful motivator for students to produce the best work they can, and they will draft and redraft almost without being directed to. Therein also lies the purpose. It is more motivating to produce work to be posted on a blog than to have it languish in an exercise book or folder. Also, the use of keyboards makes the process more accessible, especially for students whose fine motor control is poor, which makes the process of handwriting stressful.

There are a good number of blog-hosting sites available, and it will be a question of researching to see which one best suits your needs. You will need to consider aspects such as ease of setup, appearance and layout, ease of uploading materia, and if there are any cost implications, for example through subscriptions. Among the most popular are:

- www.typepad.com
- www.blogspot.com
- www.blogger.com
- www.posterous.com
- www.wordpress.com
- www.edublogs.com

The 'engine room' of the blog is the screen where you compose the blog post. In some cases this is called the 'dashboard', and offers the possibility of typing text or pasting in an embed code to allow something produced elsewhere to be imported into the blog. There may be two tabbed pages to work on, 'Rich Text', where you type in directly, and 'HTML' where you paste in an embed code from another website. This will be explored in more detail below.

Some examples of current and functioning departmental blogs in the UK are www.chilternedgemfl.typepad.com and www.nottinghamhigh mfl.co.uk.

Requirements

There are a couple of aspects to consider as we begin to put the provision in place. One of the most important concerns are the blocking and filtering protocols in place in the school or local authority. These can be a source of considerable frustration, as perfectly innocuous sites can be inaccessible owing to blanket blocking procedures that may not originate in the school itself, but might involve negotiating with information communication technology (ICT) departments housed in the civic centre or county hall. Another consideration is that of peripheral hardware. Students will need to be able to access equipment that will enable them to make digital recordings that can be converted into mp3 sound files, or digital video cameras that allow students to convert footage into mp4 files. The advent of tablet computers or mobile handheld devices such as smartphones has transformed the learning landscape and these can be easily harnessed to make language learning more accessible to students with special educational needs.

In summary, we have put our framework in place, we have investigated a viable methodology to deliver it, we have selected our blog host, we have negotiated access to the sites we want to use and we have obtained suitable equipment. We now need to consider what we want to do with these interactive resources. There are plenty available, and we need to consider what might be most appropriate, in the light of our pedagogy.

Developing Speaking and Listening Skills

For some pupils speaking a foreign language represents a significant challenge. Trying to make sounds that are alien, while at the same time trying to decode a phoneme-grapheme relationship that is not always clear, can be daunting. And if the pupil is a selective mute, there are obvious barriers to overcome. The twin drivers of audience and purpose, as mentioned above, can have a noticeable impact on pupils' motivation and engagement. It is more motivating to say to pupils 'We are going to create an avatar which will speak using your voice if you want it to, and we are going to publish your avatars on our blog so that other people can comment on your work'. This is very different from trying to persuade them by dangling a better National Curriculum level or P Scale in front of them. The Performance Scales, or P Scales as they came to be known, were the result of the work of a group of special school head teachers who were worried that their pupils would always be classified as 'working towards' Level 1 of the National Curriculum in the UK. They elaborated a set of eight performance descriptors for pupils operating below Level 1 (see http://theingots.org/community/psml), the higher ones providing teachers of modern foreign languages with another way of measuring progress.

One avatar site is www.voki.com. In using this site, pupils create a cartoon avatar and give it a voice. There is a huge variety of characters to choose from in a range of categories including dogs and cats, animals and a variety of cartoon-type characters drawn from the Japanese Manga tradition. There is also a Christmas-themed selection. It should be pointed out, however, that it is like many an American site, so the VIP and Politics sections tend to be American and as such may not be instantly recognisable to English pupils (although there are characters like Mahatma Ghandi available).

Having chosen their basic avatar, pupils can change elements, such as hair, eyes, clothing, headwear and general body shape. They can also add accessories, such as jewellery and sunglasses, through the 'bling tab'. At each step in the design process, they can finalise their choices by clicking on the 'Done tab' at the bottom right-hand side of the main work area. It is also possible to change backgrounds to match their chosen character. Once this phase has been completed, pupils move on to the process of giving the avatar a voice. There are four options for this part of the process. They can record onto a mobile phone and upload the result to the website or they can record directly into the website through a USB microphone plugged into the computer. The other two options are potentially more engaging for pupils. The text-to-speech function could be useful for reluctant speakers or selective mutes. In this mode, pupils type in the text and then choose an appropriate voice and accent from a drop-down menu. The benefits of this are two-fold; first, they need to be accurate in their spelling, or the avatar will not speak correctly. This could encourage drafting and redrafting. Second, if a pupil is a reluctant speaker, this feature may give them an accurate model to imitate, and if the pupil is a selective mute, then the avatar will voice what they want to say without putting them under pressure to speak. Admittedly, it is not as beneficial as recording their own voice, but may well be a significant step in the process of encouraging them to speak.

The fourth option is to upload a pre-recorded sound file. For many pupils this will be the most appropriate choice, as they can record their output in a calm environment away from the class, should they so wish. They can have the opportunity to reflect not only on accuracy but also on pronunciation and intonation by re-recording before committing their final product to the Voki website.

There are several good examples of digital recording devices available. One that is proving very popular in the UK because of its price, ease of use and robust design, is the Easi-speak microphone (www.tts-group.co.uk). The microphone contains a rechargeable battery that automatically recharges when connected to a computer, and a 128MB hard drive, onto which pupils record directly by pressing the red record button until the flashing yellow light turns steady and red. They then speak into the microphone as normal. Pressing the green button allows pupils to review what they have recorded. They can re-record if they feel they can improve their performance, and it affords the teacher an opportunity to coach pupils accordingly. Each recording is held as a separate mp3 sound file, so if recording a dialogue, one pupil will need to keep control of the device, otherwise each element of the dialogue will be recorded separately. Another slight wrinkle is that each mp3 file is identified on the hard drive simply as 'Voice 001', 'Voice 002' and so on, and it will make things much easier if pupils are trained to rename their files as they record them, in order that the teacher can easily identify who has recorded what.

Once the recording has been satisfactorily completed, it can be transferred to the website. Removing the base of the microphone reveals a USB connection that can be plugged directly into the computer. You then browse as you would a normal memory stick. You can then rename the files, or upload into the website. (If you want to edit the recording further before uploading, you can put it through the Audacity editing programme, in which you can edit out long gaps or extraneous noises.)

Once the avatar has been completed to everyone's satisfaction, the next step is to transfer it to your departmental or school blog. You must first obtain the embed code from the Voki website. This is found by clicking on the 'Publish tab', and then choosing 'Embed code' from the options. Highlight and copy the code, then go to your blog work area (e.g. the Typepad Dashboard) and paste the code into the HTML box. Then click on Publish your blog work area, and the finished product will be transferred into your blog. Pupils can be encouraged to listen to each other's Vokis and comment on them by writing on the blog. Obviously, you will have moderation facilities on the blog to prevent abuse, and pupils should be trained to use a format like '2 stars and a wish' (i.e. two positive comments and one thing that might be improved).

If teachers spread the word about the blog, for example through social networking sites like Twitter, they can ask colleagues in other areas (indeed in other countries) to comment, and to get their pupils to do so as well. It is very powerful for pupils in one part of the country to receive feedback on their work from hundreds of miles away, or even from countries on the other side of the world.

A website that operates in a similar fashion is www.blabberize.com, it performs a similar function to Voki, but uses photographs instead of cartoon avatars. Pupils choose a photograph and upload it to the site. They then use a drawing tool around the mouth of the subject in the photograph to determine how far the mouth should open, record their speech and upload it, and the photograph then lip-synchs with the soundtrack. Pupils could use photographs of famous people or animals to create short sound files practising various topics. Any images used should of course be copyright-free. The finished product can then be exported to a blog or wiki in the normal way, using the embed code.

For more general recording purposes, www.audioboo.fm offers the ability to make short recordings and post them on a blog. It supports smartphones, so the recordings could be made on a mobile phone, but if these devices are not available, recordings can be made through a PC. Recordings can also be made available as podcasts. A free Audioboo account gives three minutes recording time. It is possible to upgrade to gain more time, but three minutes is probably enough for most purposes.

Developing Reading and Writing Skills

In a similar fashion, pupils can be encouraged to produce written work that is not consigned to an exercise book or a worksheet in a folder. One website for helping pupils develop a more positive attitude towards writing is www.storybird.com. This is an art-led approach to creative writing. The finished product is sumptuous in appearance as it uses the work of professional graphic artists. To view the possibilities for language learning, there is www.mfl-storybirds.wikispaces.com. This site contains nearly 90 Storybird e-books in four languages. Clicking on the front cover of the chosen story takes you into the Storybird website, and you can then use the stories for reading purposes. When the pupils are ready, they click on Open at the bottom right-hand side of the front cover, and then use the right arrow to navigate through the pages. At the end of the story they have the option to read it again, read another, send it to a friend or create a Storybird.

If they decide to create a Storybird, they go into the main site and begin to choose an artist whose work they like. They will need to set up an account so that their work can be saved on the site. In terms of e-safety, Storybird are keen to advise pupils not to use their full names but rather to use first names only or a nickname. Having chosen their artist, they then look for a set of images that might support a narrative thread. The work station allows them to design their front cover and then add and remove pages. They drag and drop images into the blank page, and can design the page in four different layouts. A text box appears in the space not occupied by the image, and pupils simply type directly into the box. When they have completed their Storybird, they can save it on the site. They can also email it to themselves or to a teacher. Highlighting and copying the JPG image of the front cover means that it can be pasted into a blog, or added to the mfl-storybirds wiki. The JPG image provides the link to the story on the Storybirds site.

Again, by using the blog as a vehicle for peer assessment, pupils can comment on each other's work as described above. Some good examples of peer assessment used this way can be found on www.nottinghamhighmfl.co.uk, clicking on Y10 and Spanish, and then the post Y10 boys publish their Storybirds. The level of language will vary among the students, but they are a good example of how the principles of peer assessment can be applied using Storybird as a vehicle and a blog as a platform.

Another tool that can generate a sense of enjoyment and provide concentrated writing practice is www.starwars.com/play/online-activities/crawl-creator/ With this tool, pupils can enter up to 41 lines of text into the box, and on pressing 'Preview' can see their written production crawl away from them into deep space, just like the opening credit sequence of the *Star Wars* series of films. What is even more enjoyable is that the sequence is accompanied by the theme music to the film.

Conclusion

These examples are but the tip of an enormous iceberg of Web 2.0 tools that can be explored for the benefit of pupils with special needs, and all language students in general. The abiding principle, however, must always be that of assessing how far a particular tool can enhance an existing and effective pedagogy. If ICT is used for its own sake it may prove to be less effective, but when considered alongside the twin pillars of audience and purpose there can be no doubt as to its power in engaging and motivating pupils for whom languages might otherwise be a struggle. Factor in the impact of effective peer assessment and positive, specific feedback, and you have a powerful formula for persuading pupils (and, by extension, parents and cynical colleagues) that learning a different language can be a meaningful activity that will benefit young people far beyond the raw measurement of an examination result.

A–Z Internet Resources for Education

I am indebted to my colleague and friend José Picardo of Nottingham High School for Boys for sharing a list of internet resources. Too numerous to publish here in its entirety, it can be found at www.johnfconnor.typepad.com/meanings-that-matter by clicking on January 2012 in the Archive list.

References

Abrams, Z. (2008) Alternative Second language curricula for learners with disabilities: two case studies. *The Modern Language Journal* 92 (3), 414–430, accessed January 2012. http://neltachoutari.pbworks.com/f/Alternative+curriculum+for+students+with+learning+disabilities.pdf

Arnold, J. (1999) *Affect in Language Learning*. Cambridge: Cambridge University Press.

Arnold, J. and Fonseca, M.C. (2004) Multiple Intelligence theory and foreign language learning: A brain-based perspective. *International Journal of English Studies* 4 (1), 119–136, accessed January 2012. http://www.um.es/ijes/vol4n1/06-JArnold&MCFonseca.pdf

Asher, J. (1969) The total physical response approach to second language learning. *The Modern Language Journal* 53 (1), 3–17.

Coyle, D., Bates, M. and Laverick, A. (eds) (1994) *The Special Schools Dimension.* Nottingham: University of Nottingham.

Ofsted (2008) *The Changing Landscape of Languages. An Evaluation of Language Learning 2004/2007,* accessed January 2012. http://www.ofsted.gov.uk/resources/changing-landscape-of-languages

9 Conflicts between Real-Time Resources and the Storage of Digitized Materials: Issues of Copyright

Andreas Jeitler and Mark Wassermann

> *Only one thing is impossible for God: to find any sense in any*
> *copyright law on the planet.*
> Mark Twain (Mark Twain's Notebook, 1902–1903)

Introduction

Digital literature like e-books, e-magazines or other kinds of electronic documents form the foundation that allows people with certain disabilities to take an active and independent part in the scientific community during their student years or at school. The University of Klagenfurt, like many other universities and colleges, offers a variety of services for blind and visually impaired students and employees (University of Klagenfurt, 2012a; University of Klagenfurt, 2012b; University of Klagenfurt, 2012c). Although a large variety of impairments exist, we will focus on the special case of these groups. We will discuss why printed media represents a barrier for persons who lost their sight or have not much of it left. Could digital media be the solution? What difficulties arise if a blind or visually impaired person wants to read an e-book or surf the web? And how is accessible digital material created? In our day-to-day work we experience two sources from which electronic documents are produced: printed material that has to be scanned in the first place, and documents that are written in common office suites like Microsoft Office or Libre Office. We will cover the process of creating accessible digital documents in the second part of this chapter.

Despite the availability of self-produced documents, we are also faced with a growing number of e-books produced by publishers. This development could widen the range of literature made available to be perceived by people with a variety of disabilities, but as our experience shows, many of these materials are not as accessible as they could be. Besides the lack of accessibility, there are also legal issues regarding digitally reproduced and stored documents. Am I allowed to produce a digital copy of a work? And if so, may I store it electronically? Do I have the right to claim a digital version of a work, which I may not access otherwise because of a certain disability? We will cover these questions from our experience as employees at Klagenfurt University, where we offer services for people with disabilities and chronic illnesses.

The situation in Austria

According to the report on the situation of students with disability (Unger *et al.*, 2010) in Austria, 20% of students are impaired or have health-related issues. According to this report 3% of all students are blind or visually impaired. These numbers should be used with extreme caution owing to the fact that the report is based on self-assessment by the students. From our own experience, we suspect the figure to be nearer 10%, as that is the proportion officially supported by the University of Klagenfurt or the Personal Assistance Project (PAA, 2011). The inconsistency between these numbers may result from the method of self-assessment and the fact that only a small number of students apply for support from the university itself.

The nature and amount of support varies from student to student. For blind and visually impaired students, we need an average amount of 15 hours per week for the preparation of previously non-accessible course-related material. Universities are organized in a two semester year that differs from the school year in many ways. The two semesters are not connected; every student has to sign on for every course by two weeks after the start of term; there is no fixed timetable; and there are no single set books, but instead a list of books per course.

That means that students with disabilities have to be prepared to survive the system. New students with disabilities are invited to visit the university before the new semester to learn about the possibilities and requirements they have to expect. Most universities like the University of Klagenfurt have at least a department for the support of students with disabilities that can provide support and information. Their libraries are, as mentioned above, equipped with a special department to digitize materials for visually impaired or blind students. There is also a service offering personal assistance. In Carinthia, the service is provided by a local non-profit-organization (BMKz, 2011) that promotes the idea of independent living and is funded by federal agencies. This organization is closely related to the university, as it was founded by university employees. While the support of students with disabilities at school is an active part of the system, at the university the student has to request and coordinate the support individually according to her or his requirements. To do so, students with disabilities must be well informed, so that they can request their materials and support on time or coordinate their assistance.

Printed materials as barriers

Access to information stored on printed materials may be difficult or even impossible to achieve by blind and visually impaired people. Blindness and low vision are two distinct situations with regard to media usage; nevertheless blind and visually impaired people are often treated as one common group. To show the differences, let us discuss the individual situations.

People who are totally blind cannot access printed material. If you close your eyes, and try to get any information on a book's content by using your remaining four senses, you may use your hands to touch it. You can feel that it has some edges, pages, even a cover, but you cannot feel the letters and images printed in the book. You could smell the book and figure out if it is an old one; you even could lick the cover, to get a taste, but we strongly advise against doing so. A traditional book, then, is a medium that offers no information to blind people. This fact applies to all kinds of printed media. But how can we otherwise compensate for the loss of the visual sense? From the remaining senses, only audio and tactile are capable of transporting enough information to work with. One way could be that a sighted person reads text to the blind individual; even graphics, photos or figures could be described by words. There is one important issue involved in this approach, however, as it means that blind people rely on the help of others either for perception or transmission of information. This is against the desirable aim of independent living.

In 1825 Lois Braille developed the Braille language, which is experienced through tactile information stamped on paper. Since that date, blind people have had the possibility to read content without the help of others, and even to write down their thoughts. Writing Braille was rather time consuming in the early years, because one had to use a stylus and slate combination (Wikipedia, 2011a) and to push each dot individually, and mirror-inverted from the back of the slate. Around 1880, the first Braille typewriters appeared which eased writing (e.g. Wikipedia, 2011b), but still did not allow mass production of text in Braille. In the late 20th century Braille embossers, printers that produce Braille, were introduced. These allow automatic reproduction of all information represented digitally as text. If you compare a work printed for visual readers and the Braille version of it, you will recognize the huge difference in size. In Braille, a line may only hold around 25 to 35 letters and a page about 25 to 30 lines, while on a standard 11 point page a line may contain approximately 100 letters with around 40 lines per page. In addition, Braille paper is much thicker, to withstand the pressure enforced on it while tactile reading. All these aspects combine to create large and heavy documents that are unlikely to be easily transported.

By using a PC, a laptop, a smartphone or other similar devices, this remaining disadvantage of Braille has been eliminated. There is no difference in size regarding to digital stored information, in general it is all in the form of text. Additionally, direct use of online resources opens a whole new dimension in information acquisition. But how do blind people use a common PC? In Europe, blind people often use a combination of Braille terminal and speech synthesizer to read digital information on a PC. A Braille terminal is a device to view Braille letters. Braille terminals are quite expensive, since the market is small and the individual Braille modules (in effect, the single letters) have to be hand-made to reach the necessary level of quality and long life. Many European countries offer a more or less functioning social system, where people are funded by public services to purchase assistive technology. In this way it is possible to raise the €3000 or more needed for a Braille terminal. The comparative absence of a social care system in the US may be the reason why many blind people there use only speech synthesizers to interact with their PC. Relying only on speech synthesis works quite well, but has the negative side-effect that these people's syntactic skills may be less developed because they only hear the words, but do not see how they are spelled.

Visually impaired people (people who still have residual vision) represent a completely different group of users, with different needs. A variety of eye diseases exist that make it difficult to predict a person's need for assistive technologies. One aspect would be the size of printed text. Small text can be made perceptible by using magnifying glasses or similar device, but another issue is the level of contrast between foreground and background colours. Magazines often use text in front of a background image, which makes the text unreadable by some people. As in the case of blind people, developments in information technology significantly improve information perception. On a PC, a screen magnifier like *ZoomText* (AiSquared, 2011) or Magic (Freedom Scientific, 2011a) offers a broad range of configuration possibilities to adapt for individual requirements. For some people even the built-in zooming mechanism in common operating systems may work, though others may need higher zoom levels. Often a combination of magnification with speech output is used, where the current text being read is highlighted on screen. Even if the opportunities afforded by assistive technologies vary between the two groups of users, developments within the digital information age have significantly increased their options for dealing with information.

How may blind and visually impaired people use a library?

As we have shown, printed materials are problematic for some people to perceive. From the viewpoint of a university library, which holds thousands or even millions of books, journals, papers and other printed media, this fact may be important, since laws in many countries around the world award people with disabilities the right to access information stored in these publications. Libraries, therefore, have had to think about ways to allow their blind and visually impaired users to receive those contents.

In the late 1990s Austrian universities realized the need to offer their blind and visual impaired students and employees a way to perceive the printed materials offered by their libraries. Several institutions implemented special workstations for this audience. These workstations had to meet several minimal specifications to meet the highly different needs that come with the known visual impairments. Some of these specifications include:

- *Large screen with adjustable stand*: today a 27" screen would be more appropriate. In the late 1990s, 21" screens were state of the art, but quite expensive and rare. A combination of large-scale screen and zooming software allows high zoom factors with more oversight, and often results in larger distances between user and screen.
- *Braille terminal*: A Braille terminal is a tactile device to read Braille letters.
- *Speech synthesizer*: A piece of software or hardware that converts text to speech output.
- *Braille printer*: As the name suggests, a Braille printer (or embosser) is a device to print computer-generated text as Braille on paper, foil or similar media.
- *Common black font printer*: To allow blind users to print in a form that is readable by everyone else.
- *Screen magnifier*: A screen magnifier is software to zoom in portions of a PC screen. Besides zooming, most screen magnifiers allow using several colour combinations to fit the users need and often are combined with a speech synthesizer function.

- *Scanner*: To scan books, using A3 scanners has turned out to be a wise option, as two pages may be scanned at once. Most OCR Products allow automatic page separation.
- *Screen reader*: Software that provides an alternative, non-graphical, user interface for blind and visually impaired persons (e.g. Freedom Scientific, 2011).
- *Adjustable desk*: To best fit the working environment to a user's need, the desktop itself has to be at least adjustable in height.

At Klagenfurt University library we try to choose equipment that offers as much mobility as possible. In this way, equipment may be borrowed by our students and staff to be used in courses, at the library or during exams. Today, larger universities offer professional digitalization services that are capable of creating electronic versions of printed works in a short time. Via Uniability (2012), the national working group on equality of people with disabilities and chronic illnesses at Austria's universities and colleges, the services all over the country stay in contact, exchange their knowledge and work on common projects. Several approaches have been made to establish a nationwide online platform to store digitalized works and offer them to their users to download. One of the reasons for the failure of these initiatives was uncertainty about the legal situation. Are we allowed to produce a digital version of a printed work, store it in a central database and offer it to other blind and visually impaired people all over the country? One of the positive effects of such a system would be the reduction of duplicates and workload. The student could get needed material with less delay, but there are legal issues to surmount.

How a printed book becomes digital

Our libraries are filled with literature, which in most cases is not fully accessible to people with certain disabilities. According to Austrian law, services offered to the public have to be presented in a way that everyone, regardless of disability, may use it. In the case of a library, this creates a need for technologies and processes to transform printed media to a form that may be perceived by the widest range of individuals, if such perception is not possible in the original state. This transformation process may be split into three stages:

- *Stage 1 – Scanning*: The process of scanning results in a two-dimensional matrix of pixels, in other words a bitmap. This construct is nothing more than a picture or photography of the original page and is in this form not usable by screen readers without further processing. With today's technologies, scanning may be done automatically in a relatively short time.

Larger libraries own special book scanners, like Treventus Mechatronics GmbH (2010), which is capable of scanning entire books on its own, with up to 2500 pages per hour. But even if you use a common flatbed scanner, the result of step one stays the same.

- *Stage 2 – Optical character recognition (OCR)*: OCR creates human and machine readable characters from images, which may have been produced in Stage 1. OCR algorithms analyse the pixel patterns of a bitmap image and try to guess their meaning as characters. This stage produces text that may, for example, be read by screen readers or Braille terminals. OCR normally results in unformatted text: a book without chapters, paragraphs or pages. If you read the book sequentially from beginning to end this would not be a big problem. However, if you intend to use the work for research, you have to know the original structure of the book, or it would not be possible to cite correctly, or to jump to a specific page or chapter. Software like Abbyy (2011) FineReader automatically recognizes some aspects of a works structure, but often you have to rebuild the structure manually.

- *Stage 3 – Review and post-editing*: Most OCR Suites offered today reach a recognition rate higher than 99%. Nevertheless, small recognition failures may still happen, or entire pages may appear as scrambled characters without sense. To ensure a certain level of quality and to reproduce a document's structure, if not recognized by the OCR step correctly, a human review and post-editing stage should be applied: if necessary, this stage usually consumes most of the resources involved in the digital reworking of printed media.

After following these steps we should hold a digital representation of the original printed book, magazine or document in our hands. However, are we even allowed to produce this digital version of a publication? The Austrian copyright law preserves a special paragraph in RIS (1936: §42d), which states the right to copy content in order to adopt media in a way for people with certain disabilities that they can use the content finally. As with other media, the author has to get some compensation in this case. In Austria, a collection company for print media manages this process (Literar-Mechana, 2011). Producing a digital representation of a printed work is one story. Austrian law tells us that this is acceptable for people who may not perceive the work otherwise. Another question is how we handle the new document in its role as data. If we made a hardcopy of the work, we could hand it over to a student, and we are finished. If another student requests a copy, the process of copying has to be done again. Legally we have to follow the same procedure for a digital copy as well. First, we must produce the copy, and send it to a student via email, or put it on a USB stick. Afterwards we must delete the local copy, because the reason we were allowed to produce the copy in the first place was to allow a specific person to access the content. If another student requests a copy of the same work, the process will have to start again. While Austrian law is not quite clear in this situation, the UK (1988: S. 31A–31F) *Copyright, Designs and Patents Act* handles this in much more detail. The only legal way to permanently store a digital copy for repeated use in Austria would be through an agreement with the publisher. The Austrian University of Linz (2012) holds such agreements, and this allows them to offer a nationwide online service for blind and visually impaired students. However, students have to sign a statement that they will only use the work for their own needs, and they are not allowed to give the copy away. Therefore, the University of Linz has to maintain a detailed log of who downloaded each document and at what time.

The process of digital reproduction of printed materials in general does not come without expenses. As mentioned above, in case of the University of Klagenfurt, a blind or visually impaired student needs an average amount of 15 hours of support per week. The preparation of inaccessible materials takes up most of these 15 hours. The preparation of one book needs an average amount of 10 hours. Scanning the book takes 20% of the time, the other 80% is needed for formatting and correcting the material. This includes the description of images, the formatting of tables and the preparation of mathematical formulas. So in the end, the preparation of a book could cost more than twice the cost of the book itself. Nevertheless, who should pay? The student, because he or she wants to get access to a publication? The library or university, because it is bound to offer accessible content? Or the publisher, because he sells inaccessible material that must be transformed to an accessible representation? According to RIS (2005), people with disabilities in Austria have the possibility to claim financial compensation if they have to deal with materials that are offered to the public and yet are not accessible to them because of their impairment. UK copyright law states the right to produce accessible copies, if a visually impaired person already owns a master copy or possesses the right to use it but is not capable of doing so because of accessibility issues (UK, 1988: S31A). Authors and publishers also have a right to get paid for their work, either by compensation RIS (1936: §42d) or by the need to hold the master copy in possession, as in the UK (1988: S31A). But who is to blame, if the work being sold is not available in an accessible form?

Disability and Law

Since 1997 the Austrian constitution guarantees that people with disabilities must not be discriminated against. The federal state, the counties and all communities are bound to promote the equalization of people with disabilities in all areas of public life (RIS, 1997: B-VG Art.7). Based on this part of the Austrian constitution, the federal state and the counties have passed several laws to formulate means to achieve the above goals. The most recent laws are the federal law for the equalization of people with disabilities, the Bundes-Behindertengleichstellungsgesetz (see RIS, 2005) in short BGStG, in 2006 and the signing and ratification of the United Nations Convention on the Rights of Persons with Disabilities in 2006 and 2008 (see United Nations, 2006). The BGStG defines several terms like accessibility and gives people with disabilities the right to sue for compensation for loss suffered. This includes immaterial damages for discrimination as well.

The term accessibility is defined as follows:

Accessibility of buildings and other environments, means of transportation, technical utilities, systems of information technology and all other artificial designed living environments, relates to whether humans with disabilities can use or access it in the usual way, without difficulties and always without the help of others. (RIS, 2005: translated BGStG §6 Abs. 5)

This section is binding for all goods and services that are available for the public, and includes all services offered by schools and universities and their libraries as well. Therefore, Austrian Universities and their libraries offer the above-mentioned service of digitalization of books, magazines and other printed educational materials for students with disabilities. In light of the United Nations Convention on the Rights of Persons with Disabilities, this also fulfils Article 24:

Education

1. States Parties recognize the right of persons with disabilities to education. With a view to realizing this right without discrimination and on the basis of equal opportunity, States Parties shall ensure an inclusive education system at all levels and lifelong learning directed to. (United Nations, 2006)

E-Books – the solution?

E-books have become more and more popular. Customers want to read their books and newspapers as e-books on mobile devices, on the move or by listening to audio books.

As we explained earlier, having the content of the book as readable text is a first step, but is by no means enough. While producing e-books is much cheaper than printing a hardcopy, e-books and audiobooks are often sold for an equal or even higher price. Partly the problem is homemade in Austria by the Ministry of Finance, because e-books are treated as new media, which results in a higher rate of sale tax. This is also the case in many other European countries. According to Austrian law on the equalization of people with disabilities (RIS, 2005) this would constitute a form of discrimination, because blind and visually impaired people have to pay higher prices for the same service.

What would make an audiobook more expensive than a hard copy? If you want to produce an audiobook, the work has to be read aloud by a living person. This produces some cost, but only once. On the other hand, a printed book produces more costs because of the print process itself, which has to be repeated for each copy. Some authors complain that reading an e-book by a screen reader would violate their audio rights, because this could be compared with an audiobook. Nevertheless, anyone who has ever read a text by listening to a screen reader and compared this to an audiobook being read by a human being, would be very aware of the difference. Since no screen reader knows a text's semantics, it is not able to use the right intonation or to speak as different persons in different voices.

There are other services that offer audio- and e-books that may be useful for blind and visually impaired people. With Google's e-book service Google Books (Google, 2011), users gain the possibility of reading parts of, or entire, books online within the browser. However, Google Books offers only pictures of pages, which may be suitable for well-sighted users, but excludes others from reading the books. There is no human intervention in the digitalization process of this kind. The earlier mentioned process of digitalization mentions three stages, but only the first two are used here. Bidok is a project founded by the University of Innsbruck (2012) in Austria. It offers scientific publications around the area of disability studies, pedagogy and more. The content is available for free and published in an accessible form. Bidok content is published in the German language. Audible offers audiobooks that are purchased using their own proprietary audible (.aa) file format (Amazon, 2012). The Audible file is encoded for one unique device, on which it may be used. If a user puts an Audible file into a friend's player, it will not play. Bookshare.org is a kind of file-sharing service of audiobooks and e-books for blind and visually impaired people; since copyright laws vary over the globe, the service is not available everywhere. The quality and accessibility of the books offered here are questionable at best but most of the specific literature for university courses would not be available at such a service anyway. This list represents only a few examples to show different approaches and is far from complete.

Publisher Catalogues

Many publishers offer their e-books and other e-materials via their own web-portals under special licensing terms (de Cruyter, 2011; Springer, 2011). One approach is to sell a library the usage rights for a given amount of copies of a publication. A library's customer may download (borrow) a copy, which results in subtracting the free copies by one. If the customer returns the publication, the counter of free copies is raised again. Another approach is to offer books only chapter by chapter. For blind and visually impaired customers two possible barriers to accessibility arise. First, most of these individual publisher portals are not very usable for this group of users. Second, even the works on offer sometimes lack important accessibility aspects. While EPUB (International Digital Publishing Forum, 2011; Wikipedia, 2011) and other proprietary formats, which allow built-in copyright management, are widely used on the mainstream market, PDF is still the preferred format within the scientific community. A PDF file's accessibility depends on the process by which it was created. Therefore, many documents contain machine readable text, but in most cases lack a logical structure. One could argue that a diversion into chapters would not be necessary, if the book is offered chapter-wise anyway.

As we have already discussed, in addition to the documents themselves, even the tools to reach them (portals, databases, etc.) often lack basic accessibility. Let us examine the scenario of a library like Klagenfurt University Library when it licenses a collection of Springer e-books. A student downloads a book and states it is not accessible to him. He claims financial compensation for this discrimination. Who is to blame, the library because it offers a licensed inaccessible book, or the publisher as producer? With the idea of licensing digital materials, libraries all over the world continuously lose their position as storage for knowledge. They only buy their users the right to use books or magazines, but in most cases do not store them locally any more. If the publishers offer their publications only via their own portals, a library's customer would have to face several completely different user interfaces that may appear quite different as regards to accessibility for people with disabilities. Thankfully, several licensing models include the right to store local copies of licensed publications. In this case the library is allowed to store the publication on its own servers and to offer it to customers via its own local catalogue for direct download, reducing the amount of user interfaces to one.

The creation of accessible documents

One of the most important issues when creating accessible information for people with disabilities is awareness of the problem itself. University employees and teachers may not be aware of the needs of people with disabilities, unless they are affected themselves. We therefore offer awareness courses in regard to eAccessibility to raise knowledge in this area within our university. Beside printed media, which must be made accessible by blind and visually impaired people, the members of the University themselves produce many scientific documents like Master theses, dissertations, papers, and much more. Such documents are, in most cases, produced electronically with word processors like MS-Word, OpenOffice or LaTeX, and are published as PDF files. Sadly, PDF is a proprietary file format published by Adobe (2011). PDF holds the potential to store accessible content, but only if the file was created in a certain way. And here lies the problem, as few people seem to know how to do this.

A promising approach to improve the accessibility of office documents has been shown by the Accessible Digital Office Document Project (2011). As we teach in our courses, it is not difficult to produce quite accessible PDF documents from a standard word processor. We will use MS Word as an example, for which we defined 10 guidelines to gain an acceptable level of accessibility.

(1) *Insert appropriate headings* by using word's predefined headings styles ('Heading', 'Heading 2', etc.). Do not mark headings only by using different fonts or sizes. Screen readers do not recognize changes in font shape or size. Therefore headings marked this way will not be presented as headings to blind people. Create a content block for larger documents.

(2) *Use textual alternatives for graphics, diagrams and figures* that are relevant to understand the content. Word supports this feature. Imagine what information would be lost if you delete the graphic. Alternatively you may use captions or the document text itself to describe complex diagrams and figures.

(3) *Use bullet lists and enumerations* to structure sequential listings. One of the reasons why these structure elements should be used is that screen readers read the beginning of a bullet list or enumeration in a way like this: 'list with tree elements' and ends it with 'end of list'. This allows the user to gain information on a list quite early and therefore decide if it is worth reading or skipping.

(4) *Use links and text-marks to ease navigation.* While not quite usable in a hardcopy, hyperlinks may be used to quickly jump to other sections within the document or to open other resources, locally or on the web.

(5) *Avoid unusual font styles.* Use plan san serif fonts, because they are best to read. Avoid fonts that look like handwriting, even if they seem to look attractive.

(6) Pay attention to a *logical text flow.* If you would like to use columns, use the built in column function. Do not use tables, frames or tabs to simulate columns, because this breaks the logical text flow in most cases.

(7) You may, and should, use *data-tables* for relational data, but pay attention to how you do so. Do not use tables for design issues. Most word processors offer alternatives to design content. Mark heading rows or columns appropriately, because screen readers use this information.

(8) *Use enough contrast between text and background,* since text may be hard to read without this.

(9) *Add meta-data* like author, description, etc. to your document. The search function, on the web as well as on the local PC, is one of the most important aids for blind and visually impaired people to find needed materials. The possibility to search for authors, keywords or description is implemented in most search functionalities and should therefore be provided by each document.

(10) *Define text language.* English text read by an English voice on a screen reader sounds quite different to that read by a German voice. It even may not be understandable at all. Therefore, proper mark-up of a document's base language and language-changes for specific parts becomes an important issue.

A more detailed documentation on these hints is currently work in progress at Klagenfurt University and will soon be released.

Besides .doc, docx and .html, PDF files represents the most frequently used file format to publish content within the scientific community. On 21 June 2011 the World Wide Web Consortium (W3C) (2011) web accessibility initiative (WAI) released a new public editor's draft of the *Techniques for WCAG 2.0,* which contains techniques to create accessible PDF files (W3C 2011). This development will lead to new discussions in the field of accessible content. For many years, web accessibility has only been considered in conjunction with html, even if experts have stated that all published documents should be accessible (Thatcher *et al.,* 2006: 368–405). Office suites like Microsoft Word 2010 or LibreOffice offer export functions to produce more accessible PDF files, if the original document was created as described earlier. The print to PDF functionality offered with common PDF creation software should not be used, as the print process would render efforts toward accessibility useless as it removes a documents logical structure and other accessibility-related components.

Personal assistance

As mentioned above, there are two systems of support for students with disabilities. The older one is the support organized by schools and universities. The newer one is personal assistance. The use of personal assistance has the clear advantage that the student is not dependent on the human resources of the school or university. The student can employ her or his own assistants and organize their support. This is also in accordance with Article 19 of the UN- Convention on the Rights of Persons with Disabilities:

Living independently and being included in the community

(b) Persons with disabilities have access to a range of in-home, residential and other community support services, including personal assistance necessary to support living and inclusion in the community, and to prevent isolation or segregation from the community. United Nations (2006)

In an example of good practice, a university contacts potential new students via associations and non-profit organizations for persons with disabilities. This is done via networking between the many associations for persons with disabilities in Austria. Folders and digital information materials are available so that new students can be informed about universities and the means to get support. When the new students contact the university before the new semester, a consultation is offered in which the student will be informed about the university and the possible support. Then the student can decide if he wants to get support from the university or through an external organization. The necessary support can then be organized by the university or the organizations for personal assistance. In any case, tutors or assistants must be hired and the necessary amount of support must be specified with the student. If the assistant has to digitize material for a blind or visually impaired student the person must be trained for this task and the level and quality of the digital output must be specified. The training is organized by the staff of the department for blind and visually impaired students, or by the students themself. Most of the tutors and assistants are fellow students. It is good practice if they are hired at the beginning of term and attend to the needs of their students until the end of the term. It is not unusual that tutors or assistants support a student with disabilities for more than one term. In this case assistance is easier to organize, because the student and assistant can co-ordinate tasks and shifts before the start of term. Unfortunately not every new student contacts the university before the semester begins. Some students organize support for themselves. This support usually builds on voluntary aid by other students with no legal claim. The quality varies from case to case, because most of the volunteers involved do not have training or a full understanding of the needs of persons with disabilities.

However, this example of good practice is the exception, and only 40% of students are reached by networking efforts. This rate is even lower among exchange students. Most of the students try to study on their own and only ask for assistance in the middle of the term, when they run into problems. At this time it is very difficult to organize and fund assistance, owing to the fact that for complex tasks we need at least one to two weeks to hire assistants and train them, so that they can do their job. These two weeks do not include the time for budgeting and in-house approval for the assistance. The creation and signing of the assistants work contract takes up to four weeks or more. So most of the time we have to do our work under time pressure to compensate for the lateness of students. Even for the assistant it is difficult to adapt their timetables so they can organize to study and work side by side.

Conclusion

Austrian Universities, like those in many other countries, offer a variety of services to assist students with disabilities and chronic illnesses. The amount, type and financing of services varies between individual institutions. Especially in times of economic crises, so called *social services* are the first to be cut-back. But if society can be persuaded to see these services as a basic human right, discussions like 'do we have to finance this service' would no more arise, because it would become a natural thing, no one would doubt the need. Not every student needs the same mixture of aids. The need for personal assistance, transcription within courses or the type of accessible documents required, varies widely between individuals and must therefore be chosen wisely. Even if Austrian law establishes a person's right to gain information and services in a way he or she may be able use it, there is no way to force accessible implementations, except through the claim for financial compensation in the case of discrimination. Peer counselling and peer consulting may be identified as essential parts of the system. As we can tell from our experience, the overall accessibility and quality of services for people with disabilities and chronic illnesses improves significantly if key positions in this area are occupied by people who themselves belong to the peer group. The reason for this observation may be found in a personal and emotional involvement that leads to improved commitment. Even if a positive development regarding legal rights for people with disabilities can be observed in recent years within Austria, certain discrepancies and shortcomings remain on the path to an inclusive society.

With regard to the legal situation around copyright and accessibility for people with disabilities, we can identify several interest groups involved. First, authors and publishers expect to ensure their rights and maximize profit. They intend to use copy protection, encryption, digital signatures and similar mechanisms to prevent the creation of illegal copies. These measures complicate access to works by people with certain disabilities, or make perception impossible. Second, people with disabilities, who have the right to access information like anyone else. Third, libraries and individuals are entitled to transform otherwise inaccessible materials into a state that allows information consumption by people with disabilities. Regarding printed material, the situation seems quite straightforward. A book or magazine is a concrete object that may be protected. A copy could be produced, but usually does not have the same quality as the original document. Additionally the reproduction process often costs more than buying another original copy of the work. For each copy, the reproduction process has to be repeated at least to some extent. By using a public printer or purchasing a new one, we pay a copyright levy that compensates the original owner for the replication. When we look at digital documents, we face a more complex situation: first, digital documents are not physical objects that may be touched. The closest analogy to a physical object may be to regard a file as a sequence of bits stored on a medium. At this level, the idea of digital signatures ties in. A unique key – a signature – is calculated for a given document. If only one bit of the document changes the signature would not match anymore. The reverse works as well. For a given document, you may check if it is the original version if you have the key. It will only match if the document was not changed.

What we may not prove with a signature would be whether a document is a copy or the original, since both are the same sequence of bits. So the copy is the same document. This raises another problem of digital documents compared with printed material. A digital copy does not have to be of lesser quality than the original. It may, as we discussed, even be the same file. However, what does quality of a digital document mean? If we copy printed materials, the reproduction may lose resolution, it may be a black and white copy, the paper differs or we may not get a cover. If we extract the plain text of a document that does not contain any graphic material, we may lose layout and formatting but keep the content. In most cases, this could be achieved by simple copy to clipboard and past to a text editor or word processor. Approaches exist to prevent users from executing this process. Adobe Acrobat offers the option to allow viewing a PDF file, but deactivates the copy and paste function. Sadly, these preventions may also disallow screen readers to access the content, although workarounds exist.

Another aspect of digital documents regards the process of reproduction itself. We may not repeat the process for each copy. Even if we scan a printed document in order to transfer the copy to five blind students, the process of scanning must be executed only once. With one key press, infinite duplicates may be created. Concerning copyright levy we could argue that by using a scanner we have already paid for one copy, but what about the other reproductions?

Several copyright laws regard the situation of blind and visually impaired people and therefore offer special sections to allow legally accessible reproductions of copyright protected documents. Even the European Parliament and the Council (2001) stated the *'importance for the Member States to adopt all necessary measures to facilitate access to works by persons suffering from a disability'*. Some companies like Audible use the approach of signing a document for each buyer and only allowing it to be read on devices where digital rights management is guaranteed. While this approach works fine as long as the documents themselves are accessible (in the case of Audible we are talking about audio books), one problem still exists. What, if I bought an audio book and want to lend it to a friend, or even trade it, as I could with a printed book or even a set of CDs? If a library uses this approach, it would need methods to sign works individually for each user and borrowed document. A digital fingerprint could identify illegal duplicates or indicate if the timeframe of the loan has expired.

Much has happened over the last few years. Instruments to allow access to information by the widest number of people exist. Legislative authorities all over the world are aware of the situation, and arrangements have been made to cover the rights of people with disabilities within existing and new laws. Some countries, like Austria, took a more general approach, which leaves room for interpretation. Others, like the UK, describe copyright issues related to people with disabilities in detail. Both ideas have their pros and cons. In general, we may observe that the situation of blind and visually impaired people, concerning access to information, has improved significantly over the last decades. Never before has access to and the creation of, information been so easy for this group of people. Nevertheless, awareness of accessibility issues and copyright considerations should be improved. While rights for blind and visually impaired people have been covered in laws, people with other kinds of disabilities still have to fight for the same amount of attention. People with learning difficulties or deaf persons, for example, still face significant problems in accessing information.

References

Abbyy (2011) *FineReader*, accessed 14 August 2011. http://finereader.abbyy.com/

AiSquared (2011) *ZoomText*, accessed 14 August 2011. http://www.aisquared.com/zoomtext/

Accessible Digital Office Document Project (ADOD) (2011) *Accessibility of Office Documents and Office Applications*, accessed 14 August 2011. http://adod.idrc.ocad.ca/

Adobe (2011) *PDF Reference and Adobe Extensions to the PDF Specification*, accessed 14 August 2011. http://www.adobe.com/devnet/pdf/pdf_reference.html

Amazon (2012) *Audible*, accessed 20 January 2012. http://www.audible.com

BMKz (2011) Beratungs-, Mobilitäts- und Kompetenzzentrum, accessed 20 October 2011. http://www.bmkz.org

de Cruyter (2011) *ReferenceGlobal*, accessed 14 August 2011. http://www.reference-global.com/

European Parliamant and the Council (2001) *Directive 2001/29/EC of the European Parliament and of the Council of 22 May 2001 on the Harmonisation of Certain Aspects of Copyright and Related Rights in the Information Society*, accessed 24 November 2011. http://eur-lex.europa.eu/LexUriserv/LexUriserv.do?uri=CELEX:32001L0029:EN:HTML

Freedom Scientific (2011) *JAWS for Windows Screen Reading Software*, accessed 14 August 2011. http://www.freedomscientific.com/products/fs/jaws-product-page.asp

Freedom Scientific (2011a) *MAGic Screen Magnification Software*, accessed 14 August 2011. http://www.freedomscientific.com/products/lv/magic-bl-product-page.asp

Google (2011) *Google Books*, accessed 14 August 2011. http://books.google.com

International Digital Publishing Forum (idpf) (2011) *EPUB*, accessed 14 August 2011. http://idpf.org/epub

Literar-Mechana (2011) *Literar-Mechana*, accessed 14 August 2011. http://www.literar.at/

PAA (2011) *BAsIS Büro für Assistenz, Information und Service*, accessed 20 October 2011. http://www.basis.co.at

RIS (1936) *Bundesgesetz über das Urheberrecht an Werken der Literatur und der Kunst und über verwandte Schutzrechte (Urheberrechtsgesetz)*, accessed 14 August 2011. https://www.ris.bka.gv.at/GeltendeFassung.wxe?Abfrage=Bundesnormen&Gesetzesnummer=10001848

RIS (1997) Bundes-Verfassungsgesetz (B-VG), accessed 14 August 2011. https://www.ris.bka.gv.at/GeltendeFassung.wxe?Abfrage=Bundesnormen&Gesetzesnummer=10000138

RIS (2005) *Bundesgesetz über die Gleichstellung von Menschen mit Behinderungen (Bundes-Behindertengleichstellungsgesetz – BGStG)*, accessed 14 August 2011. https://www.ris.bka.gv.at/GeltendeFassung.wxe?Abfrage=Bundesnormen&Gesetzesnummer=20004228

Springer (2011) *SpringerLink*, accessed 14 August 2011. http://www.springerlink.com/

Thatcher, J., Burks, M.R., Heilmann, C., Henry, S.L., Kirkpatrick, A., Lauke, P.H., Lawson, B., Regan, B., Rutter, R., Urban, M. and Waddell, C. (2006) *Web Accessibility: Web Standards and Regulatory Compliance*. Friends of Ed. http://jimthatcher.com/book2.htm

Treventus Mechatronics GmbH (2010) *ScanRobot 2.0 MDS*, accessed 14 August 2011. http://www.treventus.com/buchscanner_scanrobot.html

UK (1988) *Copyright, Designs and Patents Act 1988*, accessed 22 November 2011. http://www.legislation.gov.uk/ukpga/1988/48/contents

Unger, M., Hartl, J. and Wejwar, P. (2010) *Projektbericht: Studierende mit gesundheitlichen Beeinträchtigungen*. BMWF.

Uniability (2012) *Uniability – Working Group on Equality of People with Disabilities and Chronic Illnesses at Austria's Universities and Colleges*, accessed 20 January 2012. http://www.uniability.org

University of Linz (2012) *Institute Integriert Studieren*, accessed 20 January 2012. http://www.jku.at/iis/

University of Innsbruck (2012) *bidok - behinderung inklusion dokumentation*, accessed 20 January 2012. http://bidok.uibk.ac.at

University of Klagenfurt (2012a) *Service Center for Students with Disabilities*, accessed 20 January 2012. http://is.uni-klu.ac.at

University of Klagenfurt (2012b) *Library, Services for Blind and Visually Impaired Persons*, accessed 20 January 2012. http://bsa.uni-klu.ac.at

University of Klagenfurt (2012c) *Web-Portal About the Inclusion of People With Disabilities*, accessed 20 January 2012. http://www.uni-klu.ac.at/inclusion

United Nations (2006) *CONVENTION on the RIGHTS of PERSONS with DISABILITIES*. http://www.un.org/disabilities/convention/conventionfull.shtml

Wikipedia (2011) *EPUB*, accessed 14 August 2011. http://en.wikipedia.org/wiki/EPUB

Wikipedia (2011a) *Slate and Stylus*, accessed 14 November 2011. http://en.wikipedia.org/wiki/Stylus_and_slate

Wikipedia (2011b) *Perkins Brailler*, accessed 14 November 2011. http://en.wikipedia.org/wiki/Perkins_Brailler

World Wide Web Consortium (W3C) (2011) *Techniques for WCAG 2.0*, accessed 14 August 2011. http://www.w3.org/WAI/GL/2011/WD-WCAG20-TECHS-20110621/

Conclusion

As we look forward to teaching in the years ahead, capability in languages and competence in technology are ever more important skills. There is also a groundswell of opinion that these skills are imperative for all learners, with teachers and researchers working towards the same goal of making languages a reality for all within an inclusive context. Initiatives are taking place on an international scale, and in this book we have seen examples of good practice in many different contexts that have transfer value into other arenas. However, there is still a gap that needs to be bridged between the provision of more effective training and the development of more collaborative work between languages, technology and inclusion experts: aspects of which have been explored in this volume. For inclusive education to be effective in the 21st century, these three components need to be integral parts of the languages classroom. Adapting materials and differentiating in class should be common practice and, indeed, these are hallmarks of effective practice. Using varied methods, materials and technologies does not just benefit learners with special educational needs but all learners. In the heterogeneous world in which we live, it is necessary to make provision for the different learning styles and needs that will be encountered, taking a proactive stance on these to provide an accessible curriculum. This volume provides both theoretical and practical examples to give our readers the support and resources they need.

All the contributors have a shared focus: a belief that languages matter. Some knowledge of at least one other language can not only provide very obvious practical benefits within a globalised and competitive world, but also cultural and intellectual benefits and others that might not be academically measurable, such as a sense of fulfilment, improved memory retention and higher self-esteem. Knowing a language gives a different perspective on one's first language and a broader understanding of the world.

Languages present options for all learners to have a stake. In November 2011 the mother of a girl with oral dyspraxia spoke on a radio programme about an initiative to bring Latin and Classics closer to state schools in London, and explained how her daughter had really improved in her French and Spanish after starting to learn Latin. Although the most studied language in Europe is English and, some of our contributors have focused on the teaching and learning of this language, the benefits mentioned are valid for all languages.

With regards to technology, the first years of the 21st century have seen a sudden increase in new means of communication. Social media have opened doors to the exchange of ideas and information in a way that was previously unimaginable, and have provided people with an opportunity to participate in global debates and sharing of experiences. Lessons can now be streamed, students can follow them on Twitter, materials are uploaded onto virtual environments and meetings happen in virtual worlds. New digital technologies have revolutionised the way we all communicate. The world is our technological oyster. Panellists in the 'Future of Education' debate at 'The Silicon Valley comes to Cambridge' conference held in November 2011, spoke of mobile education, online teaching, adaptive modules, digital applications, learning being created through participation and collaboration (peers teaching languages to each other by using online platforms or teachers offering language lessons through video), and tools for the classroom such as tablets or smart boards that provide an alternative to traditional teaching. Technology is a way to share knowledge, to empower teachers and students, and to give them autonomy to do things at their own pace, in their own way, recognising different needs and preferences.

It is our intention that this volume might, in some way, inspire technology specialists, language experts and SEN professionals to come together and work collaboratively to facilitate languages learning for all.

Index